Anastomosing rivers

Cover design: A. van Oudenallen, M. Stoete
Cover photos: Bart Makaske, G. van Betlehem

ISBN 90-6266-167-X (Thesis)
ISBN 90-6809-271-5 (NGS)

Gedrukt door Drukkerij Elinkwijk b.v. - Utrecht

Anastomosing rivers

Forms, processes and sediments

Anastomoserende rivieren

Vormen, processen en sedimenten

(met een samenvatting in het Nederlands)

Proefschrift

ter verkrijging van de graad van doctor aan de Universiteit Utrecht, op gezag van de Rector Magnificus, Prof. Dr. H.O. Voorma, ingevolge het besluit van het College voor Promoties in het openbaar te verdedigen op vrijdag 4 december 1998 des namiddags te 2.30 uur

door

Albertus Makaske

geboren op 8 mei 1965 te Doornspijk

Promotor: Prof. Dr. E.A. Koster
               Faculteit Ruimtelijke Wetenschappen, Universiteit Utrecht

Co-promotor: Dr. H.J.A. Berendsen
               Faculteit Ruimtelijke Wetenschappen, Universiteit Utrecht

Een deel van dit onderzoek is uitgevoerd met financiële steun van het Ministerie van Buitenlandse Zaken.

Contents

Figures

Tables

Acknowledgements

When I shot the main cover photo of this thesis, in Cambodia in the summer of 1991, I was not really aware of the fact that I was looking at an anastomosing river. At that moment, it was rather a bizarre freak of nature to me, which looked good for a pretty picture. Soon thereafter, I took up the research that led to this thesis and I learned about the logic behind anastomosing rivers. Although they were always fascinating, by times they also were fairly unreliable phenomena. This is especially true for the fossil examples, whose channel-fills tend to twist around your boreholes and may escape to places where you can not drill. Even now, after years of travelling, boating and augering, a certain part of the magic of anastomosing rivers is still intact.

The anastomosing river project was executed under supervision of Prof. Dr. E.A. Koster and Dr. H.J.A. Berendsen. I thank my promotor Ward Koster for his faith and the freedom he gave me to carry out my plans. Together with Henk Berendsen he created the unique 'Gruppo fluvial', a stimulating group of people working on diverse types of fluvial research. I admire Ward's organizational talents that keep the 'gruppo' going. Co-promotor Henk Berendsen was the always-present teacher since I started studying physical geography. I especially thank him for his continuous interest and curiosity, both scientifically and socially. I respect his energy and tenacity in tackling scientific problems. With his sense of humour he always manages to create a relaxed working atmosphere.

I owe much thanks to Prof. Dr. Derald G. Smith from the University of Calgary for the considerable interest he took in the project. Being *the* expert on anastomosing rivers, his supervision was indispensable. I am very grateful for the unforgettable introduction to the upper Columbia River and the wilds of Canada. His constructive comments on drafts of several chapters of this thesis were of great value.

Fieldwork in Mali took place within the framework of 'Projet Togué', run by Prof. Dr. Diderik van der Waals. I very much appreciated the African style of the project and Diderik's respect for Malian customs and culture. I really enjoyed the motorcycle trips through the Inland Delta and the stays in small and isolated villages.

Obviously, the field research for this thesis demanded many miles of travelling. However, also in the department I led a more or less nomadic life, having shared five different working-rooms with eight different people. I thank them all for the stimulating atmosphere, the coffee-talks and the occasional help. In particular, I want to thank Henk Weerts and Hans Middelkoop. Henk succeeded in disentangling a complex knot of sand ribbons, which was of crucial importance for my research. His very special sense of humour helped much to fight the dullness of certain phases of scientific research. Hans is thanked for lending me 50 'slibmatten' and for sharing his experience with thesis-stress in the past months.

Nathalie Asselman is thanked for the hospitable sharing of her room during long Apple-sessions and for patiently explaining once again what I had forgotten about Excel. I also much appreciated the continuous general interest ("hoe gaat-ie?") of Henk Kruse. Torbjörn Törnqvist was nearly always in the mood for a discussion about anastomosis or any other aspect of fluvial sedimentology and critically read the draft version of this thesis. Also Janrik van den Berg, André van Gelder, Leo van Rijn and Piet Hoekstra willingly shared their expertise whenever needed. All colleagues and former colleagues of the 'gruppo fluvial' and other related research groups are thanked for creating a friendly atmosphere. In particular, I mention Jaap Kwadijk, Marc Bierkens, Cees Wesseling, Hans Renssen, Esther Stouthamer, Annika Hesselink, Kathelijne Wijnberg, Aart Kroon, Birgitta van der Wateren-de Hoog, Thom Boogerd, Francisca Sival, Nico Willemse, Harry Blijenberg and Marcel van der Perk. Thanks are also due to the secretaries, Celia Roovers and Annina Koopmans.

Mark van Ree participated in various ways in the project. Mark, I enjoyed working together in the field, in all kinds of weather. I hope we will have a future opportunity to break our Van der Staay record. Thanks also for selecting material for ^{14}C-dating and, together with Eric Faessen, for compiling geological maps. 'Maatje' Gerard Ouwerkerk kindly taught me how to handle the Van der Staay suction corer and the vibracorer.

I am also much indebted to the students that helped me collecting a large part of the data discussed in this thesis. Simone van Dijck, Olga van Es and Jeroen Rijnbeek augered many deep boreholes in the Rhine-Meuse delta, now appearing in the appendices 3 and 4. Jeroen was also a pleasant companion in the Inland Niger Delta. With Arjan de Boer and Marinka Kiezebrink, I spent a summer in the quiet Beavertail Lodge in the Columbia Valley, counting mosquitos, beavers and bears.

During stays in Mali I appreciated the hospitality of Harber and Dougouma in Djenné, as well as the pleasing cooperation with the Malian partners from the 'Institut des Sciences Humaines' in Bamako, in particular Mamadi Dembelé and Daouda Diakité. Mark Terlien joined me during my first stay in Mali and drew a substantial part of the draft version of appendix 2.

The Laboratory for Physical Geography is acknowledged for the construction of a 'fish' by Jaap van Barneveld, and for the assistance in chemical and grain size analysis by Kees Klawer. Martin Konert (Free University, Amsterdam) kindly allowed me to use the laser particle sizer. Dr. Klaas van der Borg (R.J. van de Graaff Laboratory, Utrecht) and Dr. Hans van der Plicht (Centre for Isotope Research, Groningen) supervised the radiocarbon dating carried out for this study. They are acknowledged for their willingness to answer questions and to supply extra information. Also discussions with Dr. Arie de Jong (R.J. van de Graaff Laboratory) were helpful. The Netherlands Institute for Applied Geosciences (NITG) provided for three excellent undisturbed cores. Thanks for this are due to Thomas de Groot (formerly 'District West') and the field crew. I sincerely thank the people of 'KartLab' for the fine drawing. Margot Stoete, Petri Bosch and Simone Buddemeijer took care of many of the figures and the appendices. Gérard van Betlehem prepared the photos for reproduction.

I acknowledge my friends for keeping an interest in this long-lasting project. I am grateful to my parents for supporting me in many different ways throughout all the years of studying. Finally, special thanks are for Anke. Of all people mentioned, she knows best about all the ups and downs of this project, and she contributed so much to its completion with her love, moral support and good advice.

Utrecht, October 1998

Bart

1   Introduction

1.1   General background

Rivers rarely follow the shortest route on alluvial plains, and some rivers even follow more than one route at a time. This simple observation actually means that there are many river channel patterns possible. Although a channel pattern may seem accidental, it contains much information on river history, sediments, and flow strength. Since these subjects are paramount to geomorphologists, geologists and river engineers, numerous efforts have been undertaken to define river types on the basis of channel pattern (e.g. Leopold & Wolman 1957; Schumm 1968b, 1977, 1981; Brice 1964, 1984; Mollard 1973; Rust 1978; Nanson & Knighton 1996).

A very striking channel pattern is that of anastomosing rivers (figure 1.1). Remarkably, this type of river received little scientific attention until quite recently. Perhaps this is due to the inaccessibility of the swampy anastomosing river floodplains, making them less attractive as research targets. Moreover, for a long time they were considered as exceptions rather than common phenomena and it was hypothesized that their occurrence requires rare circumstances (Garner 1959, 1967; Rutten 1967). On the other hand, the similarity between inland anastomosing rivers and the widely occurring deltaic distributary rivers was already early noted (e.g. Reclus 1887).

In the last decades, a substantial number of anastomosing river systems has been reported worldwide, casting doubts on their previously presumed rarity. Now, it is known that ancient anastomosing river deposits generally have a high preservation potential in the fossil record, and that they can have much economic importance. Modern anastomosing river floodplains provide an extensive potential of arable and pasture land for rapidly growing populations in developing countries. Putting this potential into use requires control measures in the natural river system to prevent flooding and to restrain channel dynamics. In addition, some anastomosing river floodplains support rare and diverse ecosystems that need conservation. Thus, more attention to the origin and evolution of anastomosing river systems in scientific research is justifiable.

1.2   Definition and historical perspective

Strictly speaking, the Greek word *anastomosis* means 'opening'. In medical sciences the word is applied to indicate the connection between two hollow organs, like veins. In fluvial geomorphology the term is used to describe the situation where a river distributes its water over various parallel channels, which are laterally connected to form networks. For a long time the words 'braided' and 'anastomosing' were used as synonyms (e.g Leopold & Wolman 1957). Although originally describing a similar pattern, nowadays both terms have a very different meaning in fluvial geomorphology. While braided channels comprise convex-up bar-like islands often with exposed sand and gravel,

Figure 1.1   Aerial view of the Tonlé Sap River, central Cambodia (see figure 1.2 for location).

anastomosing channels are separated by concave-up islands, which consist of swampy floodbasins fringed by levees. The size of the latter islands generally exceeds the size of average braidbars by far. Most often, anastomosing rivers seem to form under relatively low-energetic conditions. In this thesis an anastomosing river is defined as: *a river composed of several interconnected channels, which enclose floodbasins*. In section 2.2, I will expand on this definition.

Systematic scientific attention for anastomosing rivers remained scant until the 1970s. Fluvial geomorphology traditionally focused on the study of both smooth regular meanders and intricate braids, which were believed to represent the basic patterns of alluvial rivers. During the 1970s and the early 1980s, awareness grew that the full morphological variability of alluvial rivers observed in nature, could no longer be forced into this simple twofold classification and many new river types were described (Mollard 1973; Rust 1978; Church 1983; Miall 1985). Most of them could be classified as transitional from meandering to braided, but at least one was fundamentally different.

From floodplains in western Canada, anastomosing rivers were reported with channels that were neither meandering nor braided. In contrast, these channels were described as: "...low-gradient, relatively deep and narrow, straight to sinuous channels with stable banks composed of fine-grained sediment (silt/clay) and vegetation" (Smith & Smith 1980, p. 157). The apparent association of laterally stable channels with an anastomosing planform, was of much interest to sedimentologists and soon an

18

'anastomosing river facies model' was born and applied to the fossil record (Smith & Putnam 1980). A major innovative aspect of this model compared to the 'traditional' facies models was the recognition of the crucial role of avulsions, i.e. the 'sudden' formation of new channels, in floodplain evolution (Smith 1983; Smith et al. 1989). At the same time the occurrence of laterally stable, low-sinuous channels was presumed to be inseparably coupled with an anastomosing (multichannel) planform. This idea is reconsidered in this thesis.

1.3   Problem definition and objectives

The anastomosing river facies model from western Canada has been applied successfully to rock sequences (e.g. Putnam 1983, 1993; Flores & Hanley 1984; Eberth & Miall 1991; Johnson & Pierce 1990; Nadon 1994), but in the meantime major controversies about the origin of anastomosing rivers have arisen from studies of modern examples in different geological and climatic settings. Especially in more arid environments, anastomosing rivers appear to exist in very different circumstances than the initial examples from western Canada, suggesting different causes and controls of river anastomosis. Reviewing fluvial facies models, Hickin (1993, p. 210), even suggested that: ".... the 'anastomosing river facies model' is an entirely premature concept, the full development of which should await much more extensive field studies of modern rivers". I will outline the major problems and controversies below.

Definition and classification
No consensus exists on the precise definition of anastomosing rivers. In fact, multiple incongruous criteria have been used for definition by different authors. What also remains unclear is the relationship between anastomosing rivers and distributary river deltas, and the relationship between anastomosing rivers and straight rivers (sensu Schumm & Khan 1972). Furthermore, confusion has been aroused by applying the term 'anabranching' to anastomosing rivers, but also to rivers more akin to the 'traditional' braided rivers (Nanson & Knighton 1996).

The role of climate
Modern anastomosing rivers have been reported from various climatic zones. However, certain controls of anastomosis (especially vegetation) seem to differ with climate. Are morphologically similar anastomosing rivers in different climates a product of convergence [or equifinality (Schumm 1988)], with different processes or causes producing similar results?

The role of base-level and floodplain sedimentation rates
Rapid base-level rise and high floodplain sedimentation rates have been mentioned as prime causes for anastomosis in modern examples from western Canada and Colombia (Smith 1983, 1986). In contrast, in central Australia anastomosing rivers exist under

relatively low floodplain sedimentation rates, resulting from a relatively stable base-level (Rust 1981; Nanson et al. 1986; Gibling et al. 1998).

Hydraulic and sedimentary processes
What we know about the processes in anastomosing rivers, is mainly induced from its sedimentary products (Smith & Smith 1980; Smith 1983; Gibling et al. 1998). Only few measurements exist on hydraulic and sedimentary processes in modern anastomosing rivers and where such data exist they have not been related to the evolution of anastomosis. Such data may illuminate the causes of anastomosis.

The above outlined problems illustrate our poor understanding of anastomosing river systems, making them one of the major challenges in current fluvial research. In this thesis the *objectives* are:

(1) To develop a consistent definition of anastomosing rivers and to classify this type of river with respect to other types.
(2) To develop a universally applicable conceptual model for the genesis of anastomosing river systems, accounting for the major controls such as climate, base-level, discharge, gradient and subsoil.
(3) To document the variability in facies and fluvial architecture of modern and subrecent anastomosing river systems to improve the interpretation of the fossil record.

1.4   Approach and organization

Rivers and their geomorphological and sedimentary processes can be studied at a number of discrete spatial scales, ranging from catchment-scale, through floodplain-scale, channel-scale and bedform-scale down to the grain-scale (e.g. Schumm 1985, fig. 1). The main focus of this thesis is on the floodplain-scale, rather than the channel-scale. Nevertheless, it is recognized that catchment-scale or channel-scale processes may help to explain floodplain-scale phenomena. In this thesis I will often refer to 'river systems' instead of just 'rivers'. The term 'river system' then applies to the river channels and their discharge (water and sediment), as well as its floodplain and subsurface alluvium. A comparable approach was adopted by Nanson & Croke (1992) in their genetic classification of floodplains.

To reach the first of the outlined goals, an extensive review of the literature on anastomosing rivers and related subjects was carried out to determine proper criteria for definition and classification. The literature review in *chapter 2* comprises the processes, morphology and sedimentary facies of anastomosing river systems and gives the reader an overview of the state-of-the-art of anastomosing river research. Subsequently, continuing on this review, hypotheses were developed and tested in the field.

20

Table 1.1 Characterization of the anastomosing river systems investigated in this study

	Upper Columbia R. (modern)	Upper Inland Niger Delta (modern)	Rhine-Meuse delta (subrecent)
Climate	temperate humid	tropical semi-arid	temperate humid
Geological setting	montane valley	intracratonic basin	coastal plain
	proximal	distal	distal
Scale	small	large	large
Floodplain sedimentation rate	high	low	variable

Obviously, comparative study of anastomosing rivers in diverse geological settings and climates is needed to solve the outlined problems. Therefore, three field studies were carried out to further elaborate the second and third objective. The three anastomosing river systems selected for study are located on very different parts of the globe (figure 1.2). They are expected to represent much of the diversity present among anastomosing rivers (table 1.1). The fieldwork took place in two modern systems and one subrecent system.

The first field study focused on the upper Columbia River, which became renowned among geomorphologists and sedimentologists as a 'textbook example' of river anastomosis since its description by Smith (1983). It is a relatively small-scale modern anastomosing river system in a temperate humid, montane setting. Smith (1983) indicated high floodplain sedimentation rates due to rapid base-level rise, and primarily was concerned with description of the sedimentology of the system. In the field study carried out for this thesis, data on hydraulic and sedimentary processes in the upper Columbia River were collected. These new data are discussed in *chapter 3*.

A second field study concentrated on the upper Inland Niger Delta. This modern river system is obviously anastomosing in morphology, but is very different from the upper Columbia in scale, setting and floodplain sedimentation rates. The Inland Delta has been relatively poorly studied. Regional geomorphological surveys (Tricart 1965; Gallais 1967) indicated low floodplain sedimentation rates. It has a tropical semi-arid, intracratonic setting. Little was known about the dynamics of this anastomosing river system due to a lack of subsurface data and poor time control. The results of the field study for this thesis are presented in *chapter 4*. They include a geomorphological map, borehole cross sections and radiocarbon dates. Paleogeographical reconstructions for the Holocene, based on these data, are discussed.

A third field study was carried out in the Rhine-Meuse delta, which is considered as a large-scale anastomosing river system in a temperate humid, coastal setting. The Rhine-Meuse delta is very well-studied (e.g. Berendsen 1982; Törnqvist 1993b; Weerts 1996)

Figure 1.2   The locations where fieldwork was carried out for this thesis [and the location of the Tonlé Sap River (figure 1.1)].

and anastomosis is known to have occurred throughout the Holocene (in this thesis a complex of delta distributaries is considered as a special type of anastomosing river). Floodplain sedimentation rates were high in the mid-Holocene (Atlantic period) and gradually decreased, due to a decreasing rate of sea-level rise. In *chapter 5* the new field data collected for this thesis are presented. They mainly include radiocarbon dates and many borehole descriptions, enabling detailed reconstruction of the morphology of three mid- to late-Holocene paleochannels in the central part of the delta. Magnitude of paleodischarge and its impact on paleochannel morphology, sand body composition, and sand body geometry are discussed.

In *chapter 6* the results of the case studies are compared, to single out the factors of local importance and to determine the universal controls and characteristics of anastomosing rivers. Next, applications of the research are briefly discussed, and point by point conclusions of the individual case studies and the comparison are drawn. Finally possible directions for future research are outlined.

2 Anastomosing rivers; a review of their classification, origin and sedimentary products

2.1 Introduction

The study of anastomosing river deposits reveals much about the behaviour of anastomosing rivers on a geological time-scale, however causes for their existence are much less understood. This is due to a lack of quantitative data on hydraulic and depositional processes from modern anastomosing rivers. Therefore, ideas on the origin of anastomosing rivers mostly resulted from inductive reasoning on the basis of geomorphology and sedimentary products.

In this chapter, the state-of-the-art of knowledge of anastomosing rivers is evaluated. Questions addressed in this chapter are: (1) when to call a river 'anastomosing', (2) what makes it anastomosing, and (3) what is preserved of such a river system on a geological time scale? First of all, the phenomenon needs to be more clearly defined and classified. Therefore, in this chapter I propose a geomorphological definition and classification of anastomosing rivers based on field characteristics mentioned in the literature. Next, processes and external controls of modern and subrecent anastomosing rivers are reviewed. This leads to a conceptual model for the origin of anastomosing rivers. The sedimentary products of modern and interpreted ancient anastomosing rivers are also discussed. Finally, it is evaluated which criteria can be used for the identification of ancient anastomosing river systems.

2.2 Definition and classification

2.2.1 Introduction

Schumm (1968b, p. 1580) is considered to be the first who pointed out the term 'anastomosing' should not be used as a synonym for braiding: "The terms braiding and anastomosing have been used synonymously for braided river channels in this country, but elsewhere, particularly in Australia, anastomosing is a common term applied to multiple-channel systems on alluvial plains (....). The channels transport flood waters and, because of the small sediment load moved through them, aggradation, if it is occurring, is a slow process. As a result, these low gradient suspended-load channels are quite stable (....)." Although Schumm's description seems to be a clear starting point, nowadays there is a bewildering array of different definitions of the anastomosing river type. Before continuing research, a clear-cut definition of this river type is needed.

Preferably, a definition of a river type should meet the following criteria: (1) It should be workable in the sense that an airphoto interpretation or a quick field survey should be sufficient to enable its application. Therefore, it should not include genetic, hydraulic or sedimentological characteristics, but instead it should be based on a limited number of visual characteristics concerning channel pattern and floodplain geomorphology, (2) It should be useful in the sense that it distinguishes a group of rivers with a similar genesis and similar sedimentological and hydraulic characteristics.

2.2.2 Channel pattern

It is generally accepted that an anastomosing river is a multi-channel river which is fundamentally different in form and process from a braided river. Can this river type be defined on the basis of channel pattern?

A channel pattern is considered as a two-dimensional, planform, configuration of river channels only, regardless of any other floodplain characteristics. In this respect, two properties are most relevant: (a) channel sinuosity (distance along the channel divided by straight line distance) and (b) channel multiplicity.

Rust (1978) defined anastomosing rivers as: high-sinuosity (> 1.5), multi-channel rivers. He applied the sinuosity and the braiding-parameter (number of braids per mean meander wavelength) to distinguish between straight, braided, meandering and anastomosing (table 2.1). He admitted that his boundary-values were arbitrary, but stated that a classification should be quantitative. Rust (1981, table 2) listed mean sinuosities of anastomosing rivers ranging from 1.51 to 1.75. Smith (1983) however, described anastomosing rivers in western Canada and found low sinuosities (1.16 and 1.4). He concluded that anastomosing rivers have a variable sinuosity (Smith & Putnam 1980). So it seems that sinuosity of the individual branches is not suitable for distinguishing anastomosing rivers (see also table 2.2), a fact also recognized by Knighton & Nanson (1993).

Table 2.1 Classification of channel patterns according to Rust (1978)

	Single-channel (Braiding parameter < 1)	Multi-channel (Braiding parameter > 1)
Low-sinuosity (P < 1.5)	straight	braided
High-sinuosity (P > 1.5)	meandering	anastomosing

Yonechi and Maung (1986) pointed out that braided channels subdivide at acute angles to the main flow direction, while anastomosing channels subdivide at a wider range of angles and even at obtuse angles. Harwood & Brown (1993) also noted the relatively large angle of subdivision of anastomosing channels. The angle of subdivision reflects a difference between the mechanisms leading to braiding (formation of mid-channel bars) versus anastomosis (avulsion, see section 2.3.2). However, the differences in angles of subdivision between braiding and anastomosing are too small to serve as a basis for a clear-cut definition [see for example Yonechi & Maung (1986, fig. 5)].

Knighton & Nanson (1993) stated that islands between anastomosing channels are large relative to the size of the channels. Some workers included a measure of the scale of channel subdivision in the definition of the term anastomosing. In this context also the term *anabranching* was frequently used. Bridge (1993, p. 21) stated that "...anastomosing channel segments (...) are longer than a curved channel segment around a single braid or point bar and their width-scale flow patterns behave substantially independent of the adjacent segments". He considered anabranching as a synonym of anastomosing. Brice (1984) used the term anabranching for channels enclosing islands having a width larger than three times channel width at average discharge. Schumm (1985) regarded anabranching rivers as being essentially braided rivers with large exposed bars in relation to channel width, as opposed to anastomosing rivers being true multi-channel systems. In addition, Schumm (1985, p. 8-9) stated that: "The individual branches of anastomosing river systems can be meandering, straight or braided; therefore, they are not considered separately from the three basic patterns (meandering, braided and straight) identified by Leopold & Wolman (1957)". Nanson & Knighton (1996) however, considered the anastomosing rivers as a subgroup of anabranching rivers. Those anabranching rivers were not defined by the size of the alluvial islands or any other channel pattern characteristic, but by the stability of riverbanks (caused by vegetation or otherwise) and continued existence of the islands up to nearly bankfull stage. Anastomosing rivers were classified as low-energy, anabranching rivers with cohesive banks (Smith & Smith 1980; Rust 1981).

In conclusion, currently there is a confusing terminology and there is no consensus on how to incorporate the scale of channel bifurcation in a useful definition of anastomosis, although there is a tendency to consider anastomosing as a hierarchically higher order of channel pattern not comparable to straight, meandering and braided (e.g. Schumm 1968b, 1985; Bridge 1993). This idea however, is hard to translate into a definition based on channel pattern only. Boundary-values for the size of islands tend to be quite arbitrary and not discriminative for a genetically, sedimentologically and hydraulically different type of river, as large islands can be coalesced braid bars (e.g. Bridge 1993, fig. 4). Following Smith & Smith (1980, fig. 6) and Nanson & Knighton (1996) it can be concluded that it is the nature of the islands, rather than their size which discriminates anastomosing rivers from braided rivers.

2.2.3 Floodplain geomorphology

The long recognised genetic association between rivers and their floodplains led Nanson & Croke (1992) to a classification of floodplains rather than rivers. It seems reasonable to assume that anastomosing rivers, if genetically, hydraulically and sedimentologically different, are characterized by a different floodplain geomorphology too. Some authors discussing anastomosing river floodplain geomorphology, also paid attention to the stabilizing effect of vegetation.

Smith (1976) suggested the stabilizing effect of vegetation is a major factor in the development of anastomosing river morphology. Rust (1981) however, described an anastomosing river in an arid environment on a scarcely vegetated floodplain and concluded that the role of vegetation is less important on arid anastomosing river floodplains. It is obvious that vegetation, being strongly climatically dependent, can not serve as a universal characteristic of anastomosing rivers.

The morphology of alluvial islands in an anastomosing reach of the Solimões River (Amazon Basin) was described by Sternberg (1959, p. 400) and Baker (1978, p. 225) as 'saucer-like' due to the bounding natural levees. Savat (1975, p. 168) described islands of his Kwilu-type rivers in the Zaire Basin likewise as: "mini alluvial plains: surrounded by levee deposits". In various papers extensive wetlands, mainly comprising the islands, and narrow prominent natural levees (figure 2.1) were mentioned as characteristics of anastomosing river floodplains in humid climates (Smith & Smith 1980; Smith & Putnam 1980; Smith 1983, 1986). Anastomosing systems in arid and semi-arid climates (Rust 1981; Nanson et al. 1986; Schumann 1989) lack these wetlands due to aridity, but the islands to some extent do have the saucer-like morphology that distinguishes them from braid bars.

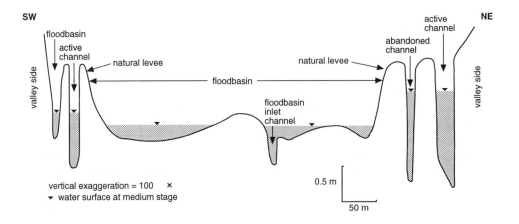

Figure 2.1   Topographic profile across the floodplain of the anastomosing Alexandra River (Alberta, Canada) (Smith & Smith 1980).

Although the rarity or absence of meander scrolls and oxbow lakes on anastomosing river floodplains was considered to be a fundamental characteristic by various workers (Smith 1983, table 2; Nanson & Croke 1992), this is not generally agreed upon. Riley (1975, p. 3), outlining the differences between distributary and braided channels in eastern Australia noted: "Cutoffs, point bars and meander scrolls can all be found in association with the individual distributaries". Later, these distributary channels were called anastomosing channels by Taylor & Woodyer (1978). The topography of the floodplain referred to by Riley however, was regarded by them as relic. Brizga & Finlayson (1990) described a recent (1952) channel avulsion of the Thomson River in Australia, leading to coexistence of two meandering channels which both showed point bars. The new channel had a narrow meander belt only. It is unclear whether anastomosis is a temporary situation in this case. Elsewhere in Australia, Bowler et al. (1978) documented a wide meanderbelt with scroll patterns for what they called 'anabranches' of the Darling River, which in turn was typified by a narrow meander belt. Nowadays, the anabranches transport floodwaters only. Schumm et al. (1996) described anastomosing channels of the Ovens and King Rivers in southeastern Australia becoming more sinuous in time. In the same region, Erskine (pers. comm. in Nanson & Knighton 1996) also identified laterally migrating anastomosing channels of the Murray River. Outside Australia, Baker (1978) also mentioned prominent scroll topography on anastomosing river floodplains of the Solimões River. It can be concluded that, although meanderbelts with ridge-and-swale topography generally are not characteristic features of anastomosing river floodplains, they may be present. Consequently, it seems that meandering and anastomosing are not mutually exclusive characteristics of a river. This gives rise to reconsider the idea of Schumm (1968b, 1985) to classify anastomosis as a higher order pattern consisting of multiple rivers which can either be straight, meandering or braided.

In short, most authors agree on the fact that floodbasins constitute a major element of the anastomosing river floodplain geomorphology. Floodbasins may also develop on braided river floodplains (e.g. Coleman 1969), but are much less common and do not occur on the islands in the river. The occurrence of meander-belts with ridge-and-swale topography on anastomosing river floodplains is not a typical feature, but it cannot be excluded.

2.2.4 Proposed definition and classification

In view of the considerations in the preceding sections, I propose a definition of anastomosing rivers based on channel pattern and floodplain geomorphology: *an anastomosing river is composed of several interconnected channels, which enclose floodbasins*. Below, I will elucidate the three basic points of the classification of river types shown in figure 2.2.

Firstly, anastomosing rivers are classified as true multi-channel rivers (having multiple channel belts), while braided rivers are regarded as single-channel (having one channel belt), multi-thread (multiple thalweg) rivers. Generally, islands in an anastomosing river are larger than islands or bars in a braided river, which genetically are

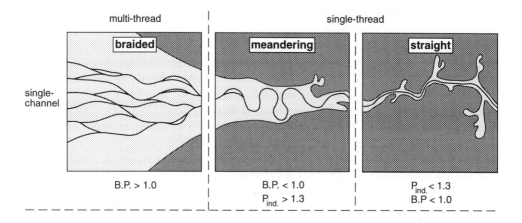

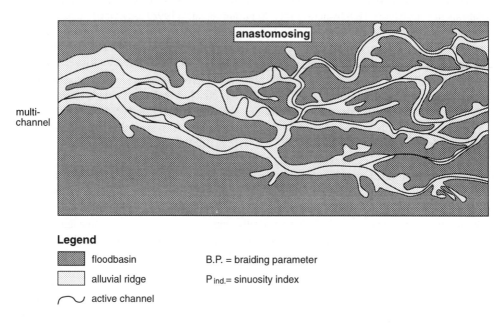

Legend

▨ floodbasin   B.P. = braiding parameter

▨ alluvial ridge $P_{ind.}$ = sinuosity index

〰 active channel

Figure 2.2   *Proposed classification of alluvial river types based on channel pattern and floodplain geomorphology.*

in-channel features. Geomorphologically, saucer-shaped islands (floodbasins) characterize anastomosing rivers, while convex-up islands (bars) characterize braided rivers. Meandering and straight rivers are classified as single-channel, single-thread rivers, as the flow in their channel is not split by in-channel bars. To distinguish between single- and multi-thread (braided) rivers the braiding parameter of Rust (1978) is applied. Braided rivers have a braiding parameter > 1.

Secondly, straight and meandering rivers are defined with respect to the alluvial ridge. Straight in this sense does not mean literally straight, but it means that the course of the channel and the course of the axis of the alluvial ridge are very similar, i.e. absence of lateral erosion and deposition. Straight channels can have a high sinuosity but this sinuosity is not the result of a meandering process involving lateral erosion and accretion. Meandering in this sense means that a reach of the channel is substantially longer than the reach of the alluvial ridge. Meandering channels do have a high sinuosity. To describe these phenomena, Brice (1964) introduced a sinuosity index, defined as the ratio of the channel length to the length of the meander-belt axis. A sinuosity index of 1.3 is proposed as a boundary value which separates straight from meandering channels. For a given channel reach, the sinuosity index will generally be lower than the sinuosity, for which 1.5 is usually accepted as a boundary value between meandering and straight (Leopold & Wolman 1957, Rust 1978).

Thirdly, multi-channel anastomosing rivers are classified as a composite form which consists of single-channel braided, meandering or straight channel reaches. This is in accordance with the classification of Schumm (1968b, 1985). An anastomosing river composed of braided channel reaches seems to be an exceptional form, with a rare example mentioned by Smith & Smith (1980, fig. 6). Meandering channel reaches are not common features of anastomosing rivers, but they may occur. Most anastomosing rivers consist of straight channel reaches (e.g. Smith & Smith 1980; Rust 1981; Smith 1983). However, there is no fundamental reason for an a priori exclusion of meandering and braided channel reaches in anastomosing rivers by definition.

An important advantage of this classification is that it can be applied at the local scale of individual channel reaches, without regard to the rest of the system. Strictly speaking, when considering isolated reaches of a channel the term anastomosing has no meaning. Especially when interpreting fluvial sediments this is important, as exposure is often limited to individual fossil channels and often the reconstruction of a multi-channel paleoriver will be impossible (see also section 2.4.5).

The classification is also meaningful with regard to the genesis and sedimentology of rivers. The hierarchical difference in the classification between the single-channel braided, meandering, and straight rivers on the one hand, and the multi-channel anastomosing river on the other hand, reflects the fundamental differences in genesis between these two categories. Straight, meandering and braided rivers all basically result from in-channel processes like lateral erosion and accretion or mid-channel bar formation. Anastomosing rivers result from an extra-channel process on the floodplain, namely avulsion (see section 2.3.2). The identification of floodbasins which is inherent to the classification is genetically significant as floodbasins provide avulsion routes and their state of preservation provides information on the lateral erosion of the channels. In addition, their identification is sedimentologically significant as they indicate major lateral differentiation in sedimentary facies from channel to floodbasin.

According to the present definition, a complex of delta distributaries can be regarded as a special form of an anastomosing river. Only the geometry of the basin determines whether the anastomosing channels will join downstream or not. Such deltaic fluvial systems are not fundamentally different from inland anastomosing rivers in form, process and sediments (compare chapter 5). In the present chapter, predominantly inland anastomosing rivers will be considered. Another category of multi-channel systems includes the radial channel patterns on alluvial fans, where floodbasins generally do not develop. An exception are the low-sinuosity meandering alluvial fans described by Stanistreet & McCarthy (1993), which have floodbasins and may be regarded as anastomosing river systems.

The focus of this thesis is on anastomomosing rivers and therefore only three basic single-channel rivers are discerned. This is a simplification as nowadays more river types are recognized in a continuum from straight (as defined above) to braided. One of them is the wandering river, which is mentioned here because the term anastomosing was frequently applied to it (e.g. Mollard 1973; Church 1983, p. 180). Wandering rivers, as described by Church (1983) and Carson (1984b), take an intermediate position between meandering and braided (e.g. Nanson & Croke 1992; Hickin 1993). Because of the presence of relatively stable vegetated islands in these rivers, they resemble the anastomosing rivers in pattern. However, there is hardly any development of floodbasins on their floodplains, as those rivers are laterally too active for floodbasins to be preserved.

It must be noted that the classification applies to alluvial rivers only. Non-alluvial rivers may to some extent resemble the classified alluvial rivers; for example, the steep-gradient ($S_{ch} \approx 12$ m/km) 'anastomosing' streams described by Miller (1991). However these degrading streams lack lateral floodbasins and moreover they are fundamentally different in process as avulsion-sites are determined by resistant bedrock strata.

Nanson & Knighton (1996) recently published an overview of *anabranching* rivers, which were defined as: "systems of multiple channels characterized by vegetated or otherwise stable alluvial islands that divide flows at discharges up to nearly bankfull". They distinguished six types of anabranching rivers on the basis of stream power, sediment texture and river morphology. These types included several types of wandering rivers as well as anastomosing rivers as defined above. The anastomosing rivers involve their types 1, 2 and 3 anabranching rivers. These are: cohesive sediment anabranching rivers (type 1), sand-dominated, island-forming anabranching rivers (type 2), and mixed-load laterally active anabranching rivers (type 3). Despite differences in sediment and channel morphology these rivers have floodbasins on their islands as a common characteristic.

A limitation of the present classification is the stage-dependency of the definition of braided and anastomosing rivers. At high stage braided rivers with submerged bars may seem single-thread channels, while at low stage anastomosing rivers will carry water in their main channel only, thereby appearing single-channel rivers. For proper classification the rivers should be observed at various stages.

2.3 The origin of anastomosing rivers

2.3.1 Introduction

Anastomosing rivers occur in a variety of environments. Climatic conditions vary from subarctic or temperate to tropical humid or arid. Geological settings include montane, foreland and intracratonic basins as well as coastal environments. The scale of anastomosing rivers also varies widely (table 2.2). However, it is not justified to conclude on the basis of this evidence that the occurrence of anastomosis is completely independent of climate and geologic setting.

The geomorphological processes acting in anastomosing rivers are of two kinds: (1) The processes creating the multi-channel pattern; e.g. the processes leading to avulsion, (2) The processes determining the morphology of the individual channels of the system. In many different ways, climate and geology are important external controls on these processes.

2.3.2 Avulsion

"Avulsion is the sudden abandonment of a part or the whole of a meander belt by a stream for some new course at a lower level on the floodplain" (Allen 1965). Sometimes this is referred to as first-order avulsion, with second and third-order avulsion relating to reoccupation of old channels and initiation of new braids within a braided channel, respectively (e.g. Nanson & Knighton 1996, p. 219). In this thesis I will use the term avulsion in the sense of Allen (1965).

Avulsion can take place in all kinds of fluvial environments. It was reported from braided rivers on alluvial fans (Gole & Chitale 1966; Knight 1975; Wells & Dorr Jr. 1987; Gohain & Parkash 1990), braided river floodplains (Coleman 1969; Nordseth 1973; Carson 1984b), meandering river floodplains (Fisk 1944; Russell 1954; Mike 1975; Brizga & Finlayson 1990; Neller et al. 1992; Mack & Leeder 1998), and deltaic plains (Fisk 1944; Kruit 1955; Elliot 1974; Berendsen 1982; Törnqvist 1994; Van Gelder et al. 1994).

Subsequent to avulsion the old channel is slowly abandoned. Törnqvist (1993b, pp. 155-157) described examples of instantaneous (period of coexistence of channels < 200 years) as well as gradual (period of coexistence 500-1000 years) avulsion in the Rhine-Meuse delta in the Netherlands. Little is known about the factors controlling the rate of capacity-loss of these channels. A high avulsion frequency generally leads to continuing coexistence of young deepening channels and old vertically infilling channels, composing an anastomosing system. An exception is the modern Yellow River delta, where in spite of a very high avulsion frequency only one distributary channel is active at any time (Van Gelder et al. 1994). This may be due to the exceptionally high aggradation rate of the alluvial ridge, that amounts to decimeters per year.

The role of avulsion in the formation of anastomosing systems was recognized by many investigators (Riley & Taylor 1978; Woodyer et al. 1979; McIntosh 1983; Smith

1983; Jacobberger 1987; Smith et al. 1989, 1997; Schumann 1989; McCarthy et al. 1992). Here, the following questions are addressed: (a) what kind of floodplain facilitates a high avulsion frequency, (b) what initiates the avulsion-process and (c) what is the evolution of the avulsion-channel after initiation of the process?

Table 2.2 Quantitative data on anastomosing rivers

River, climatic setting, and data source	Q_{ma} (m³/s)	Q_{bf} (m³/s)	Q_{max} (m³/s)	S_{ch} (cm/km)	P (-)	w/d (-)	Sed. rate (mm/yr)
Temperate humid							
Mistaya [1]		34		390		15	0.6
Alexandra [2]		66		60	1.51	13	1.8
North Saskatchewan [3]		164		100	1.62	16	1.8
Upper Columbia [4]	108	275	770	9.6	1.16	16	1.7
Lower Saskatchewan [5]	648	1400	3000	12.2	1.4		1.5
Ovens [6]		225		89	1.49	17	
Tropical humid							
Magdalena [7]	7400	8800		10.0		28	3.8
Japura [8]	11130				1.1		
Solimões [9]	36815				1.5		2.3
Magela Creek [10]		40	1580	50	1.1	10	1.5
Arid and semi-arid							
Red Creek [11]				11	1.92	<10	
Upper Darling [12]	681	200		5	2.3	8	0.02
Cooper Creek [13]	40-100		5800-25000	17.5	1.69	10	0.04
Middle Niger [14]	1330		9700	2.0	1.2		0.14
Subarctic							
Attawapiskat [15]	508		3115	52	<1.5	70	a

Q_{ma}	= mean annual discharge	P	= sinuosity
Q_{bf}	= bankfull discharge	w/d	= width/depth ratio of channels
Q_{max}	= maximum recorded discharge	Sed. rate	= average floodplain sedimentation rate
S_{ch}	= channel slope	a	= incision

Data sources:
[1] Smith (1986), Smith & Smith (1980); [2] Smith (1986), Smith & Smith (1980), Rust (1981); [3] Smith (1973, 1986), Smith & Smith (1980), Rust (1981); [4] Smith (1983, 1986), This thesis, Water Survey of Canada (1991a); [5] Smith (1983, 1986), Water Survey of Canada (1991b); [6] Schumm et al. (1996); [7] Smith (1986); [8] Baker (1978); [9] Baker (1978), Mertes (1994); [10] Nanson et al. (1993), Knighton & Nanson (1993); [11] Schumann (1989); [12] Riley & Taylor (1978); [13] Rust (1981), Knighton & Nanson (1993); [14] ORSTOM (1970a), Gallais (1967), Direction Nationale de l'Hydraulique et de l'Energie, Bamako, Mali (unpubl. data); [15] King & Martini (1984).

Bridge & Leeder (1979) stated that: "Avulsion is initiated if floodwaters travelling from an alluvial ridge to the floodbasin, through crevasses or low parts of the levees, have a gradient advantage over the main channel". Thus, the avulsion-process is caused by the formation of alluvial ridges, as the deposition rate close to the channel is generally much higher than some distance away from the channel in the floodbasin. Mackey & Bridge (1995) expressed this phenomenon mathematically as follows:

$$r_z = a\ e^{-b\ z_c\ /z_m}$$

in which: r_z = deposition rate, at distance z from the channel belt
            a = maximum net deposition rate at the edge of the channel belt
            z_c/z_m = dimensionless distance from the channel belt
            b = coefficient that describes the rapidity at which the rate of deposition decreases with distance from the channel belt

Mackey & Bridge (1995) argued that realistic values of b range from 0.35 to 1.4. Considerably higher values of b ranging between 3 and 7 were calculated by Törnqvist et al. (1996) based on borehole data from the Rhine-Meuse and Mississippi deltaic plains covering long (1500 years) time spans. Similar values of b were obtained by Törnqvist et al. (1996) from single flood data from the Rhine-Meuse delta. These high values of b suggest a relatively rapid formation of pronounced natural levees. Higher compaction rates of silty, clayey and peaty floodbasin deposits with respect to gravelly and sandy channel belt deposits, further enhances the formation of alluvial ridges. Based on theoretical considerations, Bridge & Leeder (1979) suggested that avulsion frequency increases with aggradation rate. This was confirmed by field data on the Holocene development of distributaries in the Rhine-Meuse delta, showing that the avulsion frequency was highest in the period of high sedimentation rate due to rapid sea-level rise. The number of avulsions decreased, when the rate of sea-level rise decreased and the aggradation rates slowed down (Törnqvist 1994). An example of exceptionally high avulsion frequency (avulsion every twelfth year on average), associated with very rapid vertical aggradation was described for the modern Yellow River delta (Van Gelder et al. 1994). Experimental evidence for a rise of avulsion frequency with increasing sedimentation rate was given by Bryant et al. (1995).

Two other boundary conditions control the process of avulsion. The first is the overall geometry of the floodplain. This particularly plays a role when the floodplain is situated on an alluvial fan, but also, to a lesser extent, in case of a deltaic plain. The convex cross profile of the floodplain, due to the semi-circular shape of the alluvial fan or delta, favours the avulsion-process. This effect is well documented for the Kosi River alluvial fan in Northern India (Gole & Chitale 1966; Wells & Dorr Jr. 1987; Gohain & Parkash 1990).

The second boundary condition is the overall gradient of the floodplain. At a given aggradation rate, favourable conditions for avulsion (i.e. the gradient advantage across the natural levee compared to the main channel gradient) are attained more easily on a low gradient floodplain than on a high gradient floodplain, because of the low channel gradients involved. The overall floodplain gradient however, can be strongly influenced by tectonics. Tilting of the floodplain can give rise to frequent avulsion in a preferential direction. Alexander & Leeder (1987) called this 'topographically triggered avulsion'. This effect was also quantified in simulation models for alluvial stratigraphy (Bridge & Leeder 1979; Bridge & Mackey 1993; Mackey & Bridge 1995). Field examples are the Brahmaputra River (Coleman 1969), the rivers on the Hungarian Plain (Mike 1975) and rivers in the upper Amazon foreland basins (Dumont 1994). Tricart (1965) and Gallais (1967) suggested rapid local subsidence as a controlling mechanism of the sequential eastward migration of the Bani and Niger Rivers (central Mali).

Once the conditions on the floodplain are favourable for avulsion, a trigger is needed to initiate the process. These triggers determine the time and location of avulsion. An extreme flood event usually determines the time of an avulsion (e.g. Smith et al. 1989; Brizga & Finlayson 1990; Mack & Leeder 1998). Therefore, Knighton & Nanson (1993) argued that a flow regime characterized by concentrated floods of relatively high magnitude is conducive to anastomosis. Another possible trigger is a sudden tectonic event resulting in bank collapse or breaching (Alexander & Leeder 1987). More common triggers are obstructions, blocking discharge in the main channel and forcing the water to seek a new course, starting as a crevasse through the natural levee (Smith 1983; Smith et al. 1989). Channel obstructions mentioned in the literature are: beaver dams (Rutten 1967), log jams (Smith 1983; Harwood & Brown 1993) and ice jams (King & Martini 1984; Smith et al. 1989) in cold to temperate climates, and dunes (McIntosh 1983; Jacobberger 1988b; Makaske 1994) in arid climates. Examples of weak spots in the natural levee where crevasses preferentially form, are beaver (Smith 1983) or hippopotamus trails (McCarthy et al. 1992). Not all crevasses develop into mature avulsion-channels. In fact, the majority will become plugged up again (Smith 1983).

Another possible obstruction is caused by in-channel fluvial deposition in favour of overbank deposition. This is only reported from semi-arid and arid floodplains (Riley & Taylor 1978; Taylor & Woodyer 1978; Woodyer et al. 1979; Rust 1981; Schumann 1989; McCarthy et al. 1992; Gibling et al. 1998). On the floodplains they described, flood regimes are flashy and bankfull discharge is exceeded far less than once every year (compare figures 2.3a and 2.3b). Due to this, the floodplain sedimentation rates are relatively low (table 2.2) and most sediment load is deposited within the channels during base-flow conditions. These deposits frequently have a bench morphology (Riley & Taylor 1978; Taylor & Woodyer 1978; Woodyer et al. 1979; Schumann 1989). Consequently, the channel looses capacity to accommodate the next flood and becomes liable to avulsion. Alternatively, Schumm et al. (1996) described avulsion as a response to loss of hydraulic efficiency as channels became more sinuous with time.

Generally, the chances for avulsion increase as aggradation continues. During extreme floods the outer bends seem to be the most favourable spots for avulsion, as water level there is slightly higher and erosive power is strongest. Nevertheless, the exact time and location of avulsion is impossible to predict, due to the random nature of extreme floods and the various triggers. Bridge and Leeder (1979) therefore argued that it should be treated as a stochastic process.

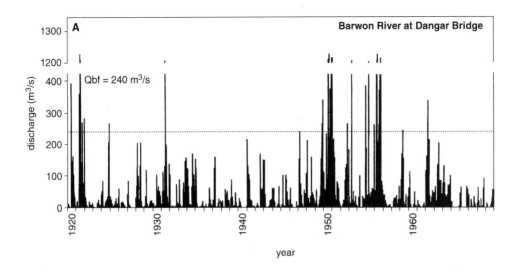

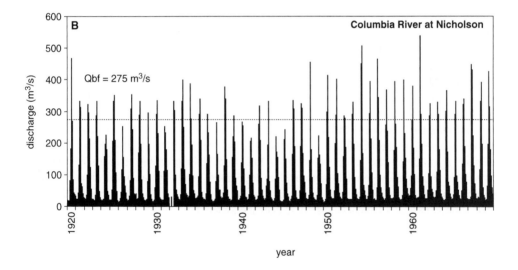

Figure 2.3　　*(a) Hydrograph of the Barwon River at Dangar Bridge, N.S.W., Australia, 1920-69 (Woodyer et al. 1979).*
(b) Hydrograph of the Columbia River at Nicholson, B.C., Canada, 1920-69 (data Water Survey of Canada 1991a).

Formation of a mature avulsion-channel from a crevasse channel was described in detail by Smith et al. (1989) for the lower Saskatchewan River. They described how the avulsion-channel developed out of an unstable multi-channel pattern on a crevasse splay. As the splay prograded into the wetlands, the channels on the older part of the splay started building natural levees and became more stable. Later on, this multi-channel system on the splay was abandoned in favour of one channel, deeply incised through the splay deposits. Splay progradation and channel formation continued until the avulsion-channel rejoined one of the main channels of the system. A similar evolution of channels was described by Van Gelder et al. (1994) for the Yellow River delta. In this area the process of avulsion involves very high sediment supply to the floodbasin during prolonged seasonal flooding.

In the arid anastomosing systems of Cooper Creek (Rust 1981) and Red Creek (Schumann 1989) however, flooding occurs less frequently and sediment supply to the floodbasin is low. In these arid regions avulsion-channels develop in a different way. Rust (1981) observed the absence of crevasse splays and the presence of poorly-developed, discontinuous natural levees in the Cooper Creek anastomosing system. He argued that avulsion here takes place without prior crevasse splay formation. Schumann (1989) described the formation of the avulsion-channel as a predominantly erosive process after minor crevasse splay formation. In contrast to the process described by Smith et al. (1989), channelization of flow starts downstream, where the avulsion flow rejoins the main channel, and gradually travels upstream to the point where the avulsion was initiated. A comparable avulsion-process was described by McCarthy et al. (1992) for the Okavango Delta. An exceptional feature in the Okavango Delta, is that water from the main channel percolates to the backswamps through permeable natural levees that are solely composed of vegetation, instead of spilling over clastic natural levees.

In summary, frequent avulsion leads to continuing existence of contemporaneously active channels on the floodplain. Frequent avulsion seems to be dependent on continuing vertical aggradation and is favoured by a low floodplain gradient. Differential vertical floodplain aggradation leads to a floodplain topography with channels on alluvial ridges perched above the floodbasins, in which future avulsion routes are located. Usually, obstructions reducing channel-capacity trigger the avulsion.

2.3.3 Lateral channel stability

The lateral stability of the individual anastomosing channels was pointed out in many studies (e.g. Smith 1976, 1983, 1986; Smith & Smith 1980; Rust 1981; Nanson et al. 1986), so there appears to be a bias towards straight channels in anastomosing rivers. What is the reason for this?

Lateral stability of river channels is generally described as a function of slope, discharge and sediment composition of the banks. A basis for this idea was provided by the classic paper of Leopold & Wolman (1957). Plotting channel slope against bankfull discharge, they found that braided and meandering channels could be separated by the line:

$$S = 0.012 \ Q_{bf}^{-0.44}$$

in which:
- S = channel gradient (-)
- Q_{bf} = bankfull discharge (m³/s)

Straight channels were also distinguished but did not appear as a separate cluster in their diagram (figure 2.4). Schumm & Khan (1972) observed a straight-meandering-braided sequence of channel patterns with increasing valley gradient at constant discharge (figure 2.5). In the same series of flume experiments, they also showed that an increase in suspended sediment load has a stabilizing effect on the river banks. Later however, it appeared that the duration of their experiments had been too short to reach equilibrium (e.g. Carson 1984a, p. 331).

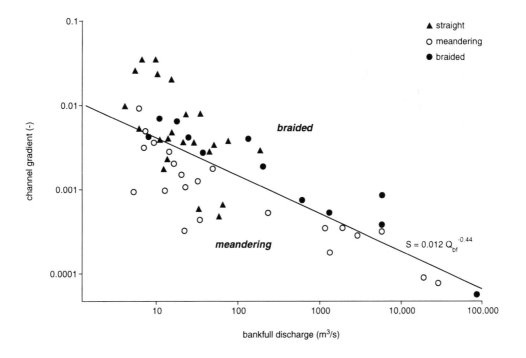

Figure 2.4   *Values of slope and bankfull discharge for various natural channels and a line defining critical values which distinguishes braided from meandering channels (Knighton 1984 after Leopold & Wolman 1957).*

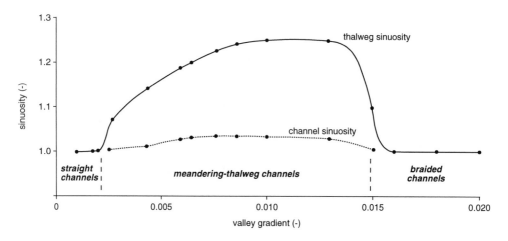

Figure 2.5   *Relation between slope of surface on which channel was formed (valley slope) and thalweg sinuosity (Schumm & Khan 1972).*

Discharge and slope can be combined in the single parameter of stream power. Stream power was often used as a tool to investigate the lateral stability of river channels (e.g. Chang 1979; Ferguson 1981; Richards 1982; Keller & Brookes 1984; Brown 1987; Nanson & Croke 1992; Van den Berg 1995; Lecce 1997). One can distinguish between gross stream power and specific stream power. Gross stream power can be defined as the rate at which potential energy of water flowing downhill is supplied to a unit wet channel length:

$$\Omega = \gamma gQS$$

in which: Ω = gross stream power (W/m)
                γ = density of water (kg/m^3)
                g   = acceleration of gravity (m/s^2)
                Q   = discharge (m^3/s)
                S   = channel gradient (-)

Specific stream power (ω) is gross stream power divided by channel width (w).

Ferguson (1981), working with a data set of 95 British rivers, concluded that inactive straight or sinuous channels tend to have low specific stream power (1-60 W/m^2), while actively-shifting low-sinuosity channels have high stream power (> 100 W/m^2). Actively meandering channels have intermediate stream power values (5-350 W/m^2). These ranges of specific stream power however, show a wide overlap.

Although certain ranges of slope-discharge combinations or stream power seem to be associated with certain channel patterns, it has been pointed out by various workers that these ranges characterize rather than predict those channel patterns (Carson 1984a, Ferguson 1987, Van den Berg 1995). This is partly due to the use of bankfull discharge and channel slope, which are dependent on channel pattern. Moreover, also the channel width, necessary to calculate specific stream power, is dependent on the channel morphology.

Stream power only represents a useful measure of the energy available to modify the channel, if it is related to the sediment to be moved (e.g. Schumm & Khan 1972; Carson 1984a; Ferguson 1987; Van den Berg 1995). It is believed that it is the excess stream power above the threshold for sediment entrainment from bed and banks, which relates to channel behaviour (Carson 1984a). Therefore, Nanson & Croke (1992) classified river floodplains on the basis of specific stream power in the channels and the texture of the sediment on the floodplain. They described anastomosing river floodplains as having gravel and sands in channels with a specific stream power < 10 W/m^2 and abundant silt and clay on the floodplains. These floodplains were classified as low-energy cohesive floodplains.

Stream power considerations can be applied to channel reaches, but not to multi-channel river systems as a whole. Knighton & Nanson (1993) plotted the bankfull discharge against channel slope (as in figure 2.4), for anastomosing, braided and meandering rivers. In their diagram most anastomosing rivers plot within a zone below the braided and meandering rivers, indicating low stream power. However, they treated the anastomosing rivers as hydraulic unities. For explaining channel processes, separate channel reaches of the anastomosing river should be considered, because each channel adapts to its discharge independently from the other channels of the system. Distribution of discharge over various channels also means distribution of stream power. This partly explains why channels in anastomosing systems tend to have high lateral stability, a fact also mentioned by Harwood & Brown (1993).

If stream power is very low, the capacity of flow to form a channel to accommodate floods will probably be insufficient and this in turn will favour overbank flooding (e.g. Lecce 1997). Knighton (1987) stated that: "Alluvial rivers with erodible boundaries in self-formed channels which, when subject to relatively uniform governing conditions, are expected to show a consistency of form, or average geometry, adjusted to transmit the imposed water and sediment discharges". One can seriously doubt whether this is true for anastomosing rivers. Knighton & Nanson (1993) regard the formation of anabranches as a response to the inability of the main channels to cope with high magnitude discharges, because "the resistivity of the banks constrains the size of the bankfull cross-sectional area". Humid climate anastomosing systems show prolonged annual flooding. For example, a mean of 45 days for the Columbia (Locking 1983, p. 35), 50 days for the Magdalena (Smith 1986) and even 100 days for the Solimões River (Mertes 1994) floodplains were recorded. In semi-arid southeast Australia, Rutherfurd (1994) described unconfined reaches of the Murray River as anastomosing where spilling overbank occurs more frequently than in the confined reaches which have a single-channel morphology. Other semi-arid and arid climate anastomosing rivers experience in-channel accretion and seem to be unable to transmit imposed sediment load (Riley & Taylor 1978; Taylor & Woodyer 1978; Woodyer et al. 1979; Rust 1981; Schumann 1989).

When considering the stable channel morphology of anastomosing systems, time is an often neglected factor. Formation of wide alluvial ridges by active meandering of channels simply needs time. Probably this played a role in the longitudinal facies architectural change of a paleochannel described by Törnqvist et al. (1993). They found evidence for rapid downstream decrease in lateral migration of a subrecent channel, together with a downstream decreasing period of activity. The frequent avulsions in anastomosing river systems, may interrupt evolution of wide laterally accreted alluvial ridges. This was described by Smith et al. (1989) for the anastomosing lower Saskatchewan River and hypothesized by Saucier (1994, p. 123-124) to explain differences in size of Holocene Mississippi River meander belts.

Climatic influence on lateral channel stability occurs through the role of vegetation or duricrusts. In humid climates, vegetation and organic deposits have a stabilizing effect on river banks (e.g. Smith 1976; Hickin 1984; Harwood & Brown 1993; Huang & Nanson 1997), although Cairncross et al. (1988) and Stanistreet et al. (1993) also described channel stabilization by extensive peat growth in a semi-arid anastomosing system. In arid environments, duricrust formation can be an important cause of channel confinement (Tricart 1959; Friend et al. 1979; Gibling & Rust 1990).

In conclusion, low stream power in combination with cohesive bank material explains the lateral stability of individual anastomosing channels. Low stream power is mainly caused by low floodplain gradients which also favours avulsion (section 2.3.2), although relatively low discharge due to distribution over various channels may be an additional factor. The resistance against erosion of the banks is related to the low stream power, as overbank deposition of clay takes place predominantly on low gradient floodplains.

2.3.4 Climatic and base-level changes

Is anastomosis a state of transition, or is it an equilibrium form? Smith et al. (1989) described anastomosis as a stage within the process of avulsion, with the single-channel stage as the final result of channel evolution. The question is whether all rivers naturally strive for a single-channel state, and if so, which conditions prevent them from reaching that state.

Some investigators regarded anastomosis as an expression of instability induced by climatic change (Garner 1959, 1967; Baker 1978). Climatic change from aridity to humidity will subject the drainage network to floods it cannot accommodate. Bowler et al. (1978) believed that avulsion of the Darling River was associated with hydrological changes from arid late glacial to more humid Holocene conditions. In the arid Inland Niger Delta, degradation of the channel network due to in-channel fluvial and eolian deposition, is believed to have been an important cause of avulsions at the onset of periods with increasing discharge (Gallais 1967, p. 55; McIntosh 1983; Makaske 1994). Little is known about the response time of river systems to altered hydrological regimes.

An important indirect climatic influence on anastomosis is the rise in sea-level in late- Pleistocene and Holocene times. Such a rapid base-level rise can be considered as a different type of instability imposed upon a fluvial system. Smith & Smith (1980) suggested: "In fluvial systems adjoining marine basins, rapid sea-level rise might provide a downstream control for upstream alluviation and possible development of channel anastomosis." The idea of downstream control (Mackin 1948) was first applied to anastomosing rivers by Smith (1973). Rapidly aggrading alluvial fans deposited by tributaries entering an alluvial valley, provided a local base-level rise and caused channel anastomosis upstream in the alluvial valley. He stated that: "Under such conditions grade should decrease with aggradation" (Smith 1973, p. 203). The combination of rapid aggradation and reduction of gradient favours both avulsion frequency and channel stability. Sea-level rise was considered a main cause for subrecent channel anastomosis in the Rhine-Meuse delta (Törnqvist et al. 1993; Törnqvist 1993a) and in the lower Mississippi Valley (Aslan 1994; Törnqvist et al. 1994). Evidence from other near-coastal areas is still very restricted. A different mechanism of base-level rise, which is important in continental arid settings, is the formation of dunes blocking the course of a river. Jacobberger (1988a, p. 356) mentioned this as a prime cause for anastomosis in the Inland Niger Delta.

Tectonic or isostatic movements provide another cause for (relative) base-level rise. Local uplift of the river bed can act as base-level rise, reducing the river gradient upstream of the uplift, thereby conducing anastomosis. Field evidence for this mechanism was obtained by Burnett & Schumm (1983). Ouchi (1985) also provided experimental evidence.

On a larger scale, rapidly subsiding foreland basins were considered ideal settings for anastomosing river systems (Smith & Putnam 1980, Smith 1986). Bakker et al. (1989) described Late Pleistocene anastomosing channel patterns in a subsiding strike-slip basin in an intramontane setting.

It can be concluded that continuing base-level rise, either climatically or tectonically caused, provides a mechanism for maintenance of low gradients under aggrading conditions and thereby creates ideal circumstances for anastomosis. Although there is evidence that some anastomosing rivers owe their existence to altered hydrological regimes associated with transition in climate from arid to humid, this is not the rule.

Whether a single channel state is the norm for alluvial rivers, with anastomosis as an expression of instability remains open, due to a lack of hydraulic understanding of anastomosis. Many anastomosing rivers are long-lived (7500 - >50,000 years according to Knighton & Nanson 1993). If the concept of anastomosis as a state of disequilibrium is right, this points either to continuous (e.g. rapid base-level rise) or repeated disturbance, or to extremely slow evolution of the river system after disturbance. Since time control on the long-term development of anastomosing rivers as yet is insufficient, no decisive conclusions can be drawn. At the moment it is most appropriate to characterize long-lived anastomosis as a state of dynamic equilibrium, with frequent avulsion continuously rejuvenating the system, while old channels are being abandoned.

2.3.5 A hypothetical genetic model

A hypothetical spatial distribution of alluvial river types which reflects the influence of a downstream reduction in floodplain gradient and a downstream increase in aggradation rate (associated with downstream control) is shown in figure 2.6. The thickness of the bars represents the probability of occurrence of a certain river type as a function of its position on a scale from proximal to distal. Because of a reduction of gradient downstream, lateral channel stability increases as well as avulsion frequency. This leads to a high probability of an anastomosing system composed of straight channels near the mouth. Moreover, conditions of base-level rise cause a high aggradation rate downstream, and enhance the chance for anastomosis. Upstream, conditions are less favourable for anastomosis.

The relationships between the factors determining the morphology of a fluvial system on an alluvial plain, are visualized in figure 2.7. On every floodplain two complexes of processes determine the morphology of the river system at the floodplain-scale and the channel-scale respectively. At the floodplain-scale, the avulsion frequency determines whether anastomosis will occur or not. At the scale of individual channels, lateral channel stability determines the place of a channel in the braided-meandering-straight sequence.

Concerning the factors 'floodplain gradient' and 'aggradation rate', table 2.2 shows essentially two groups of anastomosing rivers. (1) The temperate and tropical humid climate anastomosing rivers which all have high floodplain aggradation rates, while some of the gradients are relatively high as well. (2) The arid, semi-arid and subarctic

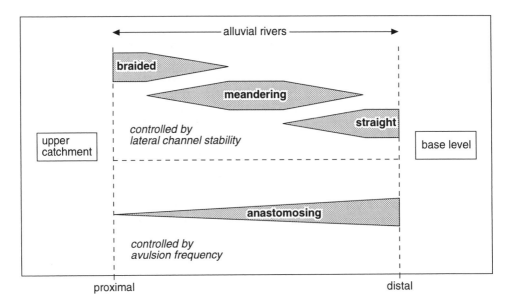

Figure 2.6   Spatial distribution of alluvial river types from proximal to distal.

42

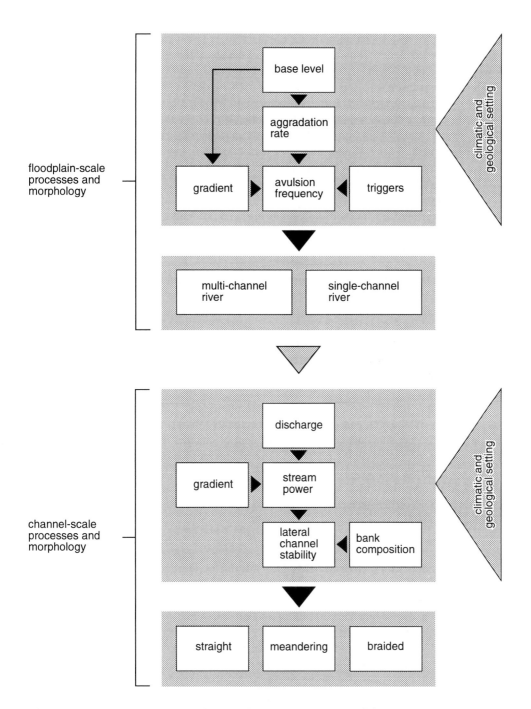

Figure 2.7   A conceptual model showing the factors determining the morphology of a fluvial system on an alluvial plain.

anastomosing rivers, which show low floodplain aggradation rates or incision as well as relatively low gradients. Thus, the reported modern anastomosing rivers either have: (1) a low gradient, or (2) a high floodplain aggradation rate, or (3) both. In the latter case, conditions for anastomosis are optimal. In the first two cases, conditions for anastomosis seem to be less favourable. The role of factors now grouped as 'triggers' is thought to be especially relevant for those anastomosing rivers. At present, these factors are still poorly documented. Additionally, in a number of anastomosing river systems in-channel aggradation might be much more important than floodplain aggradation, as a driving force behind avulsions. However, very few data exist on rates of in-channel aggradation.

2.4   The sedimentary facies of anastomosing river systems

2.4.1 Introduction

The sedimentary products of anastomosing rivers contain a wealth of long-term information on anastomosing rivers and can be expected to be relatively abundant in the stratigraphic record due to high aggradation rates. Moreover, identification of ancient anastomosis in the field gives important clues for interpretation of the large-scale paleogeographical setting (e.g. Galloway & Hobday 1983, p. 51). In this section I will deal with the question how we can recognize the sedimentary product of anastomosing rivers in the stratigraphic record. This requires analysis of sedimentary facies and fluvial architecture.

The term 'fluvial architecture' was introduced by J.R.L. Allen (at the First International Symposium on Fluvial Sedimentology in his keynote address) "...to encompass the geometry and internal arrangement of channel and overbank deposits in a fluvial sequence" (Miall 1996, p. 34). The term 'facies' is used in a purely descriptive sense in this thesis, following the definition of Reading (1986, p. 4): "A facies is a body of rock with specified characteristics. (...) If fossils are absent or of little consequence and emphasis is on the physical and chemical characteristics of the rock, then the term lithofacies is appropriate."

2.4.2 The sedimentary environments and lithofacies of modern anastomosing river systems

Information on the sedimentary facies of modern anastomosing systems is still scarce, especially with respect to sedimentary structures. The widely-used lithofacies model is mainly based on a few well-documented examples in western Canada. In this region, Smith & Smith (1980) investigated the subsurface characteristics of three anastomosing river floodplains in montane valleys. In figure 2.8 their results are summarized. In this model rapid vertical accretion in combination with very restricted lateral movement of channels, produces a network of thick and narrow sand bodies in the subsurface. The sand bodies are embedded in (sometimes organic) floodbasin fines and the lateral

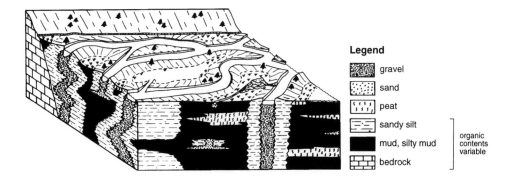

Legend

gravel

sand

peat

sandy silt

mud, silty mud

bedrock

⎫
⎬ organic contents variable
⎭

Figure 2.8　*Textural facies model of an anastomosing river system (Smith & Smith 1980) (© SEPM, reprinted by permission).*

lithological boundaries are rather abrupt. It is now realized that the vertical scale of this diagram is exaggerated far too much to give a realistic picture (D.G. Smith pers. comm. 1998).

In later publications, the core of this model remained unchanged, although the importance attached to crevasse splay deposits and avulsion was added (Smith 1983; Smith et al. 1989). The frequent avulsion was a significant addition to the model since this prevents the channel deposits from reaching an almost infinite thickness, as was suggested in figure 2.8.

On the basis of the research in western Canada, six anastomosed sedimentary environments and associated lithofacies were identified (e.g. Smith 1983). The lake, marsh and bog (mire) environments and facies are laterally extensive and show little variability. These facies were estimated to make up 60 to 90 percent (Smith 1983) of anastomosing river deposits. The channel-related environments and facies however, are laterally more restricted and internally more complex.

Aggradation in anastomosing *channels* can result in channel-fills which are remarkably thick [5-12 m in the Columbia River (D.G. Smith pers. comm. 1998)] and relatively narrow. In lateral and vertical direction, the channel deposits change abruptly into the finer grained overbank deposits. The channel-fill deposits range from gravel (Smith & Smith 1980) to silt (Smith 1975), but predominantly they consist of sand. Sets of planar tabular cross beds result from deposition by migrating sand waves. In addition, multi-storied fining-upward textural sequences were identified. These were interpreted as flood cycle deposits during channel aggradation. Locally, small-scale (1 m thick) sets of inclined heterolithic stratification (IHS), produced by narrow laterally accreting point bars, were found in the channel-fills (Smith 1983; Thomas et al. 1987, p. 138).

The *natural levees*, which flank the channels, are wedge-shaped in cross section. They consist of laminated fine sand and silt, which fine and taper out laterally in floodbasin deposits. These sediment bodies can be up to 4 meters thick and 1 km wide in the lower Saskatchewan River (Smith 1983, p. 163). Usually, they are topped by

45

floodbasin deposits such as lake or marsh deposits or peats. Directly underneath levees however, sandy crevasse splay deposits may be present. These reflect the avulsive origin of the neighbouring channel.

Crevasse splays are deposited in the floodbasin, adjacent to spots where the natural levee is eroded by a small channel drawing sediment-laden floodwaters from the main channel. Being deposited by miniature fluvial systems, their structure, texture and geometry tends to be very complex. Their planform is generally lobate but can be highly irregular. In cross section, crevasse splays are lens-shaped and up to 3 m thick. They show a coarsening upward sequence at the base and a thin fining upward sequence at the top. Their texture ranges from coarse silt to coarse sand with granules. Cross lamination as well as high-angle cross beds are the internal structures of the sandy deposits. Usually crevasse splay deposits are sandwiched between floodbasin muds or peat in a conformable fashion, however crevasse channels may incise through the splay deposits into the subsurface. This process may herald formation of an avulsion channel.

The deposits associated with avulsion in the anastomosing Saskatchewan River were described in detail by Smith et al. (1989) and Smith & Pérez-Arlucea (1994). It appeared that there is wide textural variation in avulsion belt deposits, reflecting proximal-distal relationships, location of avulsion channels, sediment supply and the stage of development of the avulsion. The sandy crevasse splay deposits as described above are the characteristic depositional unit of the proximal part of the avulsion belt only. In the more distal parts, the lens-shaped body of avulsion belt deposits is predominantly built up of silt, underlain and capped by organic-rich deposits. Vertically, the silty deposits, which are volumetrically dominant over the sandy avulsion belt deposits, are characterized by a coarsening upward sequence. Coarsening upward units of a similar origin, although typically more rich in sand, were described by Elliott (1974) from deltaic interdistributary bays. Close to the avulsion channels, natural levee deposits rest on top of the avulsion belt deposits. Infilling of these channels with sandy bed load results in stringers of sandy channel deposits which are inset in the predominantly silty body of avulsion belt deposits. The avulsion belt deposits characteristically range from 1 to 3 m in thickness. The avulsion of the lower Saskatchewan River in 1873, affecting 500 km^2 of wetlands up to today (Smith et al. 1989), suggests that avulsion belt deposits are a volumetrically important element of the bulk of anastomosing river deposits.

Marshes, *lakes* and *bogs (mires)* are the wetland environments with a low elevation relative to the natural levees and crevasse splays. In lakes and marshes suspended load is deposited, while bogs generally are too remote from the channels to receive significant amounts of clastics. Marsh deposits consist of organic and clastic mud, which may be laminated, but usually are bioturbated. Lake deposits consist of laminated clay and silt, although bioturbation may also have destroyed any structure. Bogs contain peats up to 3.5 m in thickness in the Saskatchewan marshes.

The cited examples from western Canada are by far the most complete and detailed descriptions of anastomosing river sedimentology and therefore have set the standard. However, these anastomosing systems represent a biased dataset, as they are all located in temperate humid continental settings and represent small to medium-scale anastomosing rivers.

Research in the tropical humid large-scale anastomosing system of the Magdalena River in Colombia (Smith 1986), showed that the model from western Canada has a more universal applicability. Additionally, it was found that the buried channel-fills of the Magdalena River have a vertically uniform trend in mean grain size and contain abundant organic litter, mud balls and wood. The overbank deposits of this river generally contain only thin accumulations of organic material, in contrast to the overbank deposits of the lower Saskatchewan River. This was attributed to the high clastic input because of the foreland basin setting of the system.

Work of Rust (1981) on the arid Cooper Creek anastomosing system, revealed important differences with the model from western Canada: (1) a lower ratio of channel-sands to overbank fines, due to lower channel density; (2) less organics in the overbank sediments due to much reduced plant growth, as well as desiccation cracks, duricrusts and evaporite horizons; (3) less crevasse splay and levee deposits, because aggradation predominantly takes place within the channels due to less frequent overbank flooding (see also figure 2.3a). Rust (1981) described the channel-sands as isolated sand stringers encased in a predominantly muddy sequence. The mud was commonly structureless due to bioturbation and alternate shrinkage and swelling. Internally, the sand bodies typically showed planar cross-stratification resulting from deposition as alternating side bars, underlain by trough cross-stratified sand and capped by horizontally and ripple-laminated sand.

Rust's model was extended by Gibling et al. (1998), who provided many details about the Cooper Creek sediments. They showed that the Cooper Creek channel bodies essentially comprise mud-rich channel-fills that are sandier in their lower parts. They reported lateral and vertical accretion of the channel deposits, often in the form of accretionary benches with inclined heterolithic stratification [IHS as defined by Thomas et al. (1987)] at higher levels. The dimensions of the muddy channel bodies can be: 7-10 m thick and > 100 m wide. Width/thickness ratios of these bodies were estimated at > 15 and possibly 100 or more, based on limited data. Notably heterolithic, anastomosing channel-fills were also described by Taylor & Woodyer (1978) and Woodyer et al. (1979) from semi-arid eastern Australia. The heterolithic benches can be found at different levels in the channel. The lower benches are characterized by cross-bedded fine sands with mud interbeds, while the upper benches consist of interlaminated sands and muds.

It can be concluded that the overbank deposits are a key element of anastomosing river sedimentary products as a whole. Braided, meandering or straight channels are defined on the basis of their channel characteristics and therefore it seems reasonable to expect that their paleochannels can be reconstructed on the basis of their channel deposits and geometry. Within the category of anastomosing rivers, the floodbasins are the unifying element between the multiple channels. They play a crucial role in their genesis, being the place where crevassing and avulsion take place. In short, it appears that we have to consider anastomosing river deposits at a larger scale than that of the channel deposits only.

2.4.3 The lithofacies of interpreted ancient anastomosing river systems

Knowledge on the sedimentology of modern anastomosing systems was first applied to ancient fluvial deposits by Le Blanc Smith & Eriksson (1979), Smith & Putnam (1980) and Rust & Legun (1983). At present, there is a number of well-described ancient fluvial sequences that are believed to be of anastomosing river origin (see table 2.3 for references). The lithofacies and facies geometries of these ancient systems will be dealt with together in this section. Besides 'true' ancient examples, a few subrecent anastomosing river systems are also included in this review (e.g. Bakker et al. 1989; Törnqvist 1993a).

Sandstone facies
Two geometric types of sandstone facies are distinguished: ribbon bodies and tabular bodies.

The ribbon bodies are characterized by a sharp, scoured, often concave base and a gradational or sharp flat top (figure 2.9). Their thickness ranges from a few meters to tens of meters and they have a width of tens to hundreds of meters. Internally they either show fining upward (e.g. Putnam 1983; Cairncross et al. 1988; Kirschbaum & McCabe 1992; Flores & Pillmore 1987) or they are relatively homogeneous in texture (e.g. Rust et al. 1984; Johnson & Pierce 1990; Törnqvist et al. 1993; Nadon 1994). The sand ranges from coarse to fine. Sometimes, conglomerates constitute a lag near the erosional base of those bodies (e.g Flores & Hanley 1984; Warwick & Flores 1987; Eberth & Miall 1991). These lags may contain fragments of mudstone, petrified wood and coal. In some cases the ribbon bodies are less sandy and have a notably heterolithic composition of interbedded sandstones, siltstones and mudstones (Kirschbaum & McCabe 1992). The dominant sedimentary structure is trough cross bedding with subordinate planar cross bedding, while near the top of the bodies ripple or climbing ripple lamination is usually present. The cross-bedded sets may be up to 1.2 m thick. Lateral accretion stratification is not a consistent feature of these sandstone bodies, but occasional examples were reported (Rust & Legun 1983; Rust et al. 1984; Warwick & Flores 1987; Kirschbaum & McCabe 1992; Nadon 1994). Some of these examples can be classified as inclined heterolithic stratification, due to the presence of mudstone drapes.

The tabular bodies typically have a flat, non-erosive base and sharp or gradational lower and upper contacts. Their thickness is usually limited to a few meters and often they are less than one meter thick. Laterally however, they can be very extensive, being hundreds of meters or even kilometres wide, before they grade into finer-grained deposits. Their area can be several to tens of km^2 (Putnam (1983). The documented vertical textural trends are: (1) upward fining (Smith & Putnam 1980; Nadon 1994), (2) upward coarsening (Flores & Pillmore 1987; Warwick & Flores 1987), (3) upward coarsening followed by upward fining (Rust & Legun 1983; Rust et al. 1984) and, (4) no vertical trend at all (Johnson & Pierce 1990). This variability may reflect proximal-distal relationships since Putnam (1983) found fining upward proximal to major paleochannels and coarsening upward away from them. The sand grains may be coarse but are usually medium to fine with a grading to siltstone. The dominant structures are ripple, climbing

Figure 2.9   *Ribbon sandstone body in the St. Mary River Formation (Alberta, Canada).*
The ribbon has a sharp concave base (black arrow) and a flat top (white
arrow).

ripple and parallel lamination, with occasional small-scale trough cross beds and wave ripple lamination (e.g. Nadon 1994). The top of these bodies is often heavily rooted and bioturbated and may show traces of paleo soil formation (e.g. Johnson & Pierce 1990).

The ribbon sandstone bodies are commonly interpreted as channel-fills, while the tabular bodies are taken as crevasse splay or levee deposits. The levee deposits may be heterolithic and display mudrock partings (Johnson & Pierce 1990). Frequently the tabular bodies are attached like 'wings' (figure 2.10) to the top of ribbon sandstone bodies (Eberth & Miall 1991; Kirschbaum & McCabe 1992; Nadon 1994). Natural levee and crevasse splay deposits in modern anastomosing river environments however, also have an important fine-grained component which is part of the mudrock facies (Smith & Pérez-Arlucea 1994). In fact, tabular sandstone bodies attached as wings to the ribbon sandstone bodies probably only represent proximal avulsion splay deposits instead of levee deposits. Another point is that the ribbon sandstone bodies may not represent all of the channel facies, as channels sometimes fill in with mud rather than sand.

Mudrock facies
Geometrically, the mudrock facies usually has a sheet-like appearance (figure 2.10) and is laterally much more extensive than the sandstone facies. The sheets are bounded or split by sandstone or coal facies. The thickness of the sheets is strongly variable. It may amount up to 20 m (Eberth & Miall 1991). Alternatively, mudrock may be present as plugs which are inset in the top of ribbon sandstone bodies (e.g. Rust & Legun 1983), or even (partly) replace them (e.g. Hopkins et al. 1982).

Figure 2.10　　*Close up of lateral wing attached to the right-hand margin of the ribbon sandstone body of figure 2.9. The wing is capped by a sequence of weathered mudrock sheets and erosion-resistant tabular sandstone bodies (positive relief).*

The term mudrock is used, following Lundegard & Samuels (1980), for a sedimentary rock which consists for more than 50% of grains finer than sand. Depending on silt-clay content, siltstones, mudstones, or claystones can be distinguished. The mudrocks usually consist of interbedded siltstone, mudstone, and claystone. The individual beds are either massive or horizontally laminated. The siltstone portion may be current or wave ripple laminated (e.g. Putnam 1983) and laminae of fine sand may locally be present. The colours range from gray and green to yellow, brown and red (e.g. Kumar & Tandon 1985). Gray and green mudrock may contain organic material like leaves, woodfragments and fruits. Additionally, dark, coaly intervals are typical for this type of mudrock facies, which is frequently carbonaceous (e.g. Putnam 1983). In contrast, yellow, and red mudrocks usually lack organics, but can have calcrete nodules or horizons (e.g. Rust & Legun 1983; Kumar & Tandon 1985). Desiccation cracks of 1 m deep were found in this type of mudrock facies (Rust & Legun 1983). In general, root mottling and burrows are common characteristics of mudrock facies and are often found in association with incipient paleosols, which can be traced laterally in the sheets over long distances.

Mudrock sheets are usually interpreted to represent a number of depositional environments. Interlaminated wedges of siltstones and mudstones adjacent to ribbon sandstone bodies are assumed to be levee deposits, while lenses of siltstone and mudstone, sandwiched between finer mudrock beds are likely to represent crevasse splay deposits. More finely laminated and possibly wave-rippled mudrock is usually taken as lacustrine deposits (e.g. Nadon 1994). Faunal or paleobotanical evidence (e.g. Van der Woude 1983, 1984) can be necessary to give this interpretation a firmer basis, as bioturbation may have destroyed the primary structures. Often, rather structureless and bioturbated (perhaps mottled) mudrock is assumed to be a marsh deposit (cf. Smith 1983).

Mudrock plugs are interpreted as residual channel deposits based on geometry, because lithologically they can be identical to all other mudrock facies. They may partly or sometimes almost completely consist of coal (or peat, e.g. Törnqvist et al. 1993).

The mudrock facies contains important paleoclimatic information by its colours, organics content and paleosols. Red and yellow colours, calcrete (nodules), desiccation cracks, and lack of organic matter are normally considered indicative of an arid climate. In contrast, dark gray and green colours and abundant (carbonaceous) organic matter are generally believed to point to a humid climate. Caution must be used however, in making these paleoclimatic interpretations, as these properties may show considerable local variation and they may partly represent the conditions of early diagenesis rather than the conditions of deposition. Miall (1996, pp. 437-442) gives an overview of the problems associated with paleoclimatic interpretation of overbank deposits.

Coal facies
Excluding the coal incorporated in mudrock plugs, the coal facies usually occurs in seams, which have a blanket geometry. The seams usually are laterally extensive and can be traced for up to kilometres or more. The coal seams are usually thin and frequently intercalated mudrock beds occur. In general, thickness ranges from a few decimeters to 2 m. Occasionally however, the coal facies may almost fully replace the mudrock facies (Cairncross et al. 1988). In such cases the seam thickness may amount to 8 m (Le Blanc Smith & Eriksson 1979). Coal blankets are most frequently encased in mudrock, but scoured upper or lateral contacts with ribbon sandstone bodies are also common (e.g. Putnam 1983).

The coal facies is interpreted to represent the mire [or 'bog' sensu Smith (1983)] depositional environment. Coal is not present in all ancient anastomosing river systems. Absence or rarity of coal was attributed to high clastic influx (Nadon 1994) or an inferred arid climatic setting (Rust & Legun 1983; Kumar & Tandon 1985; Eberth & Miall 1991). The thickness of coal seams is strongly influenced by compaction. They may represent significant quantities of peat. For example, the estimated pre-compaction and the measured post-compaction proportions of coal and carbonaceous mudstones differ from 40 to 11 % respectively, in sections studied by Kirschbaum and McCabe (1992). McCabe (1984, p. 20) cited peat-to-coal compaction ratios between 1.4:1 and 30:1.

2.4.4 The fluvial architecture of interpreted ancient anastomosing river systems

In this section three aspects of fluvial architecture will be discussed: (1) the proportion of overbank deposits relative to channel deposits, (2) the lateral connectedness of the channel sandstone bodies and (3) the geometry (width/thickness ratio) of the channel sandstone bodies. These properties are of considerable economic significance. Table 2.3 gives data about these aspects for fifteen interpreted ancient anastomosing river systems.

Proportion of overbank deposits
Subsurface data from modern anastomosing rivers suggest that a large amount of the overbank deposits is preserved (Smith & Smith 1980; Smith 1983, 1986). The proportion of overbank deposits preserved in the stratigraphic record is controlled by several interrelated variables, most importantly: (1) sediment load, (2) lateral mobility of the fluvial channels (Collinson 1986, p. 57), (3) channel density, and (4) basin width. Rust (1981) believed that channel density in arid anastomosing river systems is significantly lower than in humid anastomosing river systems. In this respect he quoted values of 3% of active channels on the arid Cooper Creek floodplain as opposed to 20% for the humid Alexandra River. These values however, are strongly determined by large differences in basin width. Simulation studies (e.g. Bridge & Leeder 1979; Bridge & Mackey 1993) suggested a positive correlation between aggradation rate and preservation of overbank deposits, which could be especially relevant for anastomosing river systems, since a number of them show high aggradation rates (table 2.2). The validity of this correlation however, was questioned by Bryant et al. (1995). They found experimental evidence for a rise in avulsion frequency with sedimentation rate, which decreases the proportion of overbank deposits by increasing the number of channel sandstone bodies.

The ancient river systems (table 2.3) all show a high proportion of overbank deposits, which is in agreement with the modern evidence. In case modern and ancient environments are compared, correction should be made for compaction of muds and organics. Compaction differences may explain that the proportion of overbank deposits in the Holocene Betuwe Formation (The Netherlands) is higher than in the ancient examples of table 2.3.

Lateral connectedness of channel sandstone bodies
It is obvious that the sandy channel-fills of anastomosing rivers will be preserved as a network of sandstone bodies in the stratigraphic record. For most examples in table 2.3 lateral connectedness of the studied channel sandstone bodies was reported. However, not every network of sandstone bodies encountered in the fossil record needs to be of anastomosing river origin, as contacts between sandstone bodies can be erosive and do not necessarily originate from confluence or bifurcation of contemporaneous active channels (see also Schumm et al. 1996).

The degree of connectedness of the individual sandstone bodies is an important variable in reservoir characterisation. Essential is planform information on the sandstone bodies. This means tight core control (e.g. Putnam & Oliver 1980; Hopkins et al. 1982; Putnam 1982, 1983), which may be aided by geomorphological evidence for the subsurface patterns (Bakker et al. 1989; Törnqvist 1993a; Berendsen et al. 1994). It is hard to prove whether several connected sandstone bodies were active channels contemporaneously. In the case of organic-rich Holocene to Late-Pleistocene deposits, ^{14}C-dating of the period of activity of the individual branches may provide conclusive evidence (e.g. Törnqvist 1993b, Törnqvist 1994). However in most cases, coexistence of channels can only be assumed on the basis of stratigraphic arguments (Currie et al. 1991; Bakker et al. 1989; Flores & Hanley 1984).

Table 2.3 Fluvial-architectural characteristics of interpreted subrecent and ancient anastomosing river systems

Study location and data source	Proportion of overbank deposits (in %)	Laterally connected channel sandstone bodies	w/t [a] of channel sandstone bodies
Upper Manville Subgroup (Alberta, Canada)[1]	no data	yes	9-50
Clifton Fm. (New Brunswick, Canada)[2]	70	unknown	≤73
Ft. Union Fm. (Wyoming, U.S.A.)[3]	45	yes	67
Ft. Union Fm. (Wyoming, U.S.A.)[4]	50-90	unknown	10
Cumberland Group (Nova Scotia, Canada)[5]	70	unknown	3-38
Tatrot/Pinjor Fm. (India)[6]	65	unknown	≥7-26
Wasatch Fm. (Wyoming, U.S.A.)[7]	80	yes	105-165
Raton Fm. (Colorado/New Mexico, U.S.A.)[8]	75	unknown	2-120
Vrijheid Fm. (South Africa)[9]	no data	yes	50-500
St. Mary R. Fm. (Alberta, Canada)[10]	85	inferred	8-27
Pitalito Basin (Colombia)[11]	no data	yes	no data
Cutler Fm. (New Mexico, U.S.A.)[12]	75	yes	≤40
Dakota Fm. (Utah, U.S.A.)[13]	60	unknown	7-20
Betuwe Fm. (The Netherlands)[14]	90	yes	7-25
Brazeau/Belly R. Fm. (Alberta, Canada)[15]	no data	yes	10

Data sources:
[1] Putnam & Oliver (1980), Smith & Putnam (1980), Putnam (1982, 1983); [2] Rust & Legun (1983); [3] Flores & Hanley (1984); [4] Johnson & Pierce (1990); [5] Rust et al. (1984); [6] Kumar & Tandon (1985); [7] Warwick & Flores (1987); [8] Flores & Pillmore (1987); [9] Cairncross et al. (1988); [10] Nadon (1988, 1994), Currie et al. (1991); [11] Bakker et al. (1989); [12] Eberth & Miall (1991); [13] Kirschbaum & McCabe (1992); [14] Törnqvist et al. (1993), Törnqvist (1993a); [15] Putnam (1993).

[a] Width/thickness ratio

53

Width/thickness ratio of channel sandstone bodies

The importance of the shape of channel deposits as an indicator of former lateral channel stability was stressed by Collinson (1978). Friend et al. (1979) and Friend (1983) used the width/thickness ratio of channel-fill bodies to infer former channel behaviour. Bodies with a width/thickness ratio < 15 were called ribbons and were thought to reflect fixed channels subject to switching by avulsion. Bodies with a width/thickness ratio > 15 were called sheets and were viewed as a product of lateral migration of a channel. Nadon (1994) proposed a width/thickness ratio of 30 as an upper limit of ribbons. Although both the values of 15 and 30 are arbitrary, the concept of reconstructing channel behaviour from the geometry of the channel-fill bodies is useful. The width/thickness ratio of a channel-fill body is determined by: (a) the width/depth ratio of the original channel, (b) a lateral migration component and (c) a vertical aggradation component (figure 2.11).

From table 2.3 it appears that the width/thickness ratio of the ancient and subrecent channel sandstone bodies varies widely and that many of them are not ribbons in the terminology of Friend (1983) (i.e. w/t < 15). Comparison with the width/depth ratios of modern anastomosing channels (table 2.2) shows that on average the width/thickness ratio of the channel sandstone bodies is significantly greater than the width/depth ratio of modern anastomosing channels. There are two possible explanations: (1) the width/depth ratio of the paleochannels was greater than those of modern anastomosing channels or, (2) the ribbons were partly formed by lateral accretion. In favour of this last explanation is the recognition of lateral accretion units in some of the channel sandstone bodies described by Rust & Legun (1983), Rust et al. (1984), Nadon (1994) and Kirschbaum & McCabe (1992). The data of table 2.3 do not indicate continued vertical accretion of the interpreted anastomosing paleochannels as was suggested for example by Smith & Smith (1980) (see also figure 2.8).

2.4.5 Final remarks

It must be realized that all we know about the sedimentary facies of anastomosing rivers is based on a limited number of facies descriptions of modern anastomosing rivers. These modern rivers represent a biased dataset because: (1) only small to medium-scale anastomosing rivers were investigated and (2) predominantly anastomosing rivers in humid climatic settings were investigated. Case studies of other modern anastomosing rivers are urgently needed.

Likewise, only a limited number of rock units in the stratigraphic record has been interpreted as being of anastomosing origin. This is due to: (1) the scale of anastomosing rivers and (2) the use of ambiguous definitions of this river type.

Anastomosing river systems are relatively large-scale geomorphological phenomena. Applying the term 'anastomosing' to a certain facies association in an ancient rock unit implies that the paleogeomorphology of the river system can be inferred. Problems arising from the application of geomorphological classifications to ancient fluvial sediments were discussed (among others) by Friend (1983) and Miall (1985). As exposure is limited and especially planform information on ancient river systems is generally scarce, conclusions

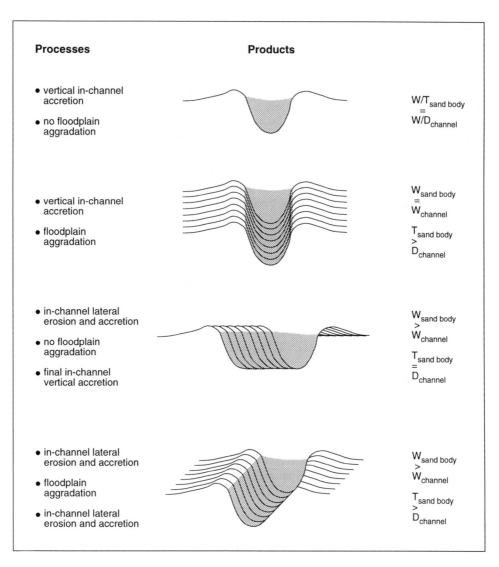

Processes	Products

• vertical in-channel accretion

• no floodplain aggradation

$W/T_\text{sand body}$
$=$
W/D_channel

• vertical in-channel accretion

• floodplain aggradation

$W_\text{sand body}$
$=$
W_channel

$T_\text{sand body}$
$>$
D_channel

• in-channel lateral erosion and accretion

• no floodplain aggradation

• final in-channel vertical accretion

$W_\text{sand body}$
$>$
W_channel

$T_\text{sand body}$
$=$
D_channel

• in-channel lateral erosion and accretion

• floodplain aggradation

• in-channel lateral erosion and accretion

$W_\text{sand body}$
$>$
W_channel

$T_\text{sand body}$
$>$
D_channel

Figure 2.11   Cross sections showing channel geometry, lateral and vertical migration determining the width/thickness ratio of a sandstone body.

on paleoriver morphology usually can only be drawn at the level of individual river branches.

In current definitions of the anastomosing river type, anastomosis (in the sense of multiple channels) and lateral stability of channels are often inseparably coupled. As was shown in the previous sections, these two properties of a fluvial system are driven by different process complexes (figure 2.7). As a result, not every laterally stable channel needs to be part of a multi-channel system (e.g. Nanson & Croke (1992, p. 477) and on the other hand, not every anastomosing, multi-channel system needs to consist of laterally stable channels (see section 2.2.3). However, in comprehensive studies on fluvial styles and facies models (e.g. Miall 1985, 1992) the single-channel straight river was neglected. As a result, ribbon sandstones often were automatically taken to represent anastomosing rivers, as no alternative model is available.

A 'straight river facies model' needs to be defined as a logical extension of the suite of braided and meandering river facies models in the low-energy domain. These models are mainly based on the lithofacies of channel sediments and can be applied at the channel-scale. In addition, the anastomosing river model should be further developed as a model for a large-scale fluvial depositional system. Reineck & Singh (1980, p. 305-306) for example, distinguish in this respect three 'fluvial associations' in which river deposits occur: (1) the alluvial fan association, (2) the floodplain association and (3) the coastal plain-delta association. Their coastal plain-delta association in fact represents the anastomosing river environment.

At present, there is no consensus on the question whether 'the anastomosing fluvial environment' includes 'the fluviodeltaic environment'. There is a tendency to consider the anastomosing river environment as a continental counterpart of the fluviodeltaic environment, but some workers applied the term anastomosing to subrecent and modern channels in deltaic environments (Peng 1990; King & Martini 1984), especially in the Rhine-Meuse delta in the Netherlands (Törnqvist 1993a; Weerts & Bierkens 1993; Bosch & Kok 1994; Weerts 1996; De Groot & De Gans 1996).

In conclusion, the application of the geomorphological term 'anastomosing' to fossil fluvial systems requires careful and often large-scale paleogeographical reconstruction. In practice, subrecent anastomosing river environments offer by far the best opportunities to realize this. In ancient rocks, geomorphological interpretation of fluvial facies will often be restricted to a classification of individual paleochannels as being braided, meandering or straight and sometimes even a less precise reconstruction will be the best attainable. In these cases a purely descriptive geometric classification of ribbon and sheet sandstone bodies (e.g. Friend 1983) is an alternative.

2.5 Summary

In presently popular definitions of anastomosing rivers, lateral stability of channels is indissolubly coupled with its multi-channel character. However, the mixing of channel-scale properties and large-scale fluvial geomorphology in one definition seems conceptually wrong. Besides, it is unpractical in sedimentological applications. Therefore I favour redefinition: (1) at the channel-scale, the term 'straight' should be used to describe laterally stable channels having a sinuosity index lower than 1.3, (2) whereas at a larger scale, rivers should be called anastomosing if: *a river is composed of several interconnected channels, which enclose floodbasins.* Furthermore, a complex of delta distributaries is considered as a special form of an anastomosing river.

Accepting these definitions, the following assumptions concerning the genesis of anastomosing rivers can be made:

1. Anastomosing rivers are formed by channel avulsion. A high avulsion frequency is necessary for the continued existence of anastomosing rivers.
2. A high avulsion frequency is favoured by a high aggradation rate and a low floodplain gradient. In addition, short-term locally acting triggers influence the process of avulsion.
3. The often observed high lateral stability of individual channels in anastomosing rivers, is caused by low stream power in combination with resistant banks.
4. The occurrence of anastomosing rivers is not tied to a certain climate.
5. In specific cases, climatic change as well as tectonic movements cause the development of anastomosing rivers.

The characteristics of anastomosing river deposits are:

1. The fluvial architecture is characterized by a large proportion of overbank deposits (probably 50 to 90%) which encase laterally connected channel sandstone bodies.
2. The geometry of the channel sandstone bodies is frequently characterized by a ribbon-shape and a flat top.
3. The channel deposits predominantly consist of sandstone which may fine upward, but also can be quite homogeneous. In the last case, the sandstone may pass abruptly into overlying mudrock. Fine-grained residual channel-fills are frequently small or absent.
4. Abundant crevasse splay deposits and thick natural levee deposits are common.
5. Lacustrine deposits and coal commonly occur in association with the overbank deposits.

It should be noted that none of these characteristics is unique to anastomosing river deposits. In arid settings, natural levee and crevasse splay deposits may be poorly developed, while lacustrine deposits and coal may be absent.

3 Channel hydraulics, sediment transport and floodplain sedimentation in a temperate humid anastomosing river system (upper Columbia River, western Canada)

3.1 Introduction

Unlike many other anastomosing rivers, the upper Columbia River in western Canada has a montane setting (figure 3.1). The narrow floodplain is flanked by glacier-capped mountains and tributary valleys from which alluvial fans protrude into the valley, obstructing the axial anastomosing river system. The system is laterally restricted ($\pm$ 1.5 km wide), but longitudinally continuous for at least 100 km. Within the anastomosing reach, the alluvial valley floor has a very gentle grade, averaging around 11.5 cm/km.

In a speculative paper, Rutten (1967) attributed the flat, gently graded valley floor to ponding behind beaver dams. In later papers, the blocking effect of cross-valley alluvial fans was held responsible for upstream aggradation and low gradients. Galay et al. (1984) believed that ponding behind the alluvial fans led to the formation of large lakes in the upper Columbia Valley, which gradually became filled up by river-dominated 'bird's-foot' deltas of which the present anastomosing river system represents the final stage. Smith (1983) proposed a more dynamic model in which the rise in base-level due to aggrading alluvial fans created a backwater effect inducing low gradients, high sedimentation rates and frequent avulsions. Smith's model was substantiated by sedimentological data, but few quantitative data on the hydraulic and sedimentary processes were provided.

My objective in this chapter is to examine the drive behind avulsions in the upper Columbia River, by a quantitative study of the hydraulic and sedimentary processes. The data on avulsion frequency and floodplain sedimentation rates result from radiocarbon dating of organic sediments and from direct measurements using sediment traps. Measurements of discharge and determination of other hydraulic variables, enabled calculations of stream power as well as sediment transport. The study site was located roughly halfway along the anastomosing reach of the upper Columbia River, 9 km upstream of Parson, British Columbia (figure 3.2). All data were collected in a cross profile which spanned the entire floodplain.

Hydraulic data for natural low-energy rivers are scarce (e.g. Van den Berg 1995, p. 269). Hydraulic and sedimentary processes in such rivers are usually inferred from measurements in flumes and irrigation ditches. Important differences however, can be expected in natural rivers, due to the effect of vegetation and variable channel morphology. Especially now that conservation practice in developed countries tends toward restoration of natural floodplain vegetation and channel morphology, hydraulic data from natural rivers are needed to evaluate the impact of such measures on discharge capacity and geomorphological processes. In this respect, the upper Columbia River offers unique opportunities: its hydrograph is not modified by man, while it has a forested catchment and an uninhabited, vegetated floodplain, where river flow is not restricted by artificial structures. Despite its natural state it is easily accessible over its full length.

Figure 3.1   *The anastomosing upper Columbia River. View looking southeast and upriver with photo taken from above the study reach.*

3.2   General background

Regional geology and geomorphology
The upper Columbia River is located in the Rocky Mountain Trench, a major valley which separates the Rocky Mountains in the northeast from the Purcell Mountains in the southwest (figure 3.2). In the anastomosing reach, the flat valley floor has an elevation of around 790 m asl (= above sea level). It is unclear, whether this part of the Trench is a truly tectonic feature or just an erosional valley (e.g. Geological Survey of Canada 1972, 1979a, 1979b, 1980).

The Columbia River has its source in Columbia Lake and flows northwestward through the Trench. To the south, near Canal Flats, a cross-valley alluvial fan forms a low divide (at $\pm$ 815 m asl) between the upper Columbia and Kootenay River catchments. The major tributaries to the upper Columbia River drain the Purcell Mountains, which primarily consist of Proterozoic shales, sandstones, conglomerates and slates. Locally, the Purcell Mountains rise above 3000 m asl and glaciers surround the highest peaks. Minor creeks drain the lower Beaverfoot and Brisco Ranges of the Rocky Mountains, which are free of ice with a number of summits around 2700 m asl. These ranges are for a large part composed of calcareous slates and shales, limestones and

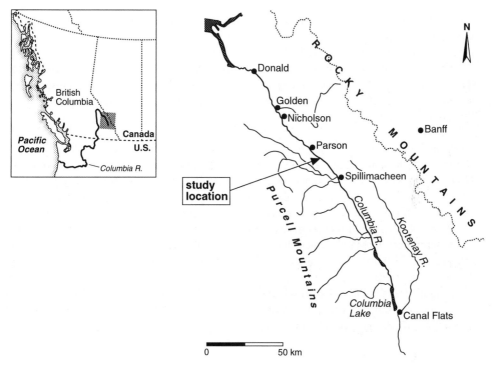

Figure 3.2   The location of the study site in southeast British Columbia, Canada.

dolomites, of Paleozoic age. These calcareous formations also crop out in a narrow band directly on the other (southwest) side of the valley floor (Geological Survey of Canada 1979a, 1979b, 1980).

The Quaternary fill of the Trench predominantly consists of unconsolidated silts, sands and gravels, partly of glacial, glaciofluvial and glaciolacustrine origin. A basal till was deposited on the Trench floor during the Late Wisconsin glaciation. Subsequently, during glacier retreat, a huge glacial lake formed in the Trench, due to ice-damming in the north near Donald and a sediment valley fill ± 25 km south of Canal Flats. Terraces of thick lacustrine silt and deltaic gravel flank parts of the present floodplain, indicating maximum paleolake levels of 900 m asl. Especially south of Spillimacheen, glaciolacustrine silts form up to 50 m high cliffs above the recent floodplain (Sawicki & Smith 1992). Lacustrine deposits, covered by deltaic deposits, also underlie the alluvium of the present anastomosing river system (Smith 1983, figs. 8 and 9).

Climate
The upper Columbia Valley has a humid continental climate with cold winters and warm summers. In January, average temperatures on the valley bottom are near -10° C, while July average temperatures are around 17° C, except for the southern part of the valley were they reach values of about 22° C. Precipitation falls all year round, but the annual

amount decreases upvalley from about 475 mm at Golden to near 300 mm at Invermere. At Golden, December and January are the wettest months, when precipitation falls in the form of snow. Upvalley, June rainfall becomes important.

Higher up in the mountains however, precipitation is much greater. The Purcell Mountains are known for deep and prolonged snow covers. At the end of most winters the equivalent of 500 to 750 mm of rain lies over the massif in snowpack form (Hare & Thomas 1974, p. 111).

Hydrology

Above the Nicholson gauging station (figure 3.2) the drainage area of the upper Columbia River is 6660 km^2, with an annual mean discharge of 108 m^3/s (Water Survey of Canada 1991a). The water discharge of the upper Columbia River principally fluctuates in response to rainfall and snowmelt, glacial meltwater constituting only a minor component of the total discharge. Minimum discharge occurs during the winter, usually in the period from December to March when there is ice in the river. Minimum monthly mean discharge is 22.9 m^3/s in February (Water Survey of Canada 1991a). In the spring, snowmelt and rains cause a sharp rise and a peak in discharge in June or July (figure 3.3). Maximum monthly mean discharge is 320 m^3/s in July (Water Survey of Canada 1991a) and bankfull conditions are reached almost yearly (figure 2.3b). During the rest of the summer, discharge gradually decreases.

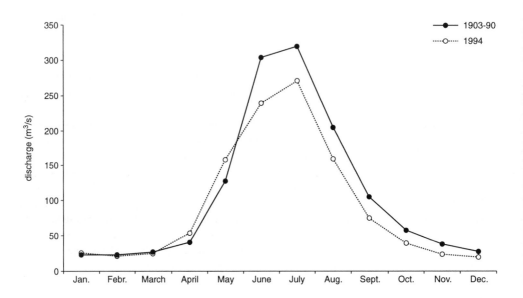

Figure 3.3   *Mean monthly discharges for the Columbia River at Nicholson (B.C.) for the period 1903-90 and for 1994 (Water Survey of Canada 1991a, unpublished data).*

3.3   Methods

Fieldwork was carried out in the Columbia Valley in 1994 during the period May-July, to enable measurements around bankfull discharge and during overbank flooding. The cross profile in which the data were collected was situated in a reach where the anastomosing morphology is best developed. The studied profile ran across the floodplain from the McKeeman Creek alluvial fan to the opposite valley side, thereby crossing six channels of variable dimensions (figure 3.4). Due to blockage by a large beaver dam, the Hogranch Channel experienced no significant discharge. Hydraulic data were gathered for the other five channels.

The floodplain topography of the profile was levelled relative to an arbitrary datum, whereas echo soundings provided data on submerged channel morphology. Apart from cross sections, longitudinal sections (80 m long) in the middle of channels were run to gather data on variation in channel depth and large bedforms. The echo sounder was mounted on an inflatable boat with outboard motor. The 192 kHz echo sounder was used with a pulse-width of 30 μs and a cone angle of 8°, providing a vertical resolution of about 2.5 cm.

Thirty-four borings were carried out in the profile, using an Edelman-auger and a gouge. Since this equipment performs poorly in water-saturated sandy sediments, five vibracores were collected later (May 1995) of the sandy channel-fill of channel 4 (figure 3.5), using the equipment described by Smith (1984). The borings were spaced such that all natural levees, crevasse splays and floodbasins traversed by the profile were covered. In the floodbasins, boreholes were probably spaced too far apart to reveal the true lithological variation in the subsurface. However, the data adequately describe the bank material of the channels and enabled strategical sampling of organic material for radiocarbon dating. Nearly all borings reached a depth of around 8.0 m below the surface, while sediment properties were described every 10 cm.

Nine samples of humic clay and peat were extracted from boreholes for ^{14}C-age determination. Seven of these samples originated from directly underneath natural levee and crevasse splay deposits genetically associated with the channels, in order to determine their age [see Berendsen (1982, p. 114-118) for a discussion of this sampling strategy] and to calculate natural levee sedimentation rates. The other two samples were taken from floodbasin peat and humic clay at greater depth (7.6-7.9 m) to enable calculation of long-term sedimentation rates. All samples were split into two or three subsamples, which were separately pretreated and dated, to check the accuracy of their ^{14}C-ages. Together the subsamples yielded twenty radiocarbon ages of which five represent bulk organic sediment, nine represent the organic residue > 425 μm, and six ages represent sets of selected terrestrial macrofossils [see section 5.3 and Törnqvist et al. (1992) for selection procedure of macrofossils]. Bulk sediment subsamples and subsamples with the organic residue > 425 μm were dated conventionally at the Centre for Isotope Research (Groningen). Terrestrial macrofossils required AMS dating, which was carried out at the Robert J. van de Graaff Laboratory (Utrecht) and the Centre for Isotope Research (Groningen).

To estimate the amount of sediment deposited during the 1994 flood season, a field method used and tested by Asselman & Middelkoop (1995) was applied. Fifty sediment traps, consisting of artificial grass mats were installed in the profile. The artificial grass was made of 1.5 cm long plastic blades attached to a pliable (plastic) base. The artificial grass was supposed to replicate the hydraulic roughness of the floodplain surface. Field observations by Asselman (pers. comm. 1998) indicate that this assumption is justified. Experiments by Mansikkaniemi (1985) show only insignificant differences in trapping efficiency between mats with different types of roughness elements. The mats measured 50×50 cm and were pinned to the floodplain, using five 20 cm long nails for each mat. Spacing between the mats in the profile varied between 4.5 and 213.5 m. Since sedimentation rates were expected to decrease exponentially away from the channels (e.g. Asselman & Middelkoop 1995), mats were spaced more closely on the natural levees than in the floodbasins. After flooding, the mats were collected, air-dried and weighed. The precisely known weight of the mats was subtracted to determine the amount of trapped sediment. The density of the upper soil layer that was used to convert the sediment weights to thicknesses was 1016 kg/m^3 (determined by measuring dry weight of undisturbed samples of surface sediments from various parts of the upper Columbia River floodplain). As a check on these sediment thicknesses, the pre-flooded surface was marked by a small patch of orange paint and a nick in a long nail pinned next to the mats, to enable direct measurement of the thickness of freshly deposited sediment.

To determine bankfull discharge as a basis for the calculation of stream power and sediment transport, flow velocity measurements were carried out in the five channels with significant discharge. Velocity profiles were measured from the inflatable boat, which was attached to a wire rope stretched across the channel. A small propeller current meter (type OTT C2) mounted on a finned probe was lowered with a winch. Stream velocities were measured at 0.25, 0.50, 1.00, 2.00 and 4.00 m above the bottom (if applicable) and often an additional measurement was carried out near the water surface. Velocity profiles were measured at breaks in the bed morphology of the channel cross sections (figure 3.14a and b). Spatial integration over the channel cross section yielded total channel discharge. The number of velocity profiles per channel ranged from four (water surface width 21.5 m) to fifteen (water surface width 56.0 m), depending on channel size, cross-sectional morphology and stage (figure 3.14a and b). For each of the channels, five series of velocity profiles were measured at five different stages near bankfull.

Figure 3.4   (facing page) Geomorphological map of the studied reach of the upper Columbia River. Flow is from right to left. (Based on 1:10,000 air photos of the British Columbia Hydro and Power Authority, taken 2 October 1978, with the river at medium stage).

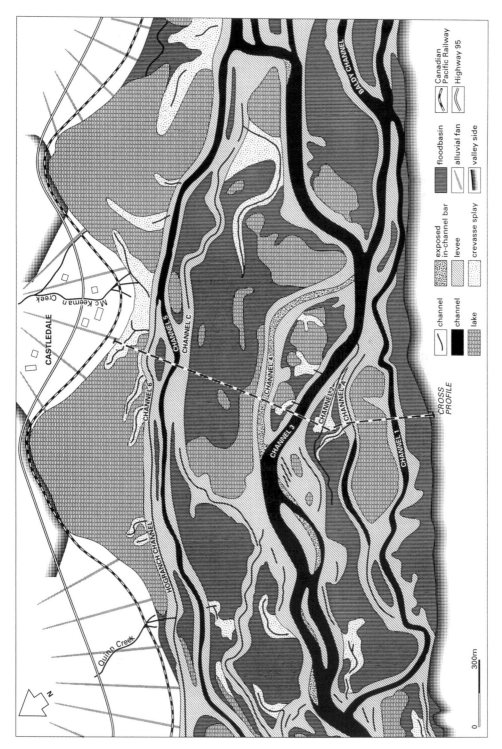

CASTLEDALE

McKeeman Creek

Quinn Creek

HOGRANCH CHANNEL

CHANNEL 6

CHANNEL 5

CHANNEL C

CHANNEL 4

CHANNEL 3

CHANNEL 2

CHANNEL 4

CHANNEL 2

CHANNEL 1

BALDY CHANNEL

CROSS PROFILE

N

0   300m

channel

channel

lake

exposed
in-channel bar

levee

crevasse splay

floodbasin

alluvial fan

valley side

Canadian
Pacific Railway

Highway 95

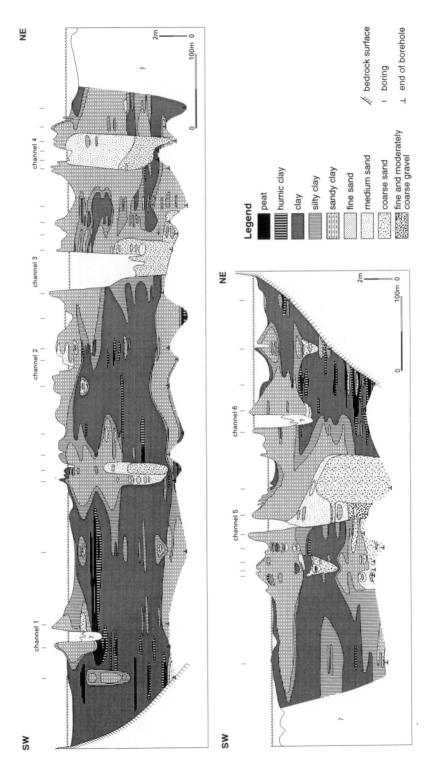

Legend

- peat
- humic clay
- clay
- silty clay
- sandy clay
- fine sand
- medium sand
- coarse sand
- fine and moderately coarse gravel

- bedrock surface
- boring
- end of borehole

Figure 3.5   Borehole cross section of the upper Columbia River floodplain. Location of the cross section shown in figure 3.4.

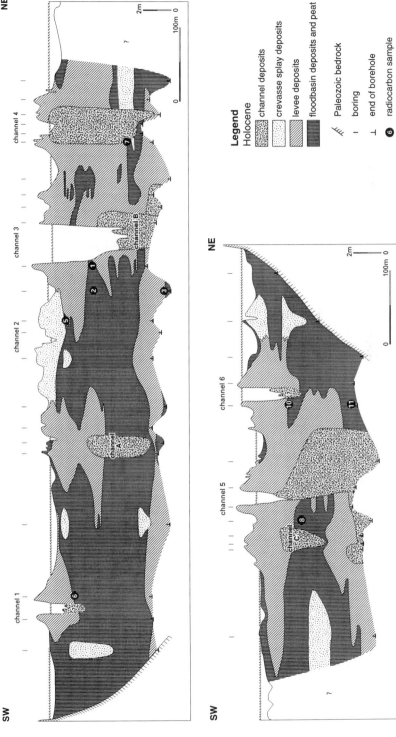

Figure 3.6   Genetical interpretation of the borehole cross section in figure 3.5. Locations of radiocarbon samples are also shown.

Grab samples of bed material were taken with a Van Veen grab sampler (Oele et al. 1983, p. 357). In each channel cross section, a series of three to seven grab samples was taken twice during the period of field research. Sampling locations were more or less evenly distributed over the wet channel perimeter, within the cross section. Laboratory grain size analysis were carried out on a total of forty-four grab samples by the standard sieving/pipette method (McManus 1988).

3.4   Results

3.4.1   Radiocarbon dates

Initially, it was attempted to obtain reliable ages of the fluvial sediments by conventional dating of bulk samples of organic sediments from the studied cross section (see figure 3.6 for sampling locations). However, the results were mistrusted because there were various inconsistencies in the data set of fourteen ages. To check the accuracy of the data set, six additional radiocarbon ages were obtained by AMS dating of selected terrestrial macrofossils from the same cores. Finally, only these dates (subsamples 2c, 3c, 5c, 6c, 8c, 10c) and the date of subsample 7b were accepted, while all the other dates were rejected (all dates are listed in table 3.1). Below I will discuss all radiocarbon dates carried out for this study.

Most of the collected samples consisted of deposits with organic material of variable nature in a predominantly clayey matrix. Carbon contents were below 5 %. In addition to the autochthonous carbon formed during deposition, Mook & Streurman (1983, p. 50-51) mention four alternative sources of carbon for this type of samples, which may cause erroneous ages: (1) resistant (allochthonous) carbon which is part of the deposited matrix, (2) reworked or eroded allochthonous organic matter, (3) infiltrated younger carbon (e.g. fulvic and humic acids), and (4) roots from higher levels. This last-mentioned source of error was believed to be relatively unimportant in our case, because of the high sedimentation rates (Smith 1983).

In addition to these four types of contamination, the hard water effect must be mentioned, which means contamination by uptake of 'old' carbon from dissolved $CaCO_3$ from the catchment by aquatic species present in the sample. Usually, this effect is considered not to lead to apparent ageing of organic deposits in shallow floodbasins and lakes, due to the fast equilibration of the dissolved inorganic carbon with the atmospheric CO_2. On the other hand, due to the proximity of the carbonate-rich hinterland (section 3.2), it was felt the situation could be different in the upper Columbia Valley.

Table 3.1 Radiocarbon dates from the upper Columbia River floodplain

Sub-sample	Laboratory nr.	¹⁴C-age (yr BP)	Depth below surface (cm)	Median cal. age [a] (yr BP)	C [b] (%)	Material
1a	GrN-18110	1330 ± 60	410-415	1241	2.9	humic clay (bulk)
1b	GrN-21194	1880 ± 200	415-420	1826	0.6	humic clay (fraction >425 μm)
2a	GrN-18111	modern [c]	244-252		1.7	humic clay (bulk)
2b	GrN-21195	1740 ± 170	252-256	1667	0.9	humic clay (fraction >425 μm)
2c	UtC-5672	1140 ± 70	256-261	1057		Coleoptera fragments, a bud and leaves
3a	GrN-18112	3900 ± 50	769-774	4325	4.8	clayey peat (bulk)
3b	GrN-21196	3790 ± 110	774-780	4170	1.3	humic clay (fraction >425 μm)
3c	UtC-5673	4026 ± 42	788-792	4495		7 *Scirpus lacustris* nuts
5b	GrN-21336	830 ± 150	185-192	783	0.3	humic clay (fraction >425 μm)
5c	GrA-4321	430 ± 80	192-200	471		2 *Carex* sp. nuts, Coleoptera fragments
6b	GrN-21337	370 ± 60	260-269	388	2.2	clayey peat (fraction >425 μm)
6c	GrA-5267	500 ± 50	269-278	533		1 *Scirpus lacustris* nut, 25 *Carex* sp. nuts
7a	GrN-18113	2600 ± 50	620-626	2703	2.6	clayey peat (bulk)
7b	GrN-21197	2650 ± 150	626-635	2754	0.7	humic clay (fraction >425 μm)
8b	GrN-21338	1350 ± 120	275-283	1261	0.4	humic clay (fraction >425 μm)
8c	UtC-5674	1452 ± 41	283-292	1342		10 *Carex* sp. nuts, 1 *Alnus* nut, 5 *Potentilla* sp. seeds
10b	GrN-21339	980 ± 100	324-331	910	1.1	humic clay (fraction >425 μm)
10c	UtC-5675	1033 ± 48	331-338	941		Coleoptera fragments, 1 *Alisma plantago-aquatica* fruit, 1 *Salix* bud, 1 *Myrica gale* nut
11a	GrN-18114	4950 ± 60	783-790	5700	4.1	humic clay (bulk)
11b	GrN-21198	4000 ± 160	790-796	4460	1.1	humic clay (fraction >425 μm)

[a] The Groningen calibration program (version CAL20) was used (Van der Plicht 1993). The degree of smoothing of the calibration curve was based on Törnqvist & Bierkens (1994). For bulk subsamples and subsamples consisting of the fraction >425 μm, $\sigma_s = 200$ was applied. For the subsamples consisting of selected terrestrial macrofossils, $\sigma_s = 60$ was applied.

[b] Carbon content by weight.

[c] 104.1 ± 0.65%

To investigate the contaminating influence of the fine-grained matrix, each sample of a first set of five was split into two subsamples: one consisting of all sampled sediment (subsamples 1a, 2a, 3a, 7a and 11a), and a second consisting of the fraction > 425 μm (subsamples 1b, 2b, 3b, 7b and 11b). Chemical pretreatment of all subsamples involved an acid treatment only (Mook & Streurman, 1983). It was hypothesized that the fine fraction contained a relatively large amount of allochthonous carbon. However, only subsample 11a had a significantly older radiocarbon age, whereas subsamples 1a and 2a even yielded much younger ages. Since the samples 1 and 2 should yield approximately the same ages (figure 3.6), the ages of the subsamples 1a and 2a seemed suspect.

Based on these results, dating of the fraction > 425 μm of the bulk samples was considered to be most accurate, although less precise due to the lower amount of carbon. Therefore, of a second series of four subsamples (5b, 6b, 8b and 10b) only the fraction > 425 μm was dated after acid treatment. However, the ages of the subsamples 5b and 6b of this series were inconsistent. As can be seen in figure 3.6, sample 6 was taken at a lower stratigraphic level than sample 5, yet subsample 5b appeared to be much older than subsample 6b. In addition, a systematic ageing effect due to the hard water effect or the presence of coarse reworked organic debris in the dated subsamples could not be excluded.

Finally, to circumvent all the above-mentioned sources of error (Törnqvist et al. 1992), AMS dating of six subsamples consisting of selected terrestrial macrofossils was carried out (subsamples 2c, 3c, 5c, 6c, 8c and 10c). In theory, terrestrial macrofossils can also be reworked. However, a study by Törnqvist et al. (1992) suggested that critical selection can minimize that risk. The results from the present study showed that there were no systematic ageing effects in the > 425 μm bulk subsamples. Two of them (5b and 2b) were apparently too old, but others were reasonably in agreement (3b, 6b, 8b and 10b) (especially when accounting for slight differences in depth within the sampled cores).

In the next sections, only the macrofossil dates (subsamples 2c, 3c, 5c, 6c, 8c, 10c) will be used for reconstruction of channel chronology and calculation of sedimentation rates. Additionally, the date of subsample 7b is accepted in absence of macrofossil dates from these samples. This is more or less justified by the very close agreement of the radiocarbon ages of the subsamples 7a and 7b and their stratigraphic position with respect to the AMS-dated subsamples 2c and 3c. Only calibrated dates (table 3.1) were used for reconstruction of channel chronology and calculation of sedimentation rates.

3.4.2 Channel morphology, bank vegetation and channel chronology

The six Columbia River channels in the cross profile have quite different dimensions (table 3.2). Although five channels have significant discharge, channel 3 is by far dominant, accounting for about 87 % of the total flow at high stage. Over most of its anastomosing reach the upper Columbia River consists of a main channel and a variable number of much smaller parallel channels.

Table 3.2 Dimensions of the studied channels

	Width [a] (m)	Depth [b] (m)	w/d ratio (-)
Channel 1	19.30	2.12	9.1
Channel 2	24.80	1.08	23.0
Channel 3	56.03	5.85	9.6
Channel 4	20.70	1.04	19.9
Channel 5	18.63	3.17	5.9
Channel 6	18.00	2.90	6.2

[a] Bankfull width.
[b] Maximum depth with respect to the bankfull level.

All of the studied channels have a low sinuosity index and can be classified as straight channels (section 2.2.4). In general, the channels are relatively deep and narrow, having width/depth ratios of less then 10, but there are notable exceptions (channels 2 and 4). The wet perimeter of the channels typically has a trapezium shape (figure 3.14a and b).

The ages of some channels were determined from radiocarbon dates of organic material sampled below the levee deposits next to the channels. Other channel ages were estimated from the stratigraphic position of their levee deposits relative to radiocarbon samples collected nearby in the cross section (figure 3.6).

The main channel at the study site is estimated to date from 750 cal. yr BP *(channel 3)*. The profile crosses a straight reach of this channel, which showed signs of active widening by slumping of its northeast bank. This process appeared to be facilitated by the structure of the bank: the cohesive levee deposits are underlain by sand of a former channel belt (channel B) into which the present channel has scoured (figure 3.6). Recent bank failure due to undercutting, resulted in a relatively low and narrow natural levee, without trees. Within the channel, totally submerged trees which had slid down to the bottom of the channel were identified by echo sounding. Little upstream, this levee is cut by two recent crevasse channels. In contrast, the southwest levee is intact and hosts trees and shrubs.

Figure 3.7   *Vegetated side-bars invading channel 4. Note the mud-draped dunes in the channel.*

This reach of the main channel has bypassed a much older channel, which has almost completely filled up with sand *(channel 4)* and accounts for only about 3% of the bankfull discharge of the system. This channel has a relatively high width/depth ratio (table 3.2), while the associated channel sand body has a low width/thickness ratio of around 7. A radiocarbon date from material below the thick southwest levee suggests a beginning of overbank sedimentation of this channel around 2750 cal. yr BP. Northeast of the channel however, its levee and basal crevasse splay deposits are finer and considerably less deep. Subsample 7b was probably overlain by a scoured contact of the coarse-grained part of the crevasse splay. Thus, channel 4 is likely to be much younger and its formation may roughly date from around 2000 cal. yr BP (when counting with long-term floodplain sedimentation rates given in section 3.4.3). The dimensions of the channel-fill suggest a former channel comparable to the present main channel. The filled-up channel is still wide, but shallow. The thalweg sways between side-bars which are overgrown with a pioneer vegetation of *Equisetum* and *Salix* shoots (figure 3.7). Mature trees grow on the narrow (10-15 m wide) levees. At the upstream entrance of the channel, the thick stem of a large fallen tree hinders the flow entering the channel. A partially buried log jam has blocked the channel. Sandy traction load continues to be deposited in the thalweg, while deposition of sandy clay dominates on the vegetated bars.

Figure 3.8   A distal sandy crevasse-splay next to the lower reach of channel 2.

A shallow crevasse channel *(channel 2)* which debouches into a floodbasin, parallels the main channel to the southwest. In the future, this relatively large crevasse may develop further and cause an avulsion of the main channel. In 1994 however, only little more than 1% of the Columbia River discharge entered this channel near bankfull stage. The channel has slightly incised the sandy splay, which is overgrown with *Salix* shrubs and grasses. An estimate of 500 years of crevasse splay sedimentation (based on subsample 5c) is obviously too high, since splay formation is known to have started only around 1970 (D.G. Smith pers. comm. 1997). The misleading age can be attributed to scour at the base of the splay, which has a concave shape (figure 3.6). Upstream of the profile, the crevasse channel is slightly narrower and up to 1 m deeper, having steeper banks with older trees. Downstream of the cross profile, an old crevasse from channel A has captured the flow (figure 3.4). Renewed splay deposition takes place along this reactivated channel (figure 3.8). In the summer of 1994, the remains of several beaver dams obstructed the flow in channel 2.

A deeper channel is located near the southwest margin of the floodplain *(channel 1)*, accounting for about 4% of the flow at high stage. The age of subsample 6c suggests that sedimentation from this channel started here soon after 530 cal. yr BP. This channel had bypassed the now abandoned channel A, and seems to be actively enlarging its capacity. In the cross profile undercutting and failure of the southwest bank was observed, while at some other places, bank scour was associated with stuck driftwood forcing the thalweg to

Figure 3.9   Log jam in channel 5.

the opposite bank. Longitudinal echo sounding profiles revealed woody debris on the bottom of the channel, which was also found in grab samples.

   Channel 5 is the oldest channel in the cross profile and its levees are the highest points of the floodplain. Near bankfull stage, this channel carries 5% of the total discharge. The profile crosses this channel in a bend, that has an asymmetrical cross section. Scroll topography characterizes the inner bend levee. The borehole data and surface morphology suggest lateral as well as vertical accretion of channel 5. The beginning of sedimentation of this channel could only be crudely estimated at 2850 cal. yr BP. At a later stage channel C, which is abandoned, has been active simultaneously with channel 5. A large log-jam was found in channel 5, 200 m downstream of the cross section. Over the full width of the channel and over a length of at least 50 m, hundreds of logs were densely packed together in all orientations (figure 3.9). At the site of the log-jam, channel width had nearly doubled, due to increased bank scour. The difference in water surface elevation over the log jam was in the order of 0.1 m.

   The levee deposits of the Hogranch Channel *(channel 6)*, which obviously overlie the deeply buried levee of channel 5, suggest a considerably younger age for this channel. Subsample 10c indicates a beginning of sedimentation soon after 940 cal. yr BP. In 1994 a large beaver dam completely blocked this channel (figure 3.10). Strange enough, water ponded behind the dam on the downstream side of the valley, indicating further blockage of the channel downstream and lateral supply of water from a small tributary draining the Beaverfoot Range. The massive dam was still actively maintained by the beavers and

Figure 3.10   Beaver dam in channel 6.

allowed very little seepage of water, with an elevation head of about one meter. The floodbasin northeast of this channel also experienced elevated water levels due to the dam.

Estimated periods of activity of the channels and paleochannels in the cross section are given in figure 3.11. It must be noted that probably not all of the paleochannels in the subsurface were identified by augering. Although figure 3.11 gives us only a crude picture, a few points are clear:

1. Coexistence of multiple channels has been a consistent feature of the upper Columbia River since at least 2850 cal. yr BP.
2. Avulsion seems to be a regularly recurring phenomenon in the upper Columbia River, with at least nine channels within the valley cross-sectional research site having formed in the past 3000 years.
3. The lifetime of channels is highly variable ranging from 800 to at least 3000 years.

Most obvious however from the data above, is the rapid aggradation of the upper Columbia River floodplain, which is the subject of the next section.

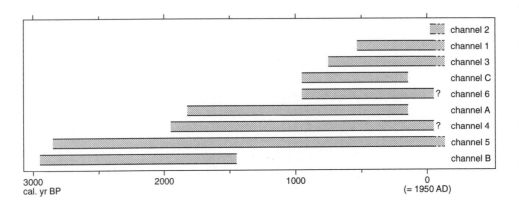

Figure 3.11   Estimated time periods of activity of active channels and paleochannels in the studied floodplain cross section.

3.4.3   Floodplain sedimentation rates

Radiocarbon dates were used to calculate long-term sedimentation rates (table 3.3). These rates include compaction, which is believed not to be too dramatic since peat is nearly absent and the organic matter content is low in the sediments considered. The long-term average floodplain sedimentation rate of 1.7 mm/yr deviates strongly from a previous value of 6 mm/yr calculated by Smith (1983). The latter value was based on the burial depth of a volcanic ash layer. The ash was encountered at a depth of 13.7 m near the present study site and was believed to be Bridge River ash which was elsewhere dated at 2500 BP. Smith (pers. comm. 1998) probably wrongly identified the ash. It is likely to have been the Mazama tephra, which dates at 6800 BP. This age would give a sedimentation rate not far from 1.7 mm/yr.

Levee sedimentation rates in the cross profile appear to be about twice as high on average as floodbasin sedimentation rates. Levee sedimentation rates vary as a function of the distance from the channel. I arrived at values of 3 to 5 mm/yr for the proximal levee environment (based on subsamples 6c and 10c) and values little higher than 2 mm/yr for the distal levee environment (based on subsamples 2c and 8c). The youngest levees (subsamples 5c and 6c) show the highest sedimentation rates and it is realized that initial rates associated with avulsion may even be higher (e.g. Smith et al. 1989; Smith & Pérez-Arlucea 1994).

Table 3.3 Long-term sedimentation rates in the cross section

Sub-sample	depth below surface (cm)	median age [a] (cal. yr BP)	2σ-age [b] (cal. yr BP)	minimum sed. rate [c] (mm/cal. yr)	median sed. rate [d] (mm/cal. yr)	maximum sed. rate [e] (mm/cal. yr)
					Average	
3c	788 - 792	4539	4414 - 4634	1.70	1.74	1.79
					Floodbasin	
3c	788 - 792	4539	4414 - 4634			
2c	256 - 261	1101	954 - 1254			
(3c - 2c):	527 - 536	3438	3160 - 3680	1.43	1.55	1.70
					Levee	
2c	256 - 261	1101	954 - 1254	2.04	2.35	2.74
5c	192 - 200	515	354 - 634	>3.03 [e]	>3.81 [e]	>5.65 [e]
6c	269 - 278	577	494 - 634	4.24	4.74	5.63
7b	626 - 635	2798	2414 - 3154	>1.98 [e]	>2.25 [e]	>2.63 [e]
8c	283 - 292	1386	1322 - 1454	1.95	2.07	2.21
10c	331 - 338	985	886 - 1074	3.08	3.40	3.81

[a] In this case: BP = before 1994.
[b] Based on minimum depth and maximum (2σ) age.
[c] Based on average depth and median age.
[d] Based on maximum depth and minimum (2σ) age.
[e] The given rates represent a minimum since the base of the levee is scoured. The radiocarbon dates from directly below the base (subsamples 5c and 7b) are considerably older than the scoured base.

The short-term sedimentation rates measured with sediment traps turned out to be much lower than the long-term rates mentioned above. This was due to the relatively low magnitude of the 1994 flood (figure 3.3), which barely exceeded the bankfull stage and did not affect higher parts of the levees. The flood level of 1994 was exceeded in 72 of the 87 years on record in the period 1903-90 (Water Survey of Canada 1991 unpubl. data). On average a 0.8 mm thick veneer of sediment was deposited on the floodplain by the 1994 flood. The measured sediment thicknesses within the profile however, were highly variable ranging from 0 to 4.7 mm (figure 3.12).

Levees that were inundated during the 1994 flood experienced a considerable amount of sedimentation immediately next to the channel, with a marked decrease further away from the channel. These peaks in sedimentation occurred on the northeast levees of channels 2 and 4. Apart from these peaks, in the rest of the profile a reversed pattern of sedimentation could be observed: most sedimentation occurred away from the channels in the floodbasins, while little or no sedimentation was recorded on the levees. Similar patterns and comparable amounts of sedimentation were measured by Asselman & Middelkoop (1995) for floods of the rivers Rhine and Meuse. Following their interpretation, the peaks in sedimentation next to the channels 2 and 4 can be attributed to

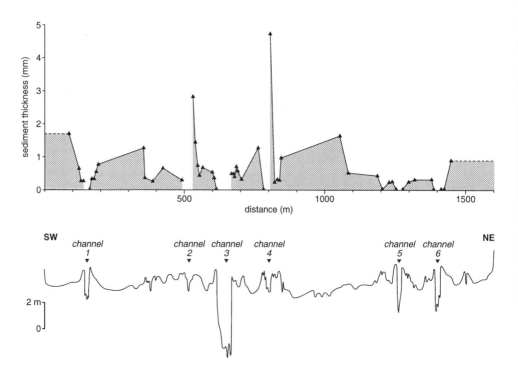

Figure 3.12   Sediment deposition from the 1994 flood in the studied cross profile.

sediment diffusion from the channels during short inundation at maximum discharge. In the remainder of the profile however, the amount of sedimentation was obviously related to inundation time which lasted longest (> 80 days) in the deepest floodbasins, while the highest levees stayed completely dry.

3.4.4   Bankfull discharge, flow velocities and bed material

In this study, bankfull discharge is used as a reference flow for calculations of stream power, channel roughness and sediment transport. Bankfull stage here is defined by the break in slope between the steep channel bank and the flatter surface of the levee (figure 3.13). In the case of a difference in elevation between the break in slope for the two banks, the lowest level was chosen. According to this definition, bankfull discharge more or less coincides with the minimum width/depth ratio of channel flow, at which maximum energy is available for in-channel geomorphological processes. On the basis of five measurements of the discharge near bankfull stage, stage-discharge graphs were constructed for each channel from which discharge at bankfull stage was interpolated. Since the graphs showed minimal hysteresis, this phenomenon was neglected and only one average value of bankfull discharge was determined for each channel (table 3.4).

Figure 3.13   Bankfull discharge in different types of channel cross sections occurring in the upper Columbia River.

Bankfull stage was reached approximately at the same moment in most channels. A notable exception was channel 5, which only just reached the bankfull stage during the field period, while at the same time stage in the main channel was about 0.4 m above bankfull. Considering the entire system, during bankfull conditions the total discharge was 220 m³/s. The peak discharge during the field period is estimated to have been 296 m³/s. The distribution of flow over the channels did not change significantly between these stages (table 3.4).

Table 3.4 Bankfull discharge and maximum discharge in 1994

	$Q_{bf,1}$	$Q_{bf,2}$		Q_{max}	
	(m³/s)	(m³/s)	(%)	(m³/s)	(%)
Channel 1	9.5	8.4	3.8	10.4	3.5
Channel 2	2.4	2.8	1.3	4.8	1.6
Channel 3	193.5	192.0	87.1	254.5	86.0
Channel 4	5.4	6.1	2.8	11.0	3.7
Channel 5	14.8	11.1	5.0	15.5	5.2
Total		220.4	100.0	296.2	100.0

$Q_{bf,1}$ = bankfull discharge for each individual channel.
$Q_{bf,2}$ = discharge when the entire anastomosing system is approximately at bankfull stage.
Q_{max} = maximum discharge in 1994.

Table 3.5 Flow velocities and flow dimensions

	u_{mean} (m/s)	u_{max} (m/s)	R (m)	h_{mean} (m)	A (m²)
Channel 1	0.32	0.49	1.4	1.54	29.8
Channel 2	0.15	0.42	0.6	0.65	16.0
Channel 3	0.79	1.31	4.1	4.37	244.8
Channel 4	0.35	0.59	0.8	0.75	15.5
Channel 5	0.40	0.60	1.8	1.99	37.0

u_{mean} = mean flow velocity in flow area at bankfull discharge in the channel.
u_{max} = maximum observed flow velocity during the measurements.
R = hydraulic radius at bankfull discharge in the channel.
h_{mean} = mean channel depth with respect to the bankfull stage in the channel.
A = flow area at bankfull discharge in the channel.

Flow velocities measured in the field were low, with a maximum of 1.31 m/s measured in the middle of main channel during falling stage. Large differences in mean flow velocity at bankfull discharge exist between the channels (table 3.5). To some extent these differences are obviously related to differences in hydraulic radius. In the case of channel 4 however, flow velocity is remarkably high and likely to be influenced by the much higher flow velocities in the neighbouring main channel.

In figure 3.14a and b the measured flow velocity patterns are given for each channel for a stage close to bankfull. The velocity patterns turned out to be fairly symmetrical. Even in channel 5, where the cross section is located just downstream of a bend apex, the thalweg is located in the middle of the channel. Steep velocity gradients occur over the full width of the flat portion of the channel beds. Over the sloping banks, velocity differences are much less pronounced. In the channels 1, 3 and 5 velocity near the surface and close to the channel margins is significantly lower than at some depth. This indicates relatively great influence of sidewall roughness, due to variable bank morphology, stuck driftwood and tree branches hanging in the water (figure 3.15). This might suppress thalweg meandering and development of (weak) secondary circulation. Such features were absent in the channels 2 and 4. In channel 2, reeds growing on the left bank retarded the flow over the full depth.

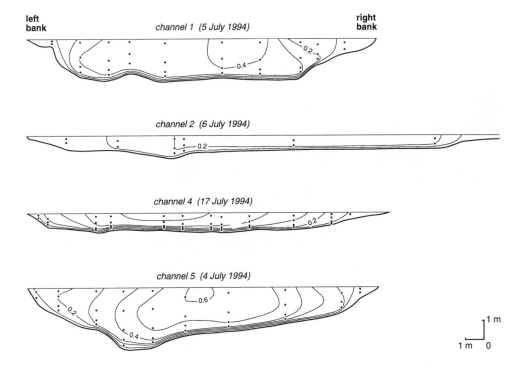

Figure 3.14a   Measured flow velocity patterns near bankfull discharge in channels 1, 2, 4 and 5. The black dots indicate flow velocity measurements. Flow is away from the observer.

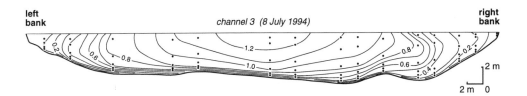

Figure 3.14b   Measured flow velocity patterns near bankfull discharge in channel 3. Black dots indicate flow velocity measurements. Flow is away from the observer.

Figure 3.15   Woody debris along the bank of channel 3, at medium flow stage.

The flat channel bed and the sloping banks are very different in grain size composition (figure 3.16). The bank material is cohesive, with low percentages of clay (around 5 %) but very high percentages of silt (typically around 50%). The silty material probably originates from the terraces of glaciolacustrine deposits, which flank the Columbia River floodplain in the south. The bed material usually consists for 85 to 95% of sand, with the exception of the crevasse channel (channel 2), where the silt and sand content of the bed material are about 40 and 60% respectively. Lumps of slumped mud, clay pebbles, leaves and wood were frequently found in the grab samples of the bed material.

The bed material of most channels consists of medium sand, which is moderately sorted on average (scale of Folk & Ward 1957). Again, the bed material of channel 2 is different, being characterized by fine, poorly sorted sand. Comparing table 3.6 with tables 3.5 and 3.7 it can be seen that the grain size of the bed material for the various channels relates well to mean flow velocity and specific stream power.

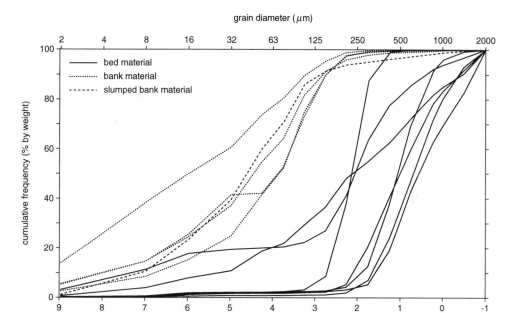

Figure 3.16   *Grain size distributions of bed and bank material of the main channel (channel 3).*

Table 3.6 Grain size of the bed material

	mean d_{50} (μm)	mean d_{90} (μm)	maximum d_{90} (μm)	σ_s (-)
Channel 1	282	680	1130	1.86
Channel 2	107	323	400	2.29
Channel 3	431	1077	1650	2.01
Channel 4	253	405	520	1.54
Channel 5	301	970	1640	2.18

d_{50}, d_{90} = grain size in a distribution for which 50 and 90 percent, by weight, respectively are finer.
σ_s = $1/2$ (d_{50}/d_{16} + d_{84}/d_{50}) representing the gradation of the bed material (based on means of d_{16}, d_{50} and d_{84}).

83

3.4.5 Channel gradients and stream power

Channel gradients are needed for the calculation of stream power, channel roughness and sediment transport. In this case, the term 'channel gradient' refers to the energy gradient in a channel which can be approximated by the water surface gradient if steady, uniform flow is assumed. It proved hard to measure channel gradients accurately by levelling, due to the swampy floodplain conditions around bankfull discharge and the abundant vegetation on the levees. Therefore, channel gradients were approximated by the valley gradient as determined from topographical maps (1:50,000) and gauge level data (Nicholson station) from the Water Survey of Canada (1991). The average valley gradient for the anastomosing reach of the Columbia River is around 11.5 cm/km. Correction factors were applied to account for the difference between the direction of maximum valley slope and the directions of the channels on the valley bottom. The resulting channel gradients are given in table 3.7.

The local channel gradients at the cross sections, may deviate from those calculated on the basis of the average valley gradient. Therefore, it was felt that for comparison another independent method should be applied to approximate the channel gradients. Brownlie (1983) presented a relationship between the hydraulic radius (or flow depth for wide channels), discharge, gradient and grain size of the bed material based on data fitting of 344 flume data and 550 field data. Since all variables except for the gradient are known and are well within the range used in Brownlie's analysis, channel gradients can be calculated. For the lower flow regime, Brownlie proposed:

$$S^{-0.2542} = R / (0.3724 \ d_{50} \ Q_*^{0.6539} \ \sigma_s^{0.1050})$$

in which:

S	=	energy gradient (-)	
R	=	hydraulic radius (m)	
Q_*	=	$Q/(w \ g^{0.5} \ d_{50}^{1.5})$ which is the dimensionless discharge (-)	
σ_s	=	$1/2 \ (d_{50}/d_{16} + d_{84}/d_{50})$ representing the gradation of the bed material (-)	
d_{16}, d_{50}, d_{84}	=	grain sizes in a distribution, for which 16, 50 and 84 percent, by weight, respectively are finer (m)	
w	=	channel width (m)	
g	=	acceleration of gravity (m/s²)	

The input data used are given in tables 3.2, 3.4, 3.5 and 3.6 and apply to bankfull discharge for each channel. The hydraulic radius was calculated by dividing the flow area by the wet channel perimeter (R = A/O) for bankfull conditions in measured cross sections. Data supplied by Brownlie (1983, table 3) that were not used in the development of his technique, were used to estimate possible errors in the gradient as calculated using the Brownlie formula. The results indicate that errors may be up to around 30 %. For the purpose of this study these errors are within acceptable limits.

Table 3.7 Channel gradients and stream power

	$S_{c,v}$ (cm/km)	$\omega_{c,v}$ (W/m^2)	S_B (cm/km)	ω_B (W/m^2)	S_v (cm/km)	ω_p (W/m^2)
Channel 1	11.3	0.54	3.3	0.16	11.5	0.74
Channel 2	10.8	0.10	1.4	0.01	11.5	0.35
Channel 3	10.0	3.38	7.6	2.57	11.5	3.36
Channel 4	11.1	0.29	5.3	0.14	11.5	0.56
Channel 5	10.8	0.84	4.5	0.35	11.5	0.93

$S_{c,v}$ = channel gradient calculated on the basis of the valley gradient.
$\omega_{c,v}$ = specific stream power based on $S_{c,v}$.
S_B = channel gradient according to Brownlie's method.
ω_B = specific stream power based on S_B.
S_v = valley gradient.
ω_p = potential specific stream power.

In table 3.7 it can be seen that the gradients as calculated according to Brownlie's technique (S_B), are lower than the channel gradient values based on the valley gradient ($S_{c,v}$). Gradient differences between the channels, are significantly greater according to Brownlie's method.

The very low gradient calculated for the crevasse channel (channel 2), might well be a better approximation of the true gradient than the one based of the valley gradient. Like in many crevasse channels of the upper Columbia River, channel depth in channel 2 considerably decreases away from its origin, leading to a negative channel bed gradient. This is due to the crevasse splay formation which preceded the scouring of channel 2. The remnants of the splay in the channel bed still cause a reduced local energy gradient.

The gradient of the main channel (channel 3) according to Brownlie's method is only slightly lower than the one based on the valley gradient and differs less than 30%. Two other methods based on shear stress analysis and requiring comparable input data, were applied to see if these yielded similar gradients. These methods were applicable for the main channel data only. The methods of Engelund & Hansen (1967) and White et al. (1979) yielded gradients of 8.5 and 8.1 cm/km respectively, in agreement with the gradient of the main channel as calculated with Brownlie's method. Remarkably, S_B for channel 4 is significantly lower than for channel 3, although over the total length of channel 4 the gradient must be the same as that over the comparable reach of channel 3.

The relatively low Brownlie-gradients for the smaller channels 1 and 5, probably reflect the relatively great influence of bank morphology, vegetation and organic debris in these channels. Brownlie's method does not account for an above-average flow resistance due to these non-sedimentary factors. Sidewall effects may be an important source of error (Brownlie 1983, p. 985). The differences in channel roughness, calculated on the basis of $S_{c,v}$ and S_B, will be further discussed in section 3.4.6.

Three sets of specific stream power values were calculated for the five Columbia River channels (table 3.7). One set is based on $S_{c,v}$, a second set is based on S_B, while a third set represents the potential specific stream power as defined by Van den Berg (1995).

The 'potential specific stream power' is a parameter that is more or less independent of channel morphology and therefore has the potential to predict rather than to characterize a channel type. To untie the stream power parameter of channel morphology, channel gradient was substituted by valley gradient, while the true width of the channel was replaced by the width according to a regime equation. In this regime equation, width is an exponential function of discharge. Bankfull discharge, although probably being dependent on channel morphology to some extent, was used as it was still considered to be the best alternative for practical reasons. Potential specific stream power for sand-bed rivers was defined as:

$$\omega_p = 2.1 \, S_v \, \sqrt{Q_{bf}}$$

in which:
ω_p = potential specific stream power (kW/m^2)
S_v = valley gradient (-)
Q_{bf} = bankfull discharge (m^3/s)

Defined as such, the potential specific stream power is a purely virtual quantity.

All values for specific stream power in table 3.7 can be classified as extremely low. Nanson & Croke (1992) suggested an upper boundary of 10 W/m^2 for low-energy river systems with laterally stable channels. Ferguson (1981) identified a range of 1 to 60 W/m^2, with a median of about 15 W/m^2, for inactive channels in Britain. With respect to these figures, the specific stream power of the upper Columbia River channels is near the bottom end, which is a result of low channel gradient and low unit discharge (= discharge divided by channel width). Potential specific stream power for most channels is very close to specific stream power on the basis of $S_{c,v}$. Since the channel gradients used are only little lower than the valley gradients, it can be concluded that the virtual channel width according to the regime equation is not far from the true channel width. The ω_p-values for the upper Columbia River are below almost all ω_p-data given by Van den Berg (1995, fig. 3), which represent predominantly braided and meandering channels (see also figure 6.4).

3.4.6 Channel roughness

The overall hydraulic roughness of a river channel can be envisaged to consist of three components: (1) the roughness of the grains of the material in the wet channel perimeter, (2) the roughness generated by bedforms, and (3) a residual roughness caused by channel vegetation, organic debris, bank morphology, bend curvature etc. The residual roughness is hard to quantify independently. Usually bedform roughness is dominant, while grain roughness is negligible if other (bigger) roughness elements are present. The effect of individual roughness elements on flow resistance however, is strongly determined by the hydraulic radius of the flow. The five studied channels showed great differences in hydraulic radius, bed material texture, bedforms, and in the presence of vegetation and stuck organic debris. To what extent do these differences cause differences in channel roughness and flow resistance?

In table 3.8 overall Chézy-coefficients (C) are given, which were computed with the Chézy equation: $Q = CA\sqrt{(RS)}$, where Q is discharge (bankfull), A is flow area, R is hydraulic radius, and S is energy gradient. Also given in table 3.8 are the equivalent Nikuradse roughness heights (k_s) derived from the Chézy-coefficients by applying $C = 18\log(12R/k_s)$. Again, two sets can be calculated applying the two different estimates of the channel gradient $S_{c,v}$ and S_B. Below, it will be evaluated to what extent the calculated roughness heights agree with the observations of the channel beds.

Table 3.8 Flow resistance and channel roughness

	Based on $S_{c,v}$		Based on S_B	
	C $(m^{0.5}/s)$	k_s (m)	C $(m^{0.5}/s)$	k_s (m)
Channel 1	25.3	0.660	47.1	0.041
Channel 2	18.6	0.667	51.8	0.010
Channel 3	39.0	0.335	44.8	0.160
Channel 4	37.0	0.084	53.8	0.010
Channel 5	28.7	0.550	44.4	0.074

C = Chézy-coefficient at bankfull discharge in the channel.
k_s = Nikuradse roughness height.

In *channel 1*, dunes were absent, while small ripples (height < 2.5 cm) may have been present on the sandy bed, but were beyond the detection limit of the echo sounding equipment. The irregular bottom topography is partly due to woody organic debris, ranging from large logs to fine twigs, which were identified on the bottom of the channel by echo sounding and in grab samples. Partially buried driftwood hindered flow near the surface just upstream of the cross section. The high estimate $k_s = 0.660$ m (based on $S_{c,v}$) represents the considerable sidewall and vegetation effects in the relatively narrow and small-scale channel. The estimate $k_s = 0.041$ m (based on S_B), seems to be much too conservative as a result of the fact that the Brownlie-method does not account for these effects. *Channel 5* closely resembles channel 1 in roughness and resistance characteristics.

The bed of *channel 2* was covered by a mud drape, which remained largely intact during the fieldwork. Where the mud drape was eroded, small ripples were formed in the underlying sand, but dunes were absent. The only influence of vegetation was that of reed growing on the left bank. Considering the scarce roughness elements present in the channel, a k_s of 0.010 m (based on S_B) seems much more acceptable than a value of 0.667 m (based on $S_{c,v}$), which even exceeds the water depth (table 3.5).

In the main channel *(channel 3)* large migrating dunes with superimposed smaller dunes were present (figure 3.17). At about bankfull discharge the dimensions of the small dunes remained fairly constant at a length of 3.9 m and a height of 0.18 m, while the large dunes averaged 60 m in length and 1.50 m in height. Van Rijn (1984c, 1993) described a method to determine the form roughness by summation of k_s-values representing the roughness imposed by ripples and dunes individually. Ripples were defined by Van Rijn (1993) as bedforms with a length smaller than the water depth. In this thesis the terminology proposed by Ashley (1990) is followed, implying that the larger ripples (sensu Van Rijn) are termed 'small dunes' based on morphometrical criteria irrespective of water depth. The following relationships apply for calculation of ripple roughness ($k_{s,r}$) (sensu Van Rijn) and dune roughness ($k_{s,d}$) respectively:

$$k_{s,r} = 20 \ \gamma_r \ \Delta_r (\frac{\Delta_r}{\lambda_r})$$

in which:
Δ_r = ripple height (m)
λ_r = ripple length (m)
γ_r = ripple presence factor ($\gamma_r = 0.7$ for ripples superimposed on dunes)

$$k_{s,d} = 1.1 \ \gamma_d \ \Delta_d \ (1 - e^{-25\Delta_d / \lambda_d})$$

in which:
Δ_d = dune height (m)
λ_d = dune length (m)
γ_d = form factor ($\gamma_d = 0.7$ for field conditions)

88

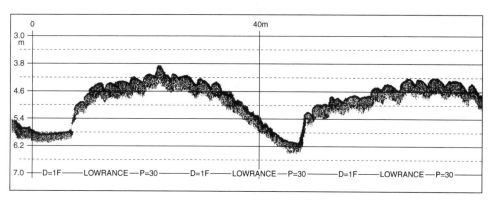

Figure 3.17   Longitudinal echo sounding profile of the main channel (channel 3). Flow is from right to left.

The use of $\gamma_d = 0.7$ is justified by the steep leeside of the dunes (figure 3.17) causing flow separation (see also Van Rijn 1993). Application of the relationships to the case of channel 3 with the input data as mentioned above, yields a $k_{s,r}$ of 0.116 m and a $k_{s,d}$ of 0.537 m and thus a k_s relating to bedforms alone of 0.653 m. The associated Chézy-coefficient is 33.8 $m^{0.5}/s$. These values suggest that the channel roughness in channel 3 is considerably underestimated on the basis of both calculated gradients, although the roughness suggested by application of $S_{c,v}$ seems to be the most realistic of the two. It should be realized that the calculated bedform roughness may be an overestimate due to the fact that bedform dimensions are derived from just one longitudinal echo sounding profile in the middle of the channel where stream velocities are highest and bedform dimensions are greatest. Laterally, the bed is likely to be smoother, although here bank vegetation and woody debris may play an additional role.

Well-developed bedforms were also found in *channel 4*, although they were less spectacular than in the main channel. Dune dimensions as identified by echo sounding averaged 11.5 m long and 0.22 m high. However, at bankfull discharge these dunes were hardly active. Ripples on the back of the dunes were too low to be detected by echo sounding, but at somewhat lower flow stages ripples of 10 cm long and 1 cm high could be observed (figure 3.18). Vegetation or woody debris were absent in the channel bed. Assuming bedform roughness to be representative for the overall roughness in this case, application of the Van Rijn (1993) relationships yields $k_{s,r} = 0.014$ m, $k_{s,d} = 0.064$ m and hence $k_s = 0.078$ m. The associated Chézy-coefficient is 37.6 $m^{0.5}/s$. In this shallow sandy channel, bedform roughness may be expected to dominate the wet perimeter. The estimate of roughness based on $S_{c,v}$ is very close to the calculated bedform roughness. For unknown reasons, the roughness estimate based on Brownlie's method is obviously much too low.

In conclusion, for channels 3 and 4 the estimates of channel roughness on the basis $S_{c,v}$ seem to match fairly well with the field observations. For channel 2, application of S_B obviously yields the best estimate of roughness. For channels 1 and 5, application of S_B yields a low roughness that probably considerably underestimates the effects of abundant

89

Figure 3.18   Ripples on the back of a small dune in channel 4. Note the mud drape.

woody debris, bank vegetation, and irregular bank morphology in these small, relatively narrow channels. Application of $S_{c,v}$ yields a much higher roughness. Overall Chézy-coefficients for the channels at bankfull discharge probably range between 35 to 55 $m^{0.5}/s$.

3.4.7 Sediment transport

Sediment concentrations in the flow were not measured in the field, but sufficient input data were collected to enable application of several sediment transport formulae to get an idea of the capacity of the various channels to transport imposed sediment load. Of the many formulae available, the functions of Engelund & Hansen (1967), Van Rijn (1984a, 1984b) and the modified Van Rijn function (Van den Berg & Van Gelder 1993) were chosen for this study. The equations are given in appendix 1.

In a verification of a number of different sediment transport functions the Van Rijn function proved to be a fairly reliable predictor (Van Rijn 1993). A computer program (TRANSPOR in Van Rijn 1993) of this method was available. Van den Berg & Van Gelder (1993) showed that at low flow velocities the Van Rijn function underestimated the transport rates. Under these conditions the Engelund & Hansen (1967) function performed better, but this was largely due to the fact that it does not account for critical bed shear stress. They proposed some modifications of the Van Rijn function, mainly concerning the Shields limit and the near bed reference concentration, which proved to enhance its predictive power.

The three sediment transport functions were used to predict sediment transport of each channel under bankfull conditions. It is important to realize that the functions only predict the transport capacity for the locally available sandy bed material assuming steady and uniform flow. Large quantities of finer material are transported as wash load, unrelated to the transport capacity of the flow as calculated with the functions.

For application of the functions the channel cross sections were schematized as being rectangular, with a depth equal to the mean channel depth and using means of the channel flow velocity and bed material. Especially for the type of channel cross sections in this study, this schematization is not far from reality. Furthermore, the objective in this study is rather to examine the sediment transport capacity of the five channels relative to each other, than to estimate the total sediment transport capacity of the upper Columbia River.

The input data used can be found in the tables 3.2, 3.4, 3.5, 3.6 and 3.8. An important input in all three functions is the overall Chézy-coefficient for the channel. Like in the previous section on channel roughness, for each channel two cases were considered. First, all three sediment transport functions were applied using a Chézy-coefficient based on $S_{c,v}$, while in a second calculation a Chézy-coefficient based on S_B was used. This resulted in six estimates of sediment transport for each channel given in table 3.9.

Table 3.9 Sediment transport according to three functions

	Engelund & Hansen		Van Rijn		Modified Van Rijn	
	Q_t^a (g/s)	Q_t^b (g/s)	Q_t^a (g/s)	Q_t^b (g/s)	Q_t^a (g/s)	Q_t^b (g/s)
Channel 1	220	34	0	0	20	7
Channel 2	43	2	0	0	0	0
Channel 3	10484	6916	4866	4603	12767	10580
Channel 4	132	43	14	12	86	35
Channel 5	417	113	39	41	117	217

[a] Total sediment transport (Q_t) was calculated using $S_{c,v}$ to calculate C and k_s. The input data apply to bankfull conditions for each channel.

[b] Total sediment transport (Q_t) was calculated using S_B to calculate C and k_s. The input data apply to bankfull conditions for each channel.

The six sets of estimates all show that the sediment transport capacity of channel 3 greatly exceeds the sediment transport capacity of all four other channels together. The results can be seen to be relatively sensitive to the chosen Chézy-coefficient. The highest sediment transport rates were predicted by the modified Van Rijn function. These are more than twice as high compared to the prediction by the original Van Rijn function. The Engelund & Hansen function predicts slightly higher transport rates for the smaller channels of the system, but this is due the fact that the critical shear stress was not taken into account.

In most of the smaller channels, the bed shear stress under bankfull conditions was only slightly above the critical shear stress required to initiate motion of the bed material. In channel 2 shear stress did not exceed the theoretical critical level, which was more or less confirmed by observations of the bed before and after the flood. Consequently, sediment transport through the smaller channels of the anastomosing system is almost negligible (table 3.9) and only stages well above bankfull can bring about substantial sediment transport outside of the main channel.

The Van Rijn function and the modified Van Rijn function make a distinction between bed load and suspended load. Predicted bed load is 18 to 41% of the predicted total load. Measurements of sediment concentrations by Locking (1983) upstream and downstream of the present study location indicated bed load to be 11% of the total load. In these measurements however, measured suspended load included wash load. The measured values therefore were much greater than the predicted quantities. Bed load transport rates predicted for the study location were amply between the rates measured by Locking with a Helley-Smith bed load sampler near bankfull discharge (table 3.10).

Table 3.10 Measured versus calculated bed load transport

Spillimacheen station (upstream)	Present study site	Nicholson station (downstream)
measured Q_b (g/s)	calculated Q_b (g/s)	measured Q_b (g/s)
7091 [a]	1904 [c]	238 [d]
5053 [b]	1904 [c]	807 [e]

[a] Measured 5 June 1982, water discharge 206.8 m³/s (Locking 1983, table 4.1).
[b] Measured 6 August 1982, water discharge 195.3 m³/s (Locking 1983, table 4.1).
[c] Calculated for the main channel at bankfull discharge (193.5 m³/s) applying the Van Rijn function (in this case the modified Van Rijn function does not yield a different solution).
[d] Measured 2 June 1982, water discharge 166.6 m³/s (Locking 1983, table 4.2).
[e] Measured 7 August 1982, water discharge 237.2 m³/s (Locking 1983, table 4.2).

3.5 Discussion

In a recent paper, Nanson & Huang (in press) stated that anabranching (including anastomosing) rivers develop in order to maintain or enhance water and sediment throughput across extensive low-gradient floodplains, where rivers are unable to increase the channel gradient. Crucial in their chain of reasoning was the observation from rivers in Australia that a substantial reduction in total water surface width for all channels together, accompanies the division of one channel into more channels. Application of basic hydraulic relationships by Nanson & Huang (in press) yielded that, with respect to the single channel upstream, the multiple channels would develop a marked increase in channel depth and naturally a decline in width/depth ratio, as well as an increase in hydraulic radius and mean flow velocity. Estimates of sediment transport rates based on these adjustments also indicated a significant increase with respect to the single-channel state. Although the present study did not focus on a transition from a single-channel to an anastomosing river, the field data to some extent do permit an evaluation of the applicability of the concept of Nanson & Huang (in press) to the upper Columbia River.

Within its anastomosing reach, the Columbia River typically has the morphology of a main channel and a number of much smaller secondary channels. Even at high flow, these secondary channels have only a modest function for the throughput of water (table 3.4). Flow velocities are much lower than in the main channel, mainly due to a much smaller hydraulic radius, so relative to their size they contribute very little to the total water discharge. Estimates of roughness indicate that the narrow and small-scale secondary channels probably have great roughness due to relatively great sidewall and vegetation effects. As conduits for sediment, the secondary channels are even less efficient (table 3.9), as bed shear stress is positively related to both the flow depth and the second power of the mean velocity. It can be concluded that although the upper Columbia River is clearly anastomosing in morphology, it can practically be considered a single-channel river as far as water and sediment discharge are concerned. In addition, bed load transport of the system appears to decrease strongly downstream (table 3.10). Therefore the multi-channel state of the upper Columbia River can not be taken as a response of the system to maximize water and sediment throughput according to the concept of Nanson & Huang (in press).

If it is not to enhance water and sediment discharge, then what is the function of the secondary channels on the floodplain? Galay et al. (1984) suggested that bed load goes into storage in the channels and indeed 66% (Smith 1986) to 85% (Locking 1983) of the bed load entering the upper Columbia anastomosing reach is deposited. Supply of bed load seems to greatly exceed transport capacity (table 3.10). A fraction of the bed load, estimated at 10-20 % (D.G. Smith pers. comm. 1998), may be trapped in crevasse splays. Crevasses however, usually tap only the shallow waters devoid of bed load but carrying sandy suspended load, although some of the large splays of the upper Columbia River obviously do tap coarse bed load. Thus, most of the sand found on crevasse splays is likely to have been transported as suspended load. From the study of Locking (1983) it becomes clear that even at stages far below bankfull, bed load goes into storage in the anastomosing system. At these stages crevasse splays are still inactive. The only place where bed load can be stored in large quantities is on the channel beds themselves. Partly, this material may be retransported during the next seasonal flood.

In meandering rivers, bed load and sandy suspended load is stored in point bars and hence storage capacity is determined by the rate of lateral channel migration. In the upper Columbia River however, lateral migration of channels is practically zero due to extremely low stream power (table 3.7) in combination with fine cohesive bank material (section 3.4.4). Therefore, storage of bed load has to take place on the channel bottom. Especially in the secondary channels, where shear stresses under bankfull conditions are on average close to the critical values (section 3.4.7) favourable spots for bed load deposition exist. In the main channel, bed load may be stored temporarily in large dunes (figure 3.17). These dunes migrate slowly as large transverse bars as commonly observed by D.G. Smith (pers. comm. 1998).

In the long term, slow bed aggradation leads to loss of channel capacity and increase in overbank flooding. Increased vertical accretion of the floodplain by deposition of suspended and wash load may (partly) restore channel capacity. It is interesting to note that vertical floodplain accretion of the upper Columbia River is rapid indeed (table 3.3) and levee deposits are very thick relative to the channel depth (figure 3.6). Floods occur almost every year and are of a long duration [45 days/year on average (Locking 1983)]. Undercapacity of the channel network also favours cutting of new channels, especially if rapid levee deposition has increased local cross-levee gradients. A similar course of events was proposed by McCarthy et al. (1992) for channels in the Okavango Delta, although here the role of overbank sedimentation is taken over by the growth of swamp vegetation.

Thus, on the basis of the data now available it is hypothesized that the inability of the river to transport the coarse sediment is what drives floodplain accretion by fine sediments and finally avulsion. In this respect, the generally low width/depth ratios of the upper Columbia River channels are misleading, because at first sight they suggest incision instead of bed accretion. It is important to realize however, that the low width/depth ratios are solely the result of the inability of the river to erode its banks and expand channels laterally. On a geological timescale, with channel lifetimes of up to 3000 years (section 3.4.2), channel bed accretion invoking bank accretion may lead to channel sand bodies having width/thickness ratios which are substantially lower than the width/depth ratios of the associated channels (figure 2.11).

Schumm et al. (1996) proposed a model in which avulsions in the anastomosing Ovens and King Rivers (Victoria, Australia) were the result of a loss of hydraulic efficiency as channel sinuosity increased and consequently channel gradients decreased with time. Is this model in conflict with the above described model for the Columbia River? The anastomosing system they studied is located in a temperate, subhumid climate similar to the upper Columbia in floodplain scale and bankfull discharge, while gradient and bed load are notably different. Potential specific stream power as calculated for the mature meandering channel reaches of the Ovens River range from 24.9 to 61.3 W/m^2 [based on Schumm et al. (1996, table 1), applying $\omega_p = 3.3 S_v \sqrt{Q_{bf}}$ (in kW/m^2) as defined by Van den Berg (1995) for gravel-bed rivers], while the bed load is gravel with a median diameter of 50 mm. Apparently, under these conditions channels are able to migrate laterally. In a stability diagram of Van den Berg (1995, fig. 3a) (see also figure 6.4) the Ovens channel reaches plot at the lower end of the range of meandering channels. Active lateral migration of channels implies storage of coarse material in point bars. On the other hand, Schumm et al. (1996, p. 1217) suggested that increase in sinuosity and resulting decrease in channel gradient, goes together with a decreasing cross sectional area and aggradation of the bed. In other words, lateral storage of bed load can not accommodate all bed load deposition and the channel shallows with time. Thus, rather than being exclusively tied to a straight channel type, the tendency for a river to become anastomosed, seems to depend on an imbalance of the lateral erosion rate, the surplus of bed material which needs to be stored, and the rate of levee growth. figure 3.19 shows a situation where bed accretion outpaces levee accretion in a straight channel and in a meandering channel. With time both channels become increasingly liable to avulsion.

Based on stratigraphic information and thermoluminescence dates, Page & Nanson (1996, p. 942) suggested a comparable course of events for the Late Quaternary Murrumbidgee paleochannels in New South Wales. In their model, separate phases of lateral and vertical accretion of bed material exist, which were supposed to depend on changes in the ratio of bed load to suspended load. It seems likely that these channels were at least partly anastomosing, although due to the level of precision of the thermoluminescence dates coexistence of channels could not be proven.

Schumm et al. (1996) suggested that channels in anastomosing river systems follow a consistent pattern in their development, with each stage having different morphological characteristics. They estimated that such a cycle, from initial formation by avulsion until final abandonment, needs hundreds to thousands of years to be completed, but they had only one radiocarbon date to support this view. The channel chronologies from the Rhine-Meuse delta (Berendsen 1982, Törnqvist 1994) and the upper Columbia River (figure 3.11) confirm their statement and clearly underscore that channel lifetimes are highly variable. One of the most important reasons for this (in temperate humid environments) is the random element introduced by the effect of log jams.

Although log jams obviously increase hydraulic resistance (Assani & Petit 1995) and cause a set up of the water table, it is perhaps more important that they greatly increase turbulence which leads to bank scour affecting the highest (near-channel) part of the levee, as was observed in channel 5 (section 3.4.2). Thus, channel development may be interrupted any time by a log jam, but small channels are more likely to become blocked than bigger channels. Additionally, beaver dams also only affect small channels. So, once a channel has reached a certain size it has a fair chance to survive much longer, probably thousands of years. One can think of a critical channel width of 30 to 50 m, which enables big floating trees to pass freely in all orientations.

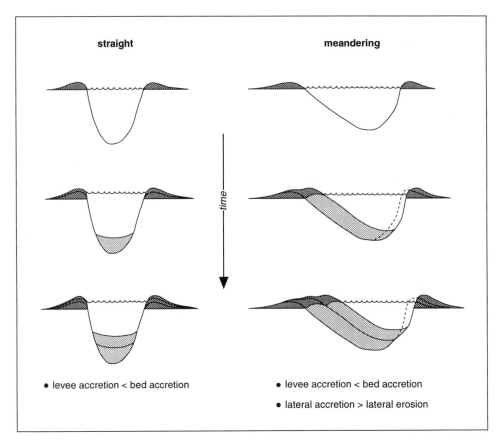

Figure 3.19 *Bed load storage in aggrading straight and meandering channels. Bed accretion outpaces levee accretion in both channels, leading to decrease of bankfull flow area with time. In the meandering channel, lateral erosion is insufficient to create the bed load storage capacity needed, resulting in bed accretion.*

3.6 Summary

The anastomosing upper Columbia River is composed of multiple, laterally stable channels, in which each channel can be classified as 'straight'. The channel morphology is the result of very low specific stream power (below 3.4 W/m^2) and cohesive silty banks. A low floodplain gradient of around 11.5 cm/km is the prime cause of the low specific stream power.

Anastomosis at the study location has persisted since at least 2850 cal. yr BP, with avulsions occurring frequently. At least nine channels have been formed in the studied floodplain-wide cross section, within the past 3000 years. Channel lifetimes appeared to be highly variable ranging from 800 to at least 3000 years. Log jams provoking avulsions are supposed to have caused this variability.

An evaluation of the radiocarbon data yielded that ^{14}C-ages of conventionally dated bulk samples may differ considerably from those of selected terrestrial macrofossils from the same location and depth. In a number of cases bulk samples were apparently much too old, mainly due to the presence of reworked organic matter. Therefore, dating of bulk samples from the upper Columbia River environment is strongly discouraged.

The long-term average floodplain aggradation rate appeared to be significantly lower than previously supposed. A long-term average of 1.7 mm/yr was based on radiocarbon data, while a short-term sedimentation rate of 0.8 mm was determined for the relatively small seasonal flood of 1994 using sediment traps.

In spite of its anastomosing morphology, the main channel of the study reach is by far dominant in the discharge of water and sediment. Mean flow velocities at bankfull discharge in the various channels are low (0.15 - 0.79 m/s). In the smaller channels sidewall and vegetation effects may cause great roughness, while shear stresses barely exceed the critical shear stress for initiation of bed material transport. Since there is a surplus of bed load while the channels are laterally stable, storage of the coarse sediment fraction takes place predominantly on the channel beds. Bed aggradation limits channel capacity, enhances overbank flooding and sedimentation, and thus promotes avulsions.

4   An anastomosing river in a tropical semi-arid climate (upper Inland Niger Delta, central Mali)

4.1   Introduction

Striking differences exist between anastomosing rivers located in humid and arid climates. In temperate humid western Canada, rapid floodplain aggradation and dense vegetation were recognized, as important controlling factors of anastomosing river morphology (e.g. Smith & Smith 1980; Smith 1983). However, anastomosing river systems in arid central Australia, have low floodplain aggradation rates and scarce vegetation (e.g. Rust 1981; Nanson et al. 1986). The very different characteristics of the anastomosing rivers in the two regions led Nanson & Croke (1992) to separate anastomosing river floodplains in an organic-rich and inorganic class, while Miall (1996, p. 52) believed the arid examples of central Australia to be anomalous. The obscure present status of arid anastomosing rivers is partly caused by the very few examples studied, Cooper Creek in central Australia being the best known. Arid anastomosing rivers however, have a wider occurrence and perhaps it is illuminating to turn to another region.

A vast anastomosing river system is located in the semi-arid Sahel zone of West Africa and fed by the Niger River (figure 4.1). This river follows a curious loop through West Africa: rising near the coast in the wet Guinea Highlands, it penetrates the arid interior, where it is seemingly deflected towards the south by the Sahara Desert, to empty into the Gulf of Guinea. Just before meeting the desert, the Niger splits into a network of channels on an extensive floodplain. The distinctive nature of this river plain was already noted by early geographers and it was called the 'Inland Niger Delta' (Reclus 1887). Being an important wetland amidst arid grounds, this region became recognized as a potential focus of prehistoric habitation and urbanisation (e.g. McIntosh 1993) and received archeological attention (e.g. Bedaux et al. 1978; McIntosh & McIntosh 1980, 1981). Nowadays, the Inland Delta is a region of economic importance for livestock breeding, rice cultivation and fishery. In the near future, a continuous increase of the human pressure on the area may be expected, due to Mali's growing population and the country's scarce natural resources.

What is the origin of this vital area? Although it would be unjust to call the Inland Delta a 'terra incognita', it remains a relatively poorly understood region from a geological and geomorphological point of view. Initially, geomorphological surveys on a regional scale were carried out by French researchers (Urvoy 1942; Tricart 1965; Gallais 1967). These studies still provide the framework for understanding the Quaternary evolution of the alluvial basin. Recent studies focused on the geomorphology of parts of the Inland Delta (McIntosh 1983; Jacobberger 1987, 1988a) and its surroundings (Jacobberger 1988a, 1988b). In spite of this work, understanding of the dynamics of the anastomosing river system is hindered by: (1) lack of subsurface data and (2) poor time control. Fieldwork carried out in the Inland Delta for this thesis aimed at filling these gaps.

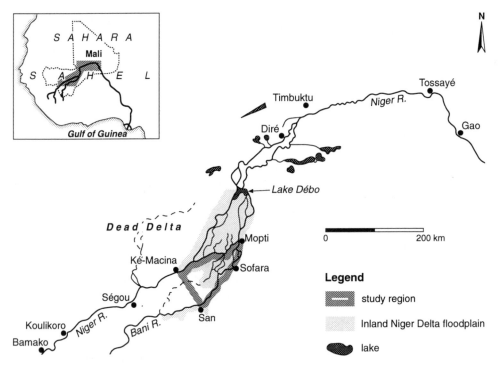

Figure 4.1   *Location of the study region and several other localities mentioned in the text.*

The purpose of this chapter is to describe the genesis and the sedimentary products of the upper Inland Niger Delta anastomosing river system. More specifically, in this chapter I address the role of the climatic setting in its genesis and the climatic signatures of its sedimentary facies. The significance of the floodplain aggradation rate is critically evaluated, as it proved to be a factor of minor importance in other arid anastomosing river systems.

The study region were fieldwork was carried out comprises the southern part of the Inland Delta where the Bani River joins the Niger (figure 4.1). In fact, this region is mainly dominated by the avulsion history of the Bani rather than the Niger. The data that I will discuss cover the geomorphology, sedimentology and hydrology of this region. Most importantly, a chronostratigraphic framework for the study region was established by AMS ^{14}C-dating of samples extracted from hand-augered borehole cross sections. A first step however, was geomorphological mapping by analysis of aerial photographs and satellite imagery as well as field survey. Data on stream discharges and water levels were supplied by the regional and the national hydrological services [Direction Régionale de l'Hydraulique et de l'Energie (DRHE) at Mopti and the Direction Nationale de l'Hydraulique et de l'Energie (DNHE) at Bamako] for three gauging stations in the study region.

The study in the upper Inland Delta was carried out within the framework of an archeological research project, named 'Projet Togué'. The purpose and organization of 'Projet Togué' were described by Dembelé et al. (1993) and Schmidt (1993). The project name refers to the local (Fulani) name of the mounds which are scattered in large numbers over the Inland Delta, representing the prime archeological sites of this region. The history of human occupation in this region is intimately related to the geomorphological history, for which reason the present study was included in the archeological project. Consequently, the choice of the study region was based on archeological interest. In this chapter I will now and then briefly refer to the archeology of the Inland Delta.

Before zooming in on the study region in the upper Inland Delta, overviews are presented of the geological and climatic setting, the hydrological characteristics and the climatic and geomorphological history of the Inland Delta since 20,000 BP.

4.2   General background

4.2.1   Geological setting

The Inland Delta is located in the Ségou basin, a wide syncline with a NNE-SSW orientation (figure 4.2). To the east and to the south, Precambrian sandstone crops out and sharply bounds the present floodplain. To the west, the floodplain boundary is less clear. Here, the Quaternary alluvium of the now abandoned 'Delta Mort' (Dead Delta) (figure 4.1) is gradually replaced by outcropping continental Tertiary deposits, which are partly unconsolidated. To the north, fault tectonics has produced the Nara Graben. A number of parallel faults, associated with this graben, is probably quite recent and is responsible for the principal lakes in this area (DNGM 1987, p. 22). North of Timbuktu, Quaternary eolian sediments dominate at the surface.

The source areas of the Bani and Niger Rivers consist of granitized gneiss and to a lesser extent of quartzites and dolerites (ORSTOM 1970a, Map 3). Downstream of the Inland Delta, folded metamorphic rocks of the Precambrian basement crop out in the bed of the Niger near the village of Tossayé (Blanck 1968). After having traversed this rock step, the river enters the Gao Graben.

According to Gallais (1967) the Inland Delta is delimited to the north by a secondary anticlinal axe with WNW-ESE orientation, just north of Lake Débo (figure 4.1). This anticline hosts the massive, E-W trending, longitudinal dunes of the Erg of Bara which dissect the floodplain.

Little is known about the intensity and nature of subsidence within the Inland Delta. Gravimetric measurements cited by Gallais (1967, pp. 13-14) indicate a relatively great depth of basement rocks near the confluence of the Bani and the Niger, while a relatively shallow depth of the basement is indicated at the bifurcation of the Niger and Diaka Rivers (see figure 4.7 for location of Diaka River). Tricart (1965) and Gallais (1967) suggested strong tectonic control on the course of the Niger and the Bani, which seem to stick to the southern and eastern border of the floodplain. This behaviour is very likely to

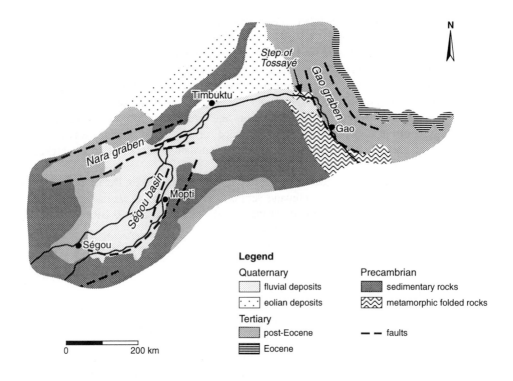

Figure 4.2   *Geological map of the Inland Delta and its surroundings (source: DNGM 1987; Keïta 1980; DNHE pers. comm. 1994).*

be caused by fault tectonics.

The DNGM (1987, fig. 3) indicated a fault running NNE-SSW a little east of Mopti (figure 4.2). Hydrogeological maps of the DNHE suggest that a fault is present between the Bani River and the edge of the present floodplain (figure 4.2). From about 25 km northeast of Mopti, this fault runs south to southwest along the Inland Delta margin for about 250 km. Well records of the DNHE show a rapid increase in thickness of unconsolidated sediments from near zero at the floodplain margin, to about 60 or 70 m a few tens of kilometres towards the centre of the Inland Delta, thereby crossing the fault. The periods and rates of activity along the fault however, are unknown.

In summary, the geological and tectonic evidence indicate an asymmetric fill and probably a half-graben structure of the Ségou Basin [see also Tricart & Blanck (1990) and McCarthy (1993)]. The indistinct western margin, consisting of Tertiary sedimentary rocks, is very different from the eastern margin which consists of steeply dipping and probably faulted Precambrian rocks. The Quaternary basin-fill becomes younger towards the eastern margin, where the present floodplain is situated. A rock step near Tossayé and an anticlinal structure just north of Lake Débo provide important base-level controls on the drainage system of the Ségou Basin.

4.2.2 Climatic setting

In the mountainous source area of the Niger River, the monsoon lasts eight months and annual rainfall amounts to 2000 mm. Northeastward along its course, the climate rapidly gets drier. The Inland Delta is located in the Sahel zone, with annual precipitation ranging from 700 mm in the south (near Ségou) to 200 mm in the north (near Timbuktu). The annual precipitation is primarily dependent on the length of the wet season, when the region is subjected to the southwest monsoon bringing in oceanic air. Within the Inland Delta, the wet season lasts three to four months (June-September), in which rainfall is concentrated in short but heavy showers.

During the rest of the year the weather is dominated by dry continental air, moving in from the northeast. This trade wind from the desert is known under the name 'Harmattan'. The Harmattan can be fierce [7-14 m/s (ORSTOM 1970b, p. 50)], especially later in the dry season. A reduced vegetation cover and desiccated soils enable the wind to pick up dust, frequently making the sky hazy in this period (see also McTainsh et al. 1997). Early in the dry season, the still inundated Inland Delta modifies the strength and direction of the Harmattan, due to differential heating and cooling of the Inland Delta relative to its surroundings (e.g. Kamaté 1980, p. 17).

Compared to the large seasonal variations in precipitation, the seasonality of the temperature is less extreme. Daily maximum temperatures vary over the year, roughly between 30 and 40°, whereas minima roughly vary between 15 and 25° C. The hottest months are April and May. Then, a marked cooling accompanies the wet season. A secondary (lower) temperature maximum follows at the end of the wet season in October. After the wet season, the inundation of the Inland Delta contributes to the lowering of temperatures during November and December. From January on, when large parts of the Inland Delta start to dry, the temperature steadily increases.

Obviously, the recurrent combination of dry winds and high temperatures, favours evaporation. Measurements by the ORSTOM (1970b, p. 58) indicated the potential annual evaporation in the Inland Delta to be 1900 mm along the south margin and 2250 mm in the northern part. These values are applicable to largely inundated areas.

The most important trait of the Sahelian climate is its unreliability with respect to the yearly amounts of precipitation (figure 4.3). How far the monsoon reaches into the West African interior, the timing of its onset, and its duration, varies significantly over the years. Naturally, these fluctuations are also felt in the discharges of the Niger and the Bani, which will be dealt with in the next section.

4.2.3 Hydrology

The distributive nature of the Inland Delta and the high evaporation, profoundly influence the Niger hydrograph in this area. The West African monsoon produces a yearly peak in the Niger discharge, which arrives in the upper Inland Delta by the end of the wet season in October. This peak is attenuated as the floodwaters are distributed over the Inland Delta floodplain by numerous crevasses and minor channels. The flood wave takes several

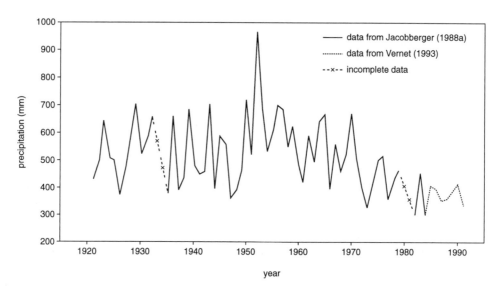

Figure 4.3   Fluctuations in annual precipitation in Mopti (1921-1990) (source: Jacobberger 1988a; Vernet 1993).

months to travel through the Inland Delta (figure 4.4).

Illustrative for the distribution of floodwater is the downstream drop in mean annual discharge of the Niger and Bani as they enter the Inland Delta. Between Koulikoro and Mopti mean annual discharge of the Niger drops from 1330 to 1010 m³/s, whereas along the Bani mean annual discharge drops from 400 to 321 m³/s between San and Sofara (data DNHE).

Due to the distribution over the floodplain, much water is lost by evaporation in the dry season. It was estimated that only little more than half of the yearly amount of water introduced into the Inland Delta in the south by the Niger and Bani, leaves the area through the Niger in the north. The loss is assumed to be mainly caused by evaporation and only for a minor amount by deep infiltration (ORSTOM 1970b, pp. 125-138).

Due to strong variability in precipitation, the interseasonal as well as the interannual fluctuations in discharge are dramatic and mean values only poorly represent the actual conditions. The Niger at Mopti (downstream of the confluence with the Bani) experiences a yearly minimum discharge in the period April-June, which may vary from a few (in 1974) to 135 m³/s (in 1954-5). It must be noted however, that during low stage, Niger discharge is modified by releases from a reservoir at Markala (30 km downstream of Ségou). During the wet season, discharge increases gradually to a maximum, usually reached in October or November, which may range from about 1400 (in 1984) to around 3850 m³/s (in 1953-5). The Bani, having a smaller catchment subjected to a less humid climate, shows even more extreme interannual differences in discharge. Its discharge distribution can be considered as completely natural. Annual minimum discharge at San

104

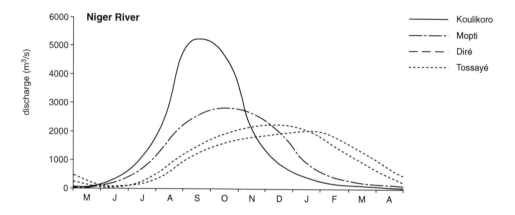

Figure 4.4   Niger River hydrographs for several stations in and near the Inland Delta for an average year (Barth 1977).

occurs in the period April-June. In this season, the river bed dried out completely in the years 1984 and 1985. In wetter years (e.g. 1954-5) discharge remained at least 20-30 m³/s. Maximum discharge usually takes place in September or October and varied from around 350 (in 1984) to a little less than 2800 m³/s (in 1964) (data DNHE).

Considering the river discharge over a period of decades, it appears that dry and wet years do come in clusters. The hydrographs of the Bani and the Niger (figure 4.5) show how wet conditions prevailed throughout the 1950s and 1960s, while the 1970s and 1980s were characterized by a drought, which continued into the 1990s. Disastrous years were 1972-3 and 1983-4, when the Sahelian drought attracted worldwide attention. Earlier this century, similar periods of low Niger discharge were recorded at Koulikoro in the 1910s and early 1920s, as well as in the 1940s (ORSTOM 1970a). In 1994, Niger River discharge peak discharge rose again above 3000 m³/s, perhaps indicating a return to wetter conditions.

Over longer time scales than decades the differences were even more spectacular and deeply influenced the geomorphological history of the region.

4.2.4   Regional climatic and geomorphological history since 20,000 BP

During the last 20,000 years, the Inland Niger Delta experienced an alternation of arid and humid periods of variable duration and intensity. Broadly speaking, in arid periods fluvial activity was significantly reduced and eolian constructional phases dominated. On the other hand, in humid periods dunes were stabilized by vegetation and affected by fluvial erosion. In these times, levees were built up and possibly lacustrine conditions ruled the interdune and interchannel areas.

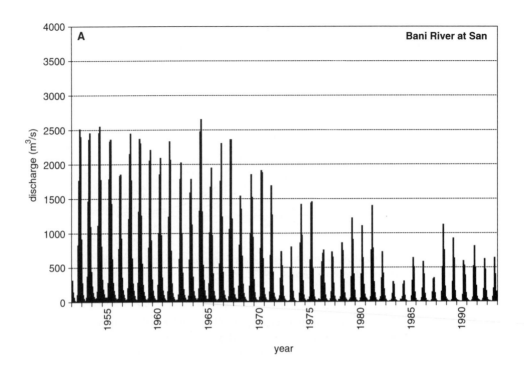

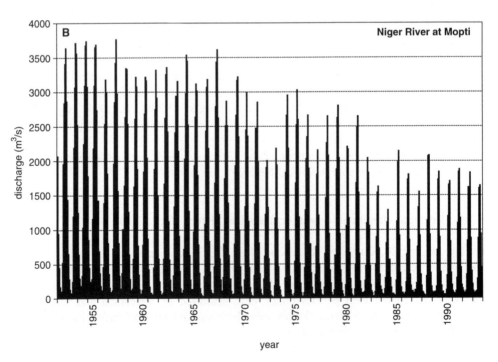

Early studies on the geomorphological history of the region were based on the concept of three (Urvoy 1942; Tricart 1959) to four Quaternary climatic oscillations (Gallais 1967). A relationship was assumed between the glacials of high latitudes and the 'pluvials' in the tropics, either as a positive (e.g. Urvoy 1942, p. 85) or a negative coupling (e.g. Gallais 1967, p. 49). Although the latter idea was confirmed by global paleoclimatic research in the tropics (e.g. Street & Grove 1979; Thomas 1994, p. 209), there proved to be important exceptions which complicate the general picture (e.g. Selby 1977). Besides, radiometric dating considerably rejuvenated the previously distinguished arid and humid periods (e.g. Blanck 1968, p.18-20). As a result climatic periods previously assumed to represent glacial-interglacial cycles, appeared to be largely Holocene (e.g. Grove & Warren 1968, p. 198). Nevertheless these periods, distinguished by Urvoy (1942), Tricart (1959, 1965) and Gallais (1967), remain crucial for understanding the geomorphological history of the Inland Delta.

Thus, although some inconsistencies remain, consensus on an African climatic chronology is growing (summarized by Thomas 1994, table 7.5). This climatic chronology is mainly based on the reconstruction of lake level fluctuations in closed basins (Street & Grove 1976), of which the Lake Chad basin (e.g. Durand 1982) is one of the most important. Pollen and phytogeographical evidence (Lézine 1989a, 1989b) underscore the observed main trends, although a delayed response of vegetation to major climatic changes of up to several thousand years seems to be the case (Lézine 1989b). In figure 4.6 the climatic periods and the chronostratigraphy for the Inland Niger Delta are summarized.

The Ogolian arid period and the early-Holocene humid period (20,000-8000 BP)
Of great importance for the geomorphological history of the study region was a late-Pleistocene arid period between 20,000 and 12,500 BP, recognized world-wide in the low latitudes [e.g. in Australia (Nanson et al. 1995)]. This was a period of extensive dune formation in West Africa (e.g. Kocureck 1996, pp. 145-146), due to precipitation significantly lower than today in combination with intensified trade winds (Talbot 1980). Aridity in Africa was probably most intense between 15,000 and 13,000 BP (Street & Grove 1976). Despite absence of geochronometric dates, massive dune cordons in and near the Inland Niger Delta are believed to stem from this Ogolian period [although Talbot (1980) dates some of them at >40,000 BP]. These late-Pleistocene dunes include the Ergs of Samayé-Djenné, Bara and Azaouad (figure 4.7).

Figure 4.5   *(facing page) (a) Hydrograph of the Bani River at San, showing mean monthly discharges (1952-93) (data DNHE). (b) Hydrograph of the Niger River at Mopti, showing mean monthly discharges (downstream of Bani-Niger confluence) (1952-93) (data DNHE).*

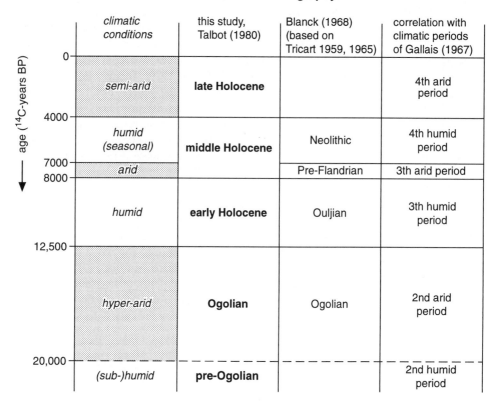

Chronostratigraphy

climatic conditions	this study, Talbot (1980)	Blanck (1968) (based on Tricart 1959, 1965)	correlation with climatic periods of Gallais (1967)
semi-arid	**late Holocene**		4th arid period
humid (seasonal)	**middle Holocene**	Neolithic	4th humid period
arid		Pre-Flandrian	3th arid period
humid	**early Holocene**	Ouljian	3th humid period
hyper-arid	**Ogolian**	Ogolian	2nd arid period
(sub-)humid	**pre-Ogolian**		2nd humid period

age (^{14}C-years BP): 0 — 4000 — 7000 — 8000 — 12,500 — 20,000

Figure 4.6   Chronostratigraphy and climatic conditions for the Inland Niger Delta (20,000 BP - present).

After 12,500 BP the climate rapidly became humid (Gasse et al. 1990) which culminated in an early-Holocene lacustrine phase between 10,000 and 8000 BP. Probably only by 9000 BP, an abrupt change to a more humid vegetation took place (Lézine 1989b). Even the nowadays hyperarid central Sahara received significantly more precipitation during this time (Petit-Maire et al. 1990). Rainfall was not only more abundant than today, but also much more evenly distributed over the year (e.g. Rognon 1976; Talbot 1980; Lézine & Casanova 1989). A matter of debate remains whether the increase in river discharge in combination with the blocking dune cordons of the previous arid period, led to permanent inundation of the entire Inland Delta. The existence of 'paleo Lake Débo', of which the present Lakes Débo and Korienzé (figure 4.7) are relics, was suggested for example by Tricart (1959, p. 336), but its extent and lifetime remains obscure. Anyway, the dunes were breached by the Bani and Niger Rivers at some stage during the early-Holocene humid period and in these times a branch of the Niger even flowed northward for 70 to 100 km through the Erg of Azaouad to feed an extensive area

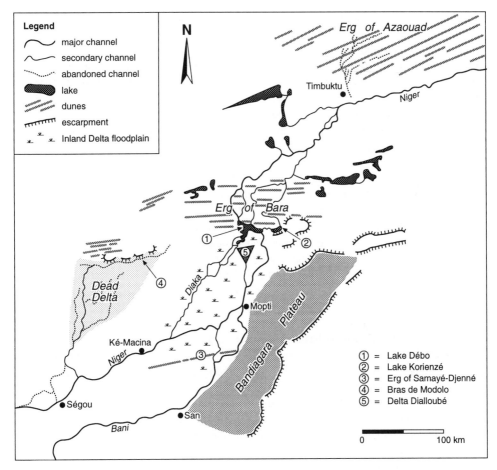

Figure 4.7   *Location map of the geomorphological features discussed in section 4.2.4 (source: Gallais 1967; Barth 1977; Riser & Petit-Maire 1986; IGN 1963, 1967).*

of interdunal lakes north of Timbuktu (figures 4.7 and 4.8) (Riser & Petit-Maire 1986; Jacobberger 1988b; Rognon 1993).

Besides the question of 'paleo Lake Débo', another controversy concerning the genesis of the Inland Niger Delta is the timing of the origin of the present course of the Niger eastward past the sill of Tossayé through which it is connected with its lower course. When abandoned channels leading into the Sahara were discovered west and north of the present Inland Delta (e.g. Furon 1929; Palausi 1955), it was suggested that until recent geological times all of the discharge of the upper Niger River flowed into an endorheic basin (Furon 1929; Urvoy 1942; Voute 1962). Overflow of the sill of Tossayé was thought to have occurred during a wet period in the Holocene (Kevran 1959). Tricart (1959) placed this event in his Ouljian period which turned out to be the equivalent of the humid early-Holocene (figure 4.6). However, an evaluation of various geomorphological evidence led Beaudet et al. (1977) to the conclusion that the unity of the present Niger drainage basin must be much older. One of their main arguments was the considerable incision (more than 30 m) of the Niger River through resistant metamorphic rocks at Tossayé. They suggested that the Niger occupied its present course at least since the Pliocene. Beaudet et al. (1977) believed that during the Pleistocene, the unity of the drainage basin was interrupted in arid periods when dunes blocked the passage to the east. Thus, it seems probable that during the wet period from 12,500 to 8000 BP the Niger occupied an already existing valley at Tossayé.

The mid-Holocene arid and humid periods (8000-4000 BP)
The early-Holocene pluvial period was terminated by a relatively short dry interval between 8000 and 7000 BP (Street & Grove 1976; Rognon 1976; Alimen 1987) in which dune remobilisation took place (Talbot 1980). Nevertheless, this mid-Holocene arid period must have been less severe than the Ogolian (Rognon 1993) and was not obvious in all studies (e.g. Lézine 1989a). Rognon (1993, p. 50) suggested that dunes dating from this period are characterized by steeper northern flanks (Gallais 1967) indicating a southern monsoonal component in the wind direction, which was absent in the Ogolian. Jacobberger (1988b) stated that the Ogolian dunes of the Azouad region were transformed in this period to such an extent that they must have obstructed the fluvial channels feeding the lacustrine basin in the north (figure 4.8). Riser & Petit-Maire (1986) dated molluscs and concluded that the paleo-lakes existed from 8500 to 3500 BP. The question remains open whether they were predominantly fed by river flow or by groundwater flow, after the mid-Holocene period of dune remobilisation.

By 6000 BP, a return to wetter conditions had taken place, but the evidence suggests that the precipitation was more seasonal than in the previous early Holocene pluvial period (Talbot 1980; Lézine 1989a, 1989b; Lézine & Casanova 1989). Maley (1982) supposed a change from fine rains with small raindrops during the early-Holocene to erosive thunderstorm rains with bigger raindrops during the mid-Holocene. The mid-Holocene humid period was mentioned 'the Neolithic humid period' by Tricart (1959). Due to the favourable conditions during this period, Neolithic man thrived around shallow lakes in now hostile Saharan environments (Petit-Maire 1988). The first neolithisation in the Sahel however, predates this period (Alimen 1987).

The late-Holocene aridification
From 4000 BP onwards, climatic conditions generally became progressively more arid, although phases wetter than today alternated with phases more arid than today. According to McIntosh (1983; 1993) a relatively long arid phase existed from 2500 to 1800 BP. Only by 2000 BP, an abrupt change to a more arid vegetation occurred throughout the present Sahel (Lézine 1989a, 1989b). Especially for this recent period, archeological evidence may contribute to the reconstruction of past hydrography. Alimen (1987, p. 222) cited radiocarbon ages between 2500 and 3500 BP from near the edge of the Dead Delta (figure 4.7), representing human bones and tools, found in association with evidence for a lake fauna including perch, crocodile and hippopotamus. The present depth of the

groundwater table at the site is 50 m below the surface! McIntosh (1993, fig. 9) suggested paludal-fluvial conditions in the Dead Delta up to 1100 AD. Large numbers of abandoned mounds along the former water courses suggest a population density once much higher than today. McIntosh (1983, p. 188) referred to abandoned Iron Age (later than $\pm$ 500 BC) mounds on the banks of watercourses now dried up. Some of the mounds were abandoned only in the 11th and 12th century AD, when people moved to the present Inland Delta (Bedaux et al. 1978), perhaps in response to continued aridification.

The abandonment of the Dead Delta, must have been a very slow process induced by (1) ongoing subsidence of the present Inland Delta (section 4.2.1) and (2) progressively increasing aridity since the early-Holocene climatic optimum. In this view, the recent wetter conditions in the Dead Delta were no more than a temporary reactivation of already long abandoned channels in response to high floods that the drainage system in the Inland Delta could not accommodate. Gallais (1967, p. 58) described the abandonment of the Dead Delta as progressively taking place from west to east. In terms of his climatic chronology the central part of the Dead Delta (Bras de Modolo) functioned until the third humid period, which is comparable to the early-Holocene wet period in a modern revised chronology (figure 4.6).

Figure 4.8   The Erg of Azaouad near Timbuktu. Clayey deposits, probably of fluviolacustrine origin (foreground), partly covered by eolian sand (background), which obstructed the fluvial channels (person on the left in the background for scale).

Linking climatic and geomorphological evolution

It is obvious that the coupling of the climatic chronology outlined above, with geomorphological events in the absence of any geochronometric dates is a hazardous enterprise. Therefore, it is not surprising that there is considerable disagreement on the chronology of the various dune generations which can be distinguished in and around the Inland Delta. The chronologies are based on relative dating and on morphological comparison with radiocarbon-dated dunes in other parts of the Sahel (e.g. Senegal Delta and Chad basin). Rognon (1993, p. 50) distinguishes four generations of dunes in the Niger bend region, based on morphology and orientation: (1) the flattened SW-NE trending dunes which he supposes to date from a pre-Ogolian arid period, (2) the massive (± 1 km wide, up to 50 km long) E-W oriented dunes, which are supposed to be of Ogolian age, (3) the much narrower (200-300 m) and shorter (few km) ENE-WSW oriented dunes, taken to be of mid-Holocene age, and (4) the small and irregular dunes believed to date from the late-Holocene. Talbot (1980) however, studying the same area, took the E-W oriented dunes to be older than 40,000 BP, while the ENE-WSW trending dunes were supposed to be of Ogolian age. The mid-Holocene arid phase is represented in his chronology by the small isolated dunes. Jacobberger (1988b) argued that the mid-Holocene reworking of the longitudinal dunes in the Erg of Azaouad, resulted in smaller transverse dunes superimposed on the longitudinal Ogolian dunes. In the upper Inland Delta, a large (80 km long, 5-20 km wide), but partly 'drowned', ENE-WSW trending cordon of massive dunes represents the core of the Erg of Samayé-Djenné (figure 4.7). It was considered to be of Ogolian age by Gallais (1967) and McIntosh (1983). Jacobberger (1987) however, proposed a more recent origin. All in all, it can be concluded that geochronometric dates are urgently needed to solve the problem of the dune chronology.

Perhaps even more difficult is the linking of fluvial forms to the climatic chronology without any independent age control. Tricart (1959, 1965) and Gallais (1967) attempted a reconstruction of the paleohydrography in the Inland Delta elaborating the idea that significant rises in base-level must have accompanied the humid climatic periods, due to the formation of large lakes upstream of the Ergs of Bara and Samayé-Djenné. Gallais (1967, p. 55) supposed the transitional periods to be the most significant for the development of the hydrography, in the following way. (1) In pre-arid phases incision took place, with levees degrading due to a decreasing vegetation cover which enabled gully erosion during intense showers. During maximum aridity, dunes occupied the desiccated river beds. (2) In the post-arid phases, stagnant water behind the fortified ergs invoked a rise in base-level. The disabled hydrographic network, still plugged up with eolian sand, was reorganized and many sandy crevasse splays were formed. Intensified rains in combination with a still not fully recovered vegetation facilitated renewed gully erosion on the levees, which aided the formation of crevasse splays.

Gallais (1967) distinguished two generations of ancient levees different in height, but both higher than levees presently formed. He linked the levee generations to the climatic periods. (1) The oldest and highest levees are clayey and were supposed to have been formed under conditions of high lake levels, which he believed to have been up to 5 m higher than today (Gallais 1967, p. 52). These levees were correlated with his third humid period (figure 4.6). Large parts of these levees are elevated above the highest present flood levels. (2) A younger generation of levees has a lower elevation than the previous generation and consist of sandy loam. These levees were supposed to be built up during the fourth humid period. Bedaux et al. (1978, pp. 100-102) documented ancient levees along the Bani supposedly of the same age.

Along with different levee generations, Tricart (1965) and Gallais (1967) distinguished a number of subdeltas (Rognon 1993, fig. 7) within the Inland Delta hydrography, which were associated with former shorelines of the presumed paleo Lake Débo. Some of these subdeltas however, can be unmasked as natural elements of the anastomosing river system [as suggested by McIntosh (1983)]. On the other hand, the Delta Dialloubé (figure 4.7), well south of the present Lake Débo, represents a clear example of a fossil lake delta adjusted to lake levels higher than today. Gallais (1967) placed the activity of this delta in his third humid period. The Niger presently enters Lake Débo east of the Delta Dialloubé, which is illustrative for the eastward shift of the hydrographic network in the paleogeographical reconstruction of Gallais (1967, fig. 5). This feature was attributed to tectonism (e.g. Gallais 1967, p. 61). A similar displacement to the east was noticed for the Bani in the present study region in the upper Inland Delta (Gallais 1967; McIntosh 1983; Jacobberger 1987).

All in all, it can be concluded that the Inland Delta anastomosing river system during the last 20,000 years, was subjected to a number of base-level rises and falls induced by fluctuations in climate. These relatively large and frequent base-level movements were probably superimposed on a slow, long-term relative base-level rise due to tectonic subsidence, which seems to have been most pronounced in the eastern part of the basin. Although this sets the crude framework of river behaviour, little is known quantitatively on: (a) magnitude and rate of base-level changes, (b) spatial distribution of sedimentation rates and (c) timing of avulsions.

4.3   Methods

Prior to the field research, an extensive study of aerial photographs was carried out. Interpretation of 130 pairs of 1:50,000 scaled stereo-photographs (IGN, 1970-1), covering the entire study region, resulted in a provisional geomorphological map. A satellite image (LANDSAT MSS, bands 4,5,7, 1988) aided in the interpretation of the large-scale features.

Two field campaigns were executed: in January-March 1990 and in October-December 1994. In 1990 the accessibility of the study region was optimal due to dry conditions. In 1994 however, large parts of the Inland Delta were inundated (section 4.2.3), limiting observation to elevated terrain, such as natural levees and dunes. Most attention was focused on the eastern half of the study region, in which the present fluvial activity is centred. The fieldwork included: (1) surveying of geomorphology, (2) hand augering, (3) sampling clastic and organic sediments. Laboratory work mainly concerned grain size analysis. In addition to the fieldwork, the Bani River gauging stations were visited and hydrological data were gathered.

The geomorphological survey was performed to check the provisional geomorphological map. Due to the remoteness of various parts of the study region (especially the western half) with respect to our fieldbases, not all of the study region has been equally visited. The results of the geomorphological survey and the air photo study are presented in section 4.4.1. and appendix 2.

Fifty-seven borings were carried out, most of them aligned in seven cross sections (section 4.4.2), covering important geomorphological units distinguished previously on the aerial photographs. The surface topography of the augered cross sections was levelled. Because of the dry and hard soils encountered, a riverside auger was most frequently used. Occasionally, in softer soils an Edelman auger and a gouge could be used. Often, hammering was needed to aid penetration. In saturated sand under the groundwater table, a Van der Staay suction-corer (Van de Meene et al. 1979) was used. A maximum boring depth of 8.0 m was reached, but often the depth ranged between 6.0 and 7.0 m. Every 10 cm, sediment properties were described. Due to the hard soils and the uncomfortable climate, hand augering in the Inland Delta proved to be very laborious and frequently we had to be content with a lesser boring depth or fewer borings than initially planned.

Seventy-five sediment samples were taken for texture analysis in the laboratory for detailed lithological description (section 4.4.2) and to aid in the interpretation of depositional history. Moreover, it was necessary to check our field classifications of the texture. The desiccated and concreted nature of the fluvial sediments considerably hampered proper field classification of texture. Therefore, sampling for laboratory grain size analysis covered a wide range of lithologies. Samples were extracted at various depths from boreholes, except for four grab samples from the Bani bed and a few samples from the surface and from an excavation. Grain size analysis was performed by the standard sieving/pipette method (McManus 1988).

Many samples were more or less concreted. However, concretions appeared to be easily pulverized during the chemical pretreatment of samples for grain size analysis. Only ferruginous and manganiferous concretions were occasionally noted as a coarse sieve fraction. Of five samples an (acid) solution containing possible cements was analyzed for its ionic composition.

Although the organic matter content of the augered sediments was very low, eleven samples were collected for AMS ^{14}C-dating (section 4.4.3). These samples constituted charcoal, wood, tree leaves, unidentifiable plant remains or dark clay. All samples received an AAA (acid-alkaline-acid) chemical pretreatment comparable to the standard procedure described by Mook & Streurman (1983). The ^{14}C-dating was carried out at the Robert J. van de Graaff Laboratory (Utrecht) and at the Centre for Isotope Research (Groningen).

Three hydrological gauging stations run by the DRHE are located along the Bani River in the study region near the towns of San, Sofara and Mopti. The elevation of the gauges is known relative to an absolute datum. A stage record for these stations, spanning the period 1952-94, was analyzed (section 4.4.4). The analyzed data consisted of 10-day means and yearly extremes of water level. A record of Bani discharge at San and Sofara is kept by the DNHE. The data used, consisted of 10-day means (until 1987) and monthly means (after 1987). For analysing flooding frequencies, the bankfull level at the three gauging stations was determined.

4.4   Results

4.4.1   Geomorphology

Physiographically, the upper Inland Delta is sharply delimited in the east and the south by the emerging Bandiagara Plateau, which was also taken as the boundary of the study region (appendix 2). To the north, the Niger River served as a practical boundary. In the west, a straight line between the towns of San and Ké-Macina, crossing predominantly higher grounds like ancient levees and dunes, was accepted as a rather arbitrary limit. The upper Inland Delta defined as such, encompasses the present lower Bani floodplain and its margins down to the Bani-Niger confluence.

The landscape in this triangular area is dominated by eolian as well as fluvial forms. Many of the dunes are part of the Erg of Samayé-Djenné, which dissects the Bani floodplain in the middle of the study region. Smaller and isolated dunes also occur scattered over the region. The fluvial forms in the region are part of the anastomosing river system of the Bani and the Niger.

Much of the geomorphology described in this section is shown in appendix 2. This map is a generalization of a 1:100,000 geomorphological map, which resulted from air photo interpretation and field survey. The 1:100,000 map (a reduced version) and a detailed description of it can be found in Makaske & Terlien (1996).

Channels
Within the study region, all morphological types of rivers distinguished in section 2.2.4 occur. Most of the channels however, can be classified as straight, their sinuosity index ranging from 1.0 to 1.2. Sharp bends are rare and lateral point bar complexes are mostly of modest extent or absent, while cut-off loops are entirely lacking. An exception to this is the meandering Siné Oualo, which traverses the dunes in the west of the study region, and has a sinuosity index between 1.4 and 1.5. This channel however, is almost totally abandoned now. Another exception is the Mayo Marou, a large crevasse channel branching off the Souman Bani, having a sinuosity index of 1.4. In contrast, the present Bani channel between San and Sofara has only slight irregular bends with narrow point bar complexes upstream, passing downstream into some remarkable straight reaches, separated by a couple of well-developed meanders with lateral scroll topography near Djenné. Another well-developed meander of the Souman Bani, a little north of Djenné, is isolated in occurrence. Downstream of Sofara, bends are open and point bars are poorly developed. The Niger displays a downstream change in morphology from a moderately braided to a straight channel. Upstream, where it enters the study region, the channel has a braiding parameter of 1.2, due to regularly spaced mid-channel sand bars as well as occasional bar-like vegetated islands of variable extent. Downstream of Koa, mid-channel

bars become rare and the Niger adopts a regular winding channel. The sinuosity index however, remains low, being near 1.1 for both the upper and the lower reach.

Dimensions of the present Bani River are variable due to bends and bifurcations. Typical bankfull widths range from 250 to 400 m, although between Sofara and Mopti, the channel narrows to 160 m in bends. Bankfull depths are 6 to 7 m, but may be more in sharp bends. In the cross section near Kouna a bankfull depth of 8.3 m was recorded in the outer bend, giving a width/depth ratio of only 20. More characteristic bankfull width/depth ratios however, range from 40 to 60. The smaller channels may have lower bankfull width/depth ratios. The Souman Bani for example, has over much of its length a width/depth ratio of around 10, being $\pm$ 50 m wide and $\pm$ 5 m deep. The same holds for the meandering Mayo Marou. The Niger is several times wider than the Bani. In its braided reach, the channel is over a kilometre wide. Gallais (1967, p. 113) reported pools in this reach of about 8 to 9 m deep at high flow stage. Downriver the channel narrows to 400-500 m. Bedforms in this reach may consist of subaqueous dunes with a height of 0.5 m and a length of 5 m, as observed on a sand flat exposed during low flow stage in the outer bend near Kouakourou.

The channel gradients are very low: a few centimetres per kilometre only. Levelled water surface gradients of the Bani River were 2.2 cm/km near Siné and 1.9 cm/km downriver, near Kouna (table 4.1). However, in very flat areas like the Inland Delta, water surface gradients are relatively stage dependent (e.g. Gallais 1967, fig. 15). Both gradients were levelled during falling stage, when water surface gradients are lower than during rising stage. Indeed, the calculated gradients of the recent levees between the gauging stations are higher (table 4.1), but they confirm the slight downstream decrease in gradient. Mean water surface gradients however, will show a stronger decrease downriver, as the flooding frequency of the recent levees increases in this direction (section 4.4.4).

Table 4.1 Gradients of the Bani River

	Levelled water surface gradient (cm/km)	Channel gradient [a] (cm/km)	Meander belt gradient [b] (cm/km)	Valley gradient [c] (cm/km)
Reach San-Sofara	2.2 [d]	3.7	3.9	4.1
Reach Sofara-Mopti	1.9 [e]	2.8	3.0	3.3

[a] Approximated by the levee gradient on the basis of the distance along the channel.
[b] Levee gradient on the basis of the distance along the meander belt axis.
[c] Levee gradient on the basis of the valley distance.
[d] Measured near Siné at 5 November 1994 during falling stage.
[e] Measured near Kouna at 18 November 1994 during falling stage.

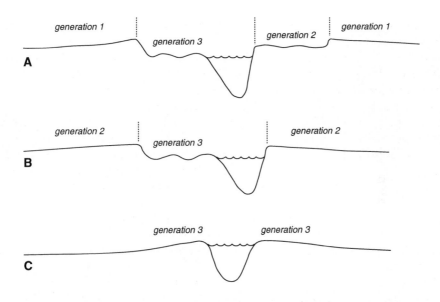

Figure 4.9   *Schematic topographic cross profiles of the Bani channel belt, showing the different levee generations near (a) San, (b) Sofara, and (c) Mopti (see figure 4.1 or appendix 2 for location of these towns).*

Levees and crevasse splays

The present river system is clearly underfit. Levees have different elevations and the highest were rarely or never inundated during this century. In the upper part of the study region, near the San gauging station, three generations of levees were recognized. The numbering of the levee generations is from high to low elevation, and is illustrated in figure 4.9. Near the San station (figure 4.9a), the highest levees *(generation 1)* occur at 9.1 m above the present Bani channel bed. An intermediate levee surface *(generation 2)* occurs at 7.5 m above the channel bed, while the lowest levees *(generation 3)* have an elevation of 6.7 m above the channel bed.

About 50 km downriver, the generation 1 levees approach the level of the generation 2 levees and gradually become covered by them downstream. Further downriver (figure 4.9b), the levee generations 2 and 3 (up to 1 m elevation difference), remain recognizable along the Bani down to Kouna. Downstream of Kouna, the higher generation 2 levees flank the abandoned Potekolé, especially on the right side, down to Mopti, which was founded on these elevated terrains. The present Bani channel between Kouna and Mopti is bordered by lower generation 3 levees (figure 4.9c).

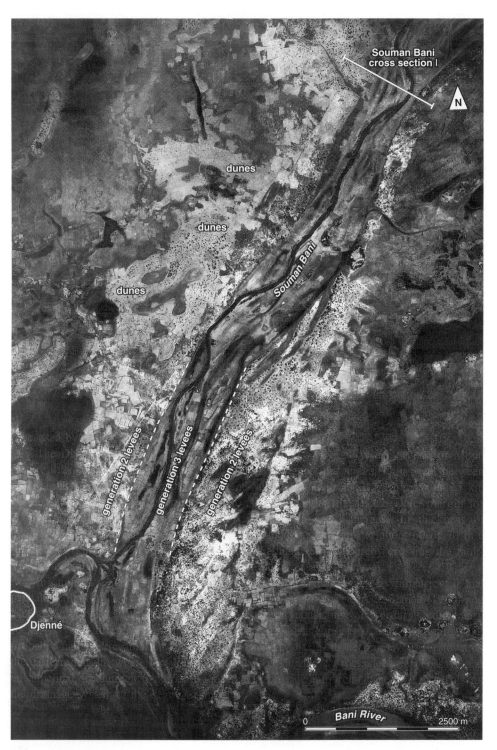

Souman Bani
cross section I

N

dunes

dunes

dunes

Souman Bani

generation 2 levees

generation 3 levees

generation 2 levees

Djenné

0   2500 m
Bani River

The Bani and Souman Bani Rivers over much of their length have a narrow scrolled floodplain ($\pm$ 1 km wide), enclosed between relatively straight superelevated generation 2 levees, varying in width from a few hundred meters to well over a kilometre (figure 4.10). In the latter case often subdued scroll topography can be recognized (e.g. right bank of the Souman Bani, figure 4.10). The generation 2 levees generally slope down rapidly into floodbasins, above which they may be elevated up to 1.5 to 2 m. A distinct step in the terrain separates these levees from the scrolled floodplain, which hosts the lower generation 3 levees (figure 4.9b).

The Niger has a similar morphology, although the generation 2 levees are generally less pronounced. In fact, these levees are morphologically quite different from the Bani levees, which can be easily delimited (e.g. figure 4.11). In contrast, the Niger levees, very gently grade into the floodbasins. In places they seem to be absent, while elsewhere they may be kilometres wide.

The surface of the levees is occupied by scattered trees and shrubs, predominantly *Acacia* species. Grasses only grow in local depressions and swales. Where the ground is bare, the surface is indurated. Termite mounds are fairly typical for the levees of the upper Inland Delta, floodbasins and eolian dunes generally being less hospitable for termites. Usually the mounds occur scattered and are of different types and dimensions (from $\pm$ 0.5 to several meters high). Locally however, spectacular monospecific concentrations of mounds exist (figure 4.12).

The river banks are steep and often near vertical in the upper part, for one or a few meters. Disintegration of the indurated levee surface takes place during high water by detachment of blocks (figure 4.13). Next to the channels, the levees may be heavily dissected by gullies (figure 4.14), which can be up to 1 m deep. In places, the levee surface is obviously lowered a few centimetres by deflation (figure 4.15). Small eolian sediment accumulations entrapped by vegetation can be found.

Crevasse splays are very common in the upper Inland Delta, although few of them are still active today. Distinct finger-shaped patterns can be seen along the Bani river south of Djenné (figure 4.11). Some of the crevasse channels in the study region are tens of kilometres long; for example the Mayo Marou (appendix 2). Another long crevasse channel branches from the Souman Bani at Djenné and can be traced westward, where it follows for some distance the abandoned channels of the Siné Oualo and Mayo Manga (appendix 2). Throughout the study region crevasse splays tend to have lobate forms. Frequently, levees and crevasse splays are amalgamated, giving a freakish plan-view.

Figure 4.10   *(facing page) Aerial photograph of the Souman Bani northeast of Djenné, where the river crosses the Erg of Samayé-Djenné. River flow is to the north. The scrolled floodplain is flanked on both sides by generation 2 levees. Especially west of the river, eolian dunes crop out. The Souman Bani cross section I (figure 4.22) is located in the north. Locations of Djenné (southwest) and the cross section are also shown in appendix 2. (Photo taken in 1970 by IGN; © DNCT, Bamako)*

Figure 4.11   *Aerial photograph of the Bani south of Djenné. River flow is to the north. Finger-shaped crevasse splays branch off into the floodbasins. One of them developed further and resulted in a major avulsion of the Bani to the east, reducing the Souman Bani to a minor channel. The Siné cross section (figure 4.19) is located in the middle of the photograph. The location of this cross section is also shown in appendix 2. (Photo taken in 1970 by IGN; © DNCT, Bamako)*

Figure 4.12   Dense concentration of termite mounds in the Korori region.

An exceptionally wide complex of elevated levees and crevasse splays is situated on the right bank of the Souman Bani. The Mayo Marou is obviously incised through this higher terrain, which is named the Korori. The local people know the Korori as a dry and desolated area covered by dense shrubwood. An abandoned channel with large meanders (wavelength $\pm$ 5 km, sinuosity index 1.3), traverses this terrain in a northwesterly direction. On closer inspection of the air photos it can be seen that downstream this meander belt gradually becomes submerged under other fluvial forms to fade away totally. Between the levees and crevasse splays of the Korori, floodbasins can be discerned which are seldom or never inundated under present conditions. Shrubs in the abandoned channels, trees in the floodbasins and abundant termite mounds (figure 4.12), testify to the dry conditions. The surface of the levees is strongly indurated. It is striking that these high grounds are restricted to the east bank of the Souman Bani. In contrast, the lower west bank is flanked by a deep floodbasin.

Floodbasins
Deep floodbasins, inundated several months per year, are   concentrated in three areas within the study region, which are poorly connected to each other. Morphologically, the three areas are quite different.

The most extensive floodbasin is the Pondori, south of the Erg (appendix 2). Enclosed by irregular shaped crevasse lobes and dunes, this is a featureless plain, which

Figure 4.13   Disintegration of an indurated river bank during falling stage.

remarkably escaped more fluvial activity. The Yongary (appendix 2) however, west of the Korori and north of the Erg, is dissected by various abandoned channels. In the south of this area, the floodbasins exhibit subdued dune topography of the drowned Erg. Minor channels and semi-permanent lakes in rounded depressions (mostly about 0.5 km in diameter) are common in these floodbasins. In the Sébéra (appendix 2), northeast of the Korori, the floodbasins are traversed by many small and tortuous channels, while lakes are common, a number of them measuring more than a kilometre across.

The Inland Delta floodbasins are totally covered by grasses. In the wettest parts the so-called 'bourgou' vegetation dominates, a typical association of different species of tall savanna grasses. Trees and shrubs normally do not occur in the floodbasins.

Dunes
Three morphological types of dunes can be recognized within the study region, on the basis of their size and orientation: (1) massive dunes (kilometres wide, kilometres to tens of kilometres long) aligned in a ENE-WSW trending cordon, (2) smaller longitudinal dunes (hundreds of meters wide, kilometres long) with orientations between ENE-WSW and NNE-SSW and (3) isolated dunes with no preferred orientation. The height of all of these dunes is modest: usually they rise no more than a few meters above the surrounding floodplain. Nowadays, many dunes are under cultivation. Trees, often palms, occur scattered.

Figure 4.14   Gullies in the generation 2 levee of the Souman Bani, near Djenné.

The core of the Erg of Samayé-Djenné consists of a cordon of massive dunes. The Femaye (3.5 km wide, 20 km long) in the east of the study region is the most conspicuous part of this cordon (appendix 2). More to the west, the massive dunes (up to 7 km wide) can be less easily delimited, because they are flanked by smaller longitudinal dunes and modified by fluvial erosion and deposition (figure 4.16).

In the western half of the study region, regular fields of longitudinal dunes (figure 4.16) occur to the north and to the south of the massive dunes. North of the massive dunes they occur west of the Souman Bani and northward they gradually disappear in the floodbasins about halfway between the massive dunes and the Niger. In this area they generally have a ENE-WSW orientation. The dunes are discontinuous and often surrounded by floodbasins. South of the massive dunes, the longitudinal dunes occur west of the Pondori and north of the Bani levees. In this area, the longitudinal dunes generally have a NNE-SSW orientation. This dune field is more coherent and interdune depressions are not connected to the present floodbasins, except along the eastern rim.

Isolated dunes of variable dimensions, which are not a part of the above described dune complexes, occur throughout the study region. South of Djenné for example, a row of dunes can be identified, which is part of the scrolled floodplain along the Bani. From boreholes it appears that these dunes are founded in the floodplain instead of being superimposed on it (e.g. figure 4.19b: highest elevation feature). In other cases however, isolated dunes are smaller and may be superimposed on the levees.

Figure 4.15   Deflation scar on a levee (knife measures ± 23 cm).

Plateau margin and alluvial fans

The emerging Bandiagara Plateau sharply stands out along the east margin of the Bani floodplain. The western part of the plateau consists of inselbergs, glacis (pediment) and extensive terraces and floodplains of rivers descending from the plateau. Low-gradient alluvial fans were deposited by these rivers and protrude into the Inland Delta floodplain. A relatively large fan was deposited by the Diama River (appendix 2). In contrast to the Inland Delta floodplain, the geomorphology of the plateau underwent the influence of lateritisation and the subsequent formation of 'cuirasses' (ferricretes). The cuirasses cap weathered sandstone as well as the associated glacis.

Figure 4.16   (facing page) Aerial photograph of the Siné Oualo and the Erg of Samayé-Djenné near Mounia in the western part of the study region. River flow is to the east. An abandoned fluvial channel eroded the massive dune. In this channel (arrow) and to the north, younger longitudinal dunes can be seen. The location of Mounia is also shown in appendix 2 (Photo taken in 1970 by IGN; © DNCT, Bamako)

124

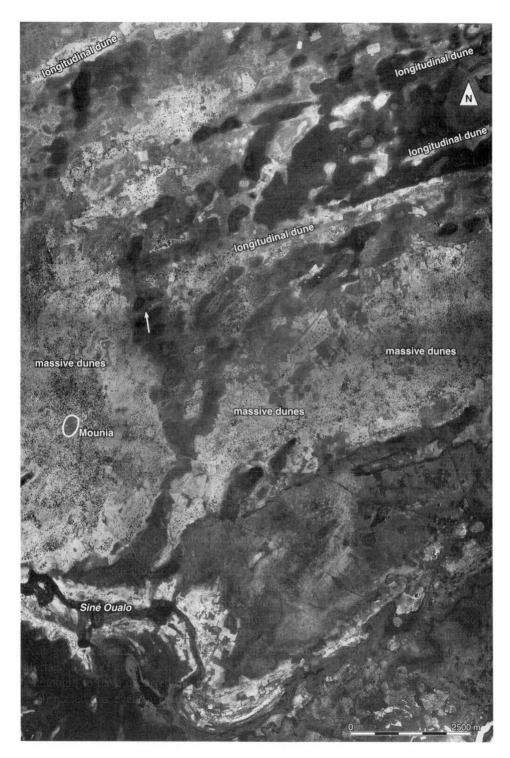

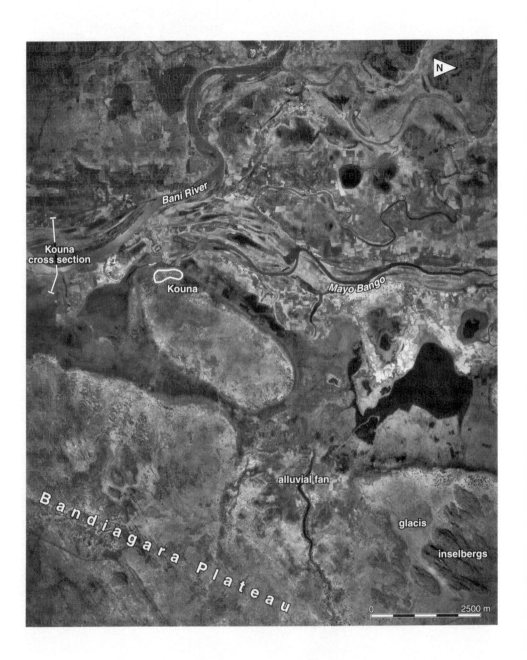

The various geomorphological units bordering the Inland Delta floodplain are illustrated in figure 4.17. In the northeast, inselbergs with their glacis can be identified. The glacis are dissected by a river, which deposited an alluvial fan in the Inland Delta floodplain. A little to the south, the village of Kouna is located on a patch of cuirasse-capped glacis which occurs isolated in the floodplain. The river on the alluvial fan probably excised this 'island' from the plateau.

Togué

Well over 1000 anthropogenic mounds occur in the study region. These togué (plural of toguéré) are mostly situated on levees. Generally they are circular in form, having steep flanks and a flat top, although more rounded cross sections occur as well. Their dimensions are variable, with heights ranging from 0.4 to 8 m and lengths between 25 to 758 m (Schmidt 1993). The surface of the togué is usually covered with pottery fragments and may be dissected by gullies. The most spectacular toguéré is Jenné-Jenno (see figure 4.11 for location), having a surface area of 330,810 m^2 and a height of 8 m (McIntosh & McIntosh 1981).

The togué are not depicted on the geomorphological map (appendix 2). Some of them were augered and appear in the cross sections discussed in section 4.4.2 (e.g. figures 4.22 and 4.25). During the 1994 field campaign, eight atypical togué were investigated with regard to their morphology and lithological composition. The results of these investigations are beyond the scope of this chapter, but were described in extension by Rijnbeek (1996). For more information on the togué and their occupational history the reader is referred to Bedaux et al. (1978), McIntosh & McIntosh (1980, 1981), Dembelé et al. (1993) and Schmidt (1993).

Figure 4.17   *(facing page) Aerial photograph of the Bani and the eastern margin of the floodplain near Kouna. River flow is to the north. The most recent avulsion of the Bani river to the west led to abandonment of the Potékolé. The Mayo Bango occupies the former bed of the Potékolé. The Kouna cross section (figure 4.21) is located in the south. The locations of Kouna and the cross section are also shown in appendix 2. (Photo taken in 1970 by IGN; © DNCT, Bamako)*

A

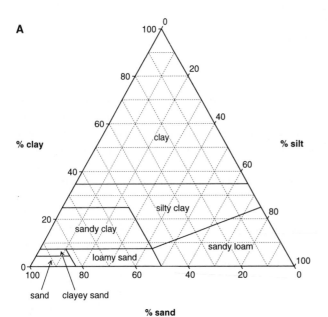

B

- o floodbasin deposits
- + levee deposits
- ▲ dune deposits

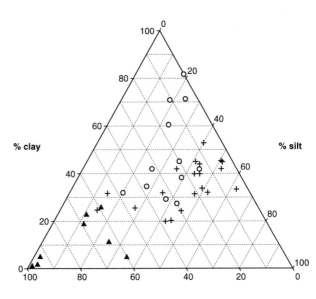

128

4.4.2 Lithology

Borings were carried out for lithological characterization of geomorphological units and to unravel the depositional history of the study region. Most of the borings were aligned in seven transects in order to enable the construction of lithological cross sections. At few places in the study region sedimentary structures were exposed. Therefore, the lithological description almost completely relies on auger data. The field and laboratory classification of the sediment texture was based on the texture triangle of the Nederlands Normalisatie Instituut (1989) (figure 4.18a). The position in the texture triangle of grain size samples from various environments in the study region (figure 4.18b) is discussed further on in this section. The verbal scale for sorting of Folk & Ward (1957, p. 13) is used in the lithological description of the sandy samples. All described sediments were poor in carbonates.

In the figures 4.19 - 4.25 the lithological cross sections and their interpretation in terms of genesis and age are shown. The location of all cross sections is indicated in appendix 2. Additionally, the Siné (figure 4.19), Kouna (figure 4.21) and Souman Bani (I) (figure 4.22) cross sections are also indicated on the air photos (figures 4.10, 4.11 and 4.17). It should be noted that the lithological cross sections depict the field descriptions of sediment texture, which may differ from laboratory determination of the sediment texture. In many cases, the sediment texture turned out to be slightly finer than initially estimated in the field. Grain size analyses were used together with the surface morphology and radiocarbon dates for the interpretation of the lithological cross sections. In this section I will focus on the lithological characterization of the geomorphological units, whereas the chronostratigraphic interpretation will be dealt with in section 4.5.1.

(the text of this chapter is continued on page 144, after the figures 4.19 - 4.25)

Figure 4.18   *(facing page) (a) Texture triangle showing classes according to NEN 5104 (Nederlands Normalisatie Instituut 1989). (b) Textural composition of levee, floodbasin and dune deposits.*

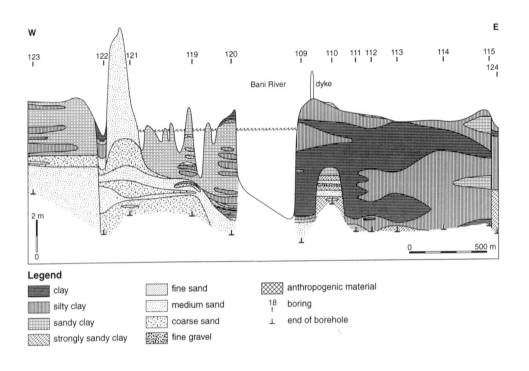

W   E

123   122 121   119   120   109   110 111 112   113   114   115
                                                                                                124

Bani River   dyke

2 m

0   0   500 m

Legend

▮ clay   ▦ fine sand   ▨ anthropogenic material

▥ silty clay   ▦ medium sand   18 boring

▤ sandy clay   ⫶ coarse sand   ⊥ end of borehole

▨ strongly sandy clay   ▩ fine gravel

Figure 4.19a   Siné cross section: lithology.

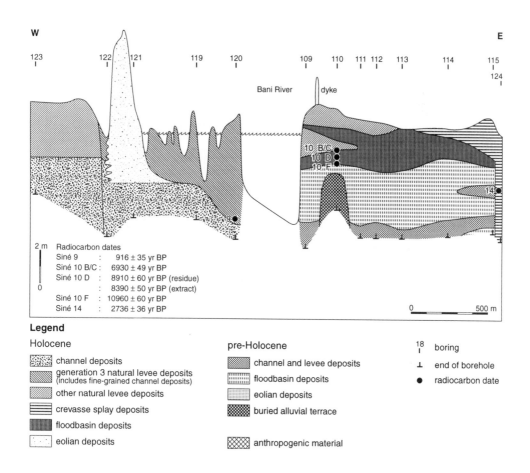

W   E

123   122 121   119   120   109   110   111 112   113   114   115

124

Bani River   dyke

10 B/C
10 D
10 F

14

2 m   Radiocarbon dates
      Siné 9   :   916 ± 35 yr BP
      Siné 10 B/C :   6930 ± 49 yr BP
      Siné 10 D   :   8910 ± 60 yr BP (residue)
0   :   8390 ± 50 yr BP (extract)
      Siné 10 F   :   10960 ± 60 yr BP
      Siné 14   :   2736 ± 36 yr BP

0   500 m

Legend

Holocene

   channel deposits
   generation 3 natural levee deposits
   (includes fine-grained channel deposits)
   other natural levee deposits
   crevasse splay deposits
   floodbasin deposits
   eolian deposits

pre-Holocene

   channel and levee deposits
   floodbasin deposits
   eolian deposits
   buried alluvial terrace

   anthropogenic material

18   boring
⊥   end of borehole
●   radiocarbon date

Figure 4.19b   Siné cross section: genetical and chronological interpretation.

131

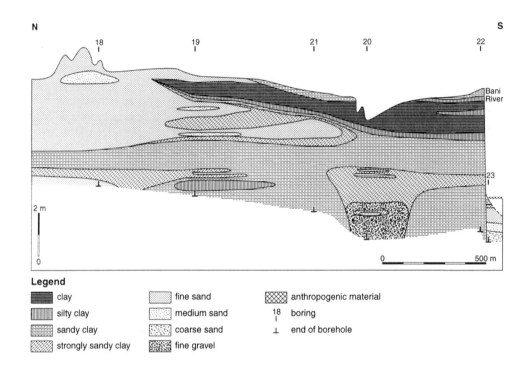

Figure 4.20a   Femaye cross section: lithology.

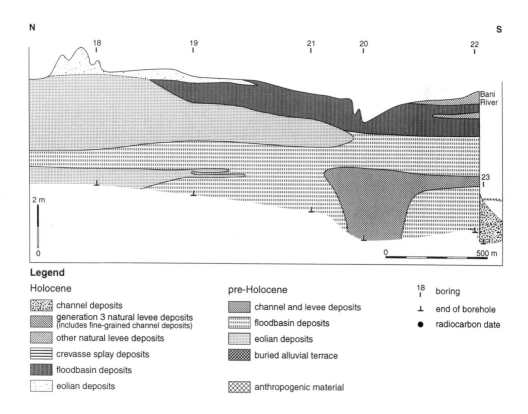

N   S

18   19   21   20   22

Bani
River

23

2 m

0   0   500 m

Legend

Holocene   pre-Holocene   ¹⁸ boring

[channel deposits]   [channel and levee deposits]   ⊥ end of borehole

[generation 3 natural levee deposits
(includes fine-grained channel deposits)]   [floodbasin deposits]   ● radiocarbon date

[other natural levee deposits]   [eolian deposits]

[crevasse splay deposits]   [buried alluvial terrace]

[floodbasin deposits]

[eolian deposits]   [anthropogenic material]

Figure 4.20b   Femaye cross section: genetical and chronological interpretation.

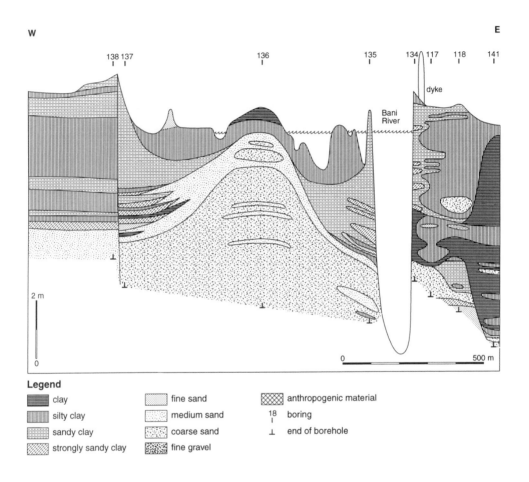

W   E

138 137   136   135   134 117   118   141

dyke

Bani
River

2 m

0

0   500 m

Legend

clay	fine sand	anthropogenic material
silty clay	medium sand	18 boring
sandy clay	coarse sand	⊥ end of borehole
strongly sandy clay	fine gravel	

Figure 4.21a   Kouna cross section: lithology.

134

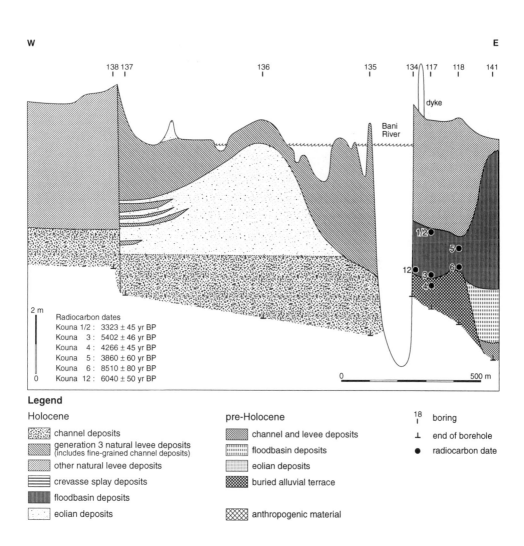

W   E

138 137   136   135   134 117   118   141

dyke

Bani River

2 m

Radiocarbon dates
Kouna 1/2 : 3323 ± 45 yr BP
Kouna   3 : 5402 ± 46 yr BP
Kouna   4 : 4266 ± 45 yr BP
Kouna   5 : 3860 ± 60 yr BP
Kouna   6 : 8510 ± 80 yr BP
Kouna   12 : 6040 ± 50 yr BP

0   0   500 m

Legend

Holocene

- channel deposits
- generation 3 natural levee deposits (includes fine-grained channel deposits)
- other natural levee deposits
- crevasse splay deposits
- floodbasin deposits
- eolian deposits

pre-Holocene

- channel and levee deposits
- floodbasin deposits
- eolian deposits
- buried alluvial terrace
- anthropogenic material

18
| boring

⊥   end of borehole

●   radiocarbon date

Figure 4.21b   Kouna cross section: genetical and chronological interpretation.

135

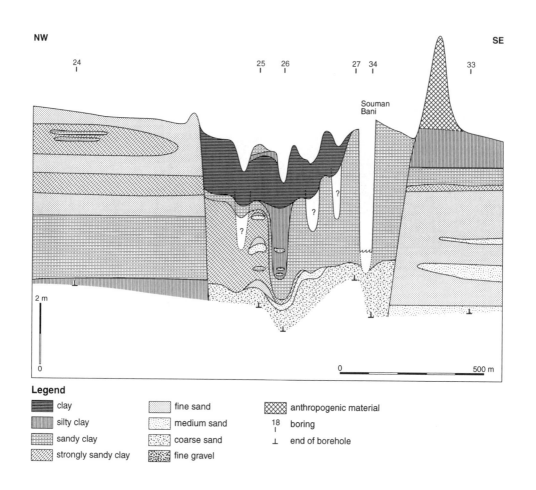

Figure 4.22a   Souman Bani cross section I: lithology.

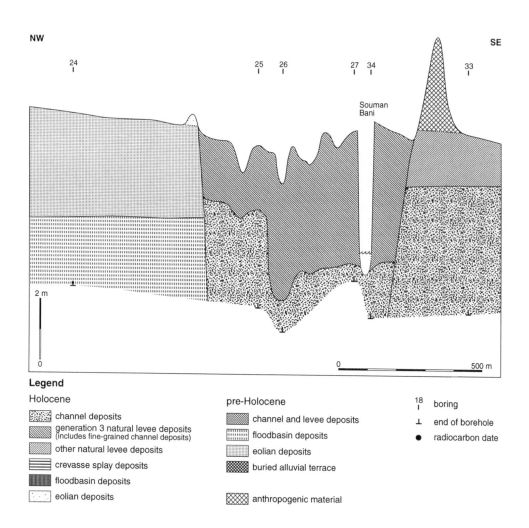

Figure 4.22b   Souman Bani cross section I: genetical and chronological interpretation.

137

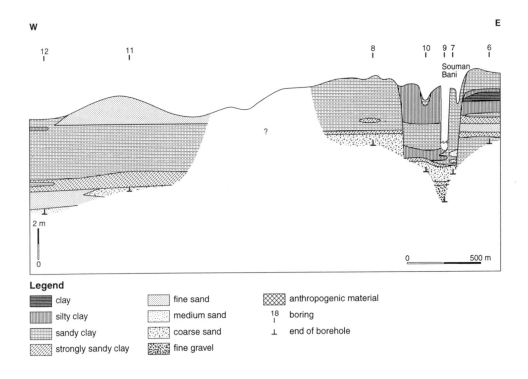

W   E

Figure 4.23a   Souman Bani cross section II: lithology.

138

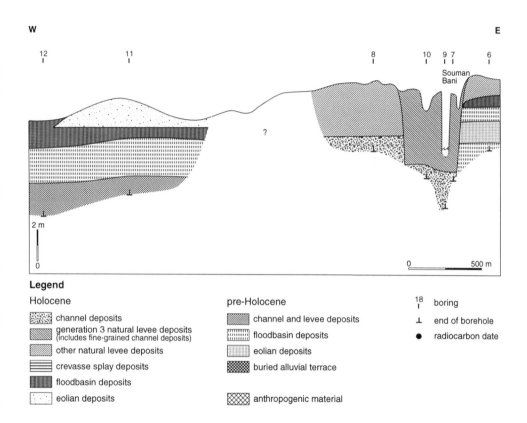

W   E

12   11   8   10 9 7   6

Souman
Bani

?

2 m

0   0   500 m

Legend

Holocene   pre-Holocene ^{18} boring

▦ channel deposits   ▦ channel and levee deposits   ⊥ end of borehole

▧ generation 3 natural levee deposits   ▦ floodbasin deposits   ● radiocarbon date
  (includes fine-grained channel deposits)

▨ other natural levee deposits   ▦ eolian deposits

▤ crevasse splay deposits   ▦ buried alluvial terrace

▥ floodbasin deposits

▦ eolian deposits   ▦ anthropogenic material

Figure 4.23b   Souman Bani cross section II: genetical and chronological interpretation.

139

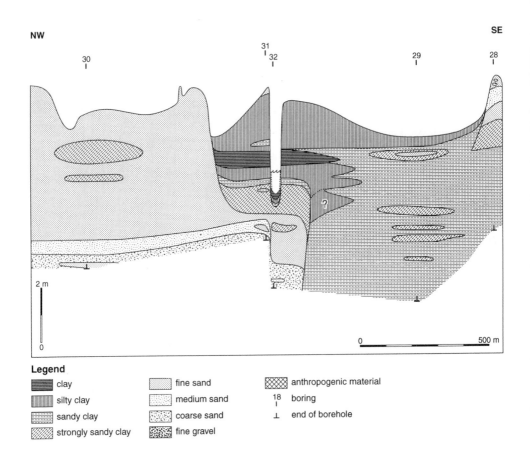

NW   SE

Legend

	clay		fine sand		anthropogenic material
	silty clay		medium sand	18	boring
	sandy clay		coarse sand	⊥	end of borehole
	strongly sandy clay		fine gravel		

Figure 4.24a   Siné Oualo cross section: lithology.

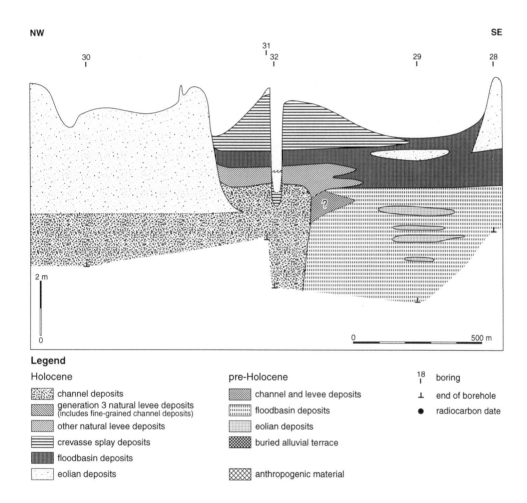

NW   SE

30   31 32   29   28

Legend

Holocene

- channel deposits
- generation 3 natural levee deposits (includes fine-grained channel deposits)
- other natural levee deposits
- crevasse splay deposits
- floodbasin deposits
- eolian deposits

pre-Holocene

- channel and levee deposits
- floodbasin deposits
- eolian deposits
- buried alluvial terrace
- anthropogenic material

- 18 boring
- ⊥ end of borehole
- ● radiocarbon date

Figure 4.24b Siné Oualo cross section: genetical and chronological interpretation.

141

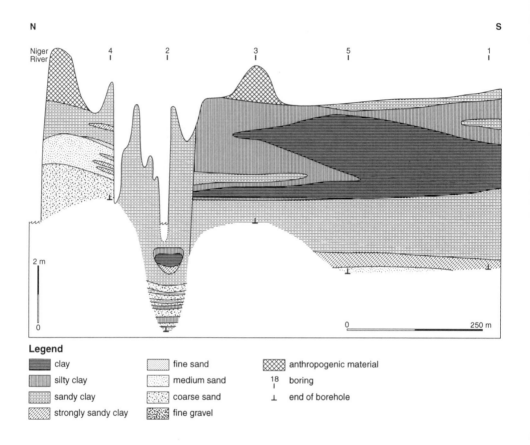

N   S

Figure 4.25a   Niger River cross section: lithology.

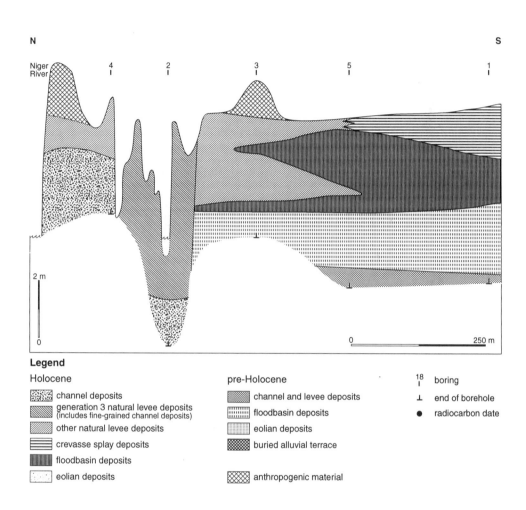

Legend

Holocene

- channel deposits
- generation 3 natural levee deposits (includes fine-grained channel deposits)
- other natural levee deposits
- crevasse splay deposits
- floodbasin deposits
- eolian deposits

pre-Holocene

- channel and levee deposits
- floodbasin deposits
- eolian deposits
- buried alluvial terrace
- anthropogenic material

$^{18}_{\,|}$ boring

⊥ end of borehole

● radiocarbon date

Figure 4.25b   Niger River cross section: genetical and chronological interpretation.

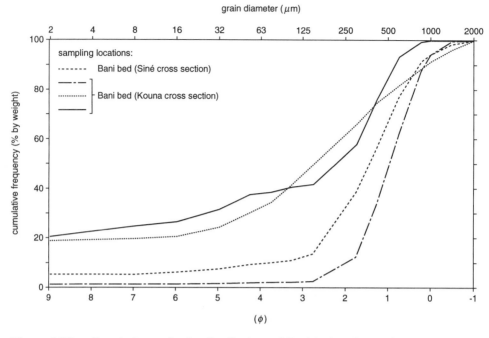

Figure 4.26   Cumulative grain size distributions of Bani bed grab samples.

Channel deposits

Grab samples from the bed of the Bani are moderately to extremely poorly sorted, while the median grain size varies from 150 to 500 μm (figure 4.26). The method used limited sampling depth to 5 metres, thereby excluding the deepest part of the channel where sediments may be coarser. The high percentage of clay fraction in some of the samples can be attributed to the presence of clay pebbles. The sand is very rich in quartz, whereas a subordinate fraction is composed of rounded ferruginous concretions, probably cuirasse fragments. Organic material was not found in these samples.

In juxtaposition to the base of the Bani and Souman Bani channels, channel sands are found below levee deposits (figures 4.19, 4.21 - 4.23). These sands vary in colour between gray and reddish-brown, are moderately to poorly sorted and have a median grain-size of 250 to 450 μm (figure 4.27). However, the sands fine upward, thus grain sizes may be coarser below boring depth. The transition to the overlying levee deposits is usually rather abrupt. Occasionally, wood fragments, tree leaves or gravel are present. The depth of the base of the channel deposits is unknown. Eolian dunes, which will be described later in this section, may rest on the channel sands.

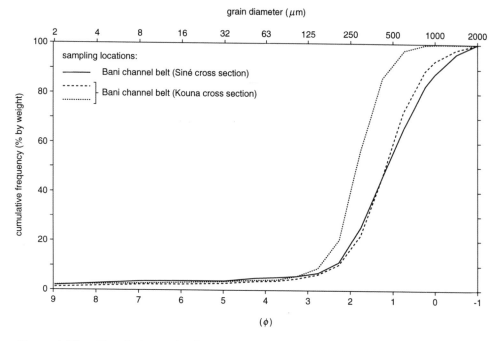

Figure 4.27   Cumulative grain size distributions of Bani channel deposits.

Levee and crevasse splay deposits

The levee deposits in the study region are relatively fine-textured. They consist of clay and silty clay and generally have a relatively low sand content (figure 4.18b). Cumulative graphs and histograms (figure 4.28) show that especially the coarse silt fraction (32-53 μm) is well represented in most of the levee samples. A sample from a crevasse splay has essentially the same grain size distribution, but is at the finer end of the range (figure 4.28a).

The sediment is brown-gray mottled, with subordinate red, light brown and dark gray colours. Ferruginous and manganiferous concretions are common, but irregularly distributed. Also locally, impressive concentrations of redbrown ferruginous concretions may cover the bare surface of the levees (figure 4.29). These concretions consist of quartz and clay stained by ferric oxides (McIntosh & McIntosh 1981, p. 19). The enrichment of these concretions at the surface may be caused by deflation of the finer material. The sediment near the surface is indurated by strong desiccation. During chemical analysis, no evidence was found for cementation of the levee surface by evaporites. Tricart (1959) and Gallais (1967) documented cementation in the subsurface by precipitation of ferric oxides in the phreatic zone [even described as 'cuirasse de nappe embryonnaire' (Gallais 1967, p. 101-102)]. The thickness of the levee deposits may be up to 5 m.

145

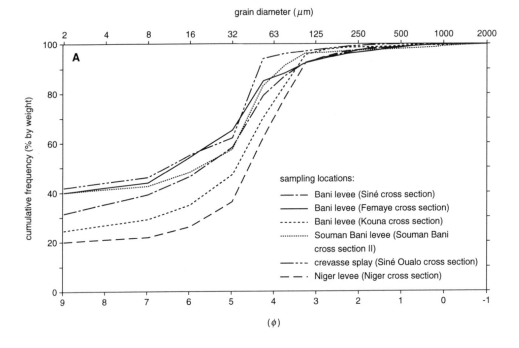

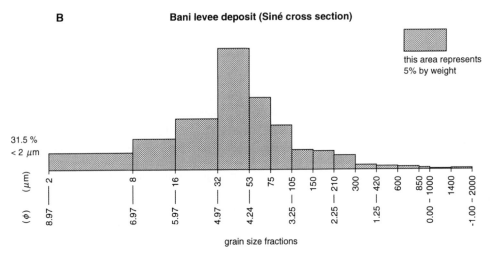

Figure 4.28   Grain size distributions of levee deposits: (a) cumulative graphs, (b) histogram of a typical sample.

Figure 4.29   Concentration of ferruginous concretions on the levee surface (knife measures 23 cm).

Termites are known to preferentially take up the finer sediment fractions (e.g. Goudie 1988). This is confirmed by comparison of the grain size distributions of a termite mound and the underlying levee (figure 4.30). The clay content of the termite mound is 5% higher, while sorting significantly decreased. The action of termites does not only result in upworking of the levee deposits into the mounds, but also in the formation of chambers (diameter up to 30 cm) and passages in the subsurface. Consequently, levee deposits may be severely bioturbated.

Floodbasin deposits
The floodbasin deposits in the study region are heterogeneous in composition and like the levee deposits, they consist of clay and silty clay. In a texture triangle the clusters of floodbasin and levee samples show large overlap (figure 4.18b). In cumulative graphs however, the difference in grain size distribution between levee and floodbasin deposits is obvious (compare figures 4.28a and 4.31a).

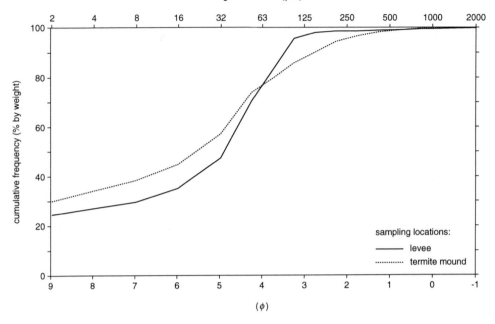

Figure 4.30   *Cumulative grain size distributions of material from a termite mound and the underlying levee.*

The upper layer of floodbasin deposits near the surface, usually is poorer in sand than the floodbasin deposits underneath. In a large part of the study region, the floodbasin deposits more or less abruptly become sandier between 1 and 3 m below the surface. In figure 4.20a (borings 20 and 22) for example, this can be recognized as a rapid change from clay to sandy clay. Most frequently however, this change is more subtle. In figure 4.31b and c the grain size distributions of the two types of floodbasin deposits are compared. The chronostratigraphic interpretation of the two types, which are believed to represent Holocene and pre-Holocene floodbasins deposits, will be discussed in section 4.5.1.

The young floodbasin deposits are usually brown-gray mottled and sometimes dark gray. Ferruginous and manganiferous concretions may occur but are not abundant. The old floodbasin deposits generally show more oxidation. Ferruginous and manganiferous concretions are more common, whereas brown-gray mottling is dominant.

Peat is absent in the floodbasins. Some of the dark gray shallow floodbasin deposits are slightly humic, but macroscopic organic remains are rarely present (section 4.4.3). Locally, a gypsum horizon may be present. Thickness of floodbasin deposits may be up to 6 or 7 m and maybe deeper if coring could penetrate deeper.

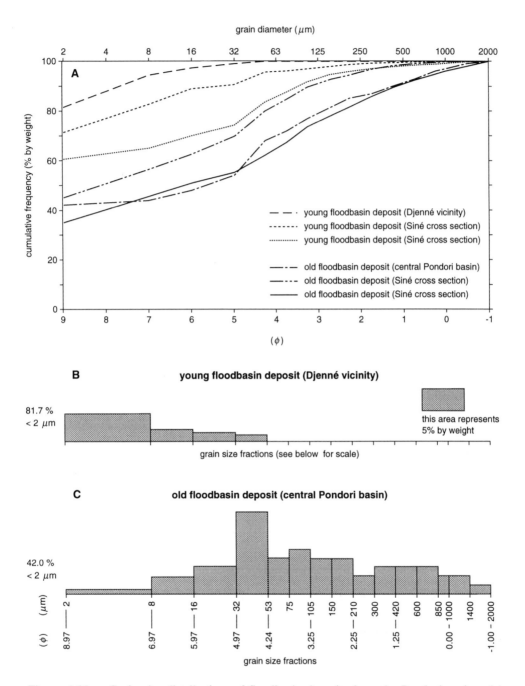

Figure 4.31 *Grain size distributions of floodbasin deposits from the Pondori region: (a) cumulative graphs, (b) histogram of a typical sample of young floodbasin deposits, (c) histogram of a typical sample of old floodbasin deposits.*

149

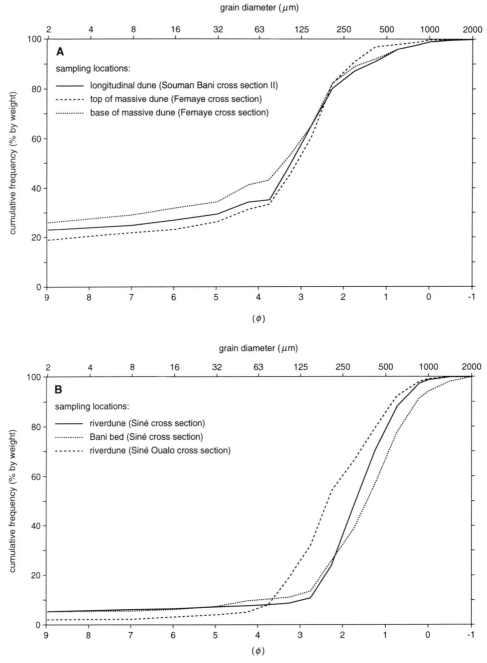

Figure 4.32   (a) *Cumulative grain size distributions of eolian deposits from massive and longitudinal dunes.* (b) *Cumulative grain size distributions of eolian deposits from river dunes on channel deposits.*

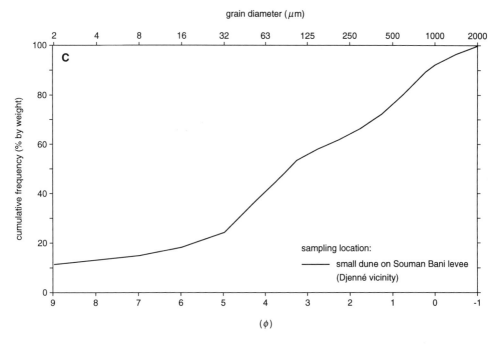

Figure 4.32   (c) Cumulative grain size distributions of eolian deposits from a small dune on a levee.

Eolian dune deposits

Eolian deposits can have variable textural compositions (figure 4.18b), according to the type of dune. The cross sections in figures 4.20 and 4.22 show a part of the massive E-W trended dune, which appeared to have its base several meters below the present floodplain. Grain size distributions (figure 4.32a) of samples taken near the top and the base of this dune in boring 18 reveal a considerable clay fraction (19 and 26%) and a very poor to extremely poor sorting. The deposits have a median grain size of around 105 μm. Figure 4.23 (boring 11) shows a smaller longitudinal dune located in a floodbasin. A sample from this dune is similar in grain size to the other two dune samples (figure 4.32a). In figure 4.24 (boring 28) another dune of this type is shown. The colour of these dune sands is reddish-brown to yellow with subordinate gray-brown colours. Ferruginous concretions commonly occur. The thickness of these deposits exceeds the present dune height, and may be up to 5 m.

Typical phenomena in the study region are eolian river dunes that rest on sandy channel deposits (figure 4.19, 4.21 and 4.24). These dunes are (partly) covered by levee deposits with which they may interfinger on their west flank. The median grain size of these dunes is 200 to 300 μm, they are poorly sorted and the clay fraction is only 2 to 5%. In fact, the grain size characteristics of these dunes are nearly identical to those of the channel sands in the vicinity (figure 4.32b). The dominant colour of these dune sands is reddish-brown, although light brown and graybrown colours may also occur. Ferruginous concretions were not found in these deposits. Thickness of these deposits exceeds the present dune height by far and ranges from 4 to 9 m in the cross sections.

Very different in textural composition are the very small dunes (tens of cm high) around the stems of shrubs on bare levees. The gray-brown deposits are very poorly sorted, whereas the median grain size is 90 μm (figure 4.32c).

Alluvial fan deposits

In the lower part of the cross sections of figure 4.19 (borings 109 - 115) and figure 4.21 (borings 117 - 118, 141), the floodbasin clays gently grade into coarse sands. These deposits are generally very poorly to extremely poorly sorted (figure 4.33). The sand may contain abundant (abraded) ferruginous concretions. The deposits are gray, brown-gray or reddish-brown and may be gravelly. The top of these deposits shows steps of about 3 m in the cross sections. These deposits are interpreted as terraced alluvial fan deposits from the nearby Bandiagara Plateau (section 4.4.1).

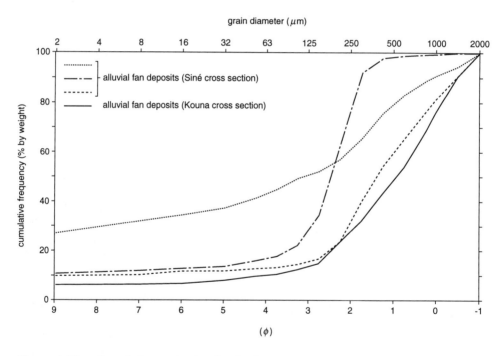

Figure 4.33   Cumulative grain size distributions of alluvial fan deposits.

152

4.4.3 Radiocarbon dates and sedimentation rates

Twelve radiocarbon dates were obtained, enabling age interpretation of the sediments described above. The two most important goals were: (1) to establish a chronological framework for the geomorphological evolution of the study region, and (2) to calculate sedimentation rates.

All radiocarbon samples (table 4.2) were extracted from the Siné and Kouna cross sections (figures 4.19b and 4.21b). Most samples were taken in clusters of stratigraphically related samples, to be able to check the consistency of the data set. A series of three samples (Siné 10B/C, 10D and 10F) was taken of a dark, strongly reduced clay bed in the Siné cross section in order to calculate sedimentation rates and to determine the beginning of sedimentation of the overlying levee. Additionally, two samples were taken from the base of generation 3 levee deposits (Siné 9) and from the base of a clayey residual channel-fill (Siné 14). These two samples represent the end of coarse clastic sedimentation. In the Kouna cross section, two samples (Kouna 1/2 and 5) were collected directly underneath (generation 2) levee deposits of the Bani to determine the age of beginning of its activity. Four radiocarbon samples (Kouna 3, 4, 6 and 12) were taken lower, near the top of a buried coarse-grained terrace to enable calculation of average sedimentation rates for the overlying sediments.

Application of Accelerator Mass Spectrometry (AMS) enabled dating in spite of the very low amount of carbon in the samples. The very small size of the organic fragments hardly allowed selection of specified organic matter, and therefore most of the samples (except for Kouna 5 and Siné 9 and 14) were dated as bulk sediment samples. It is realized that due to the low organic matter content (table 4.2), most samples are very sensitive for contamination. Therefore the radiocarbon ages should be considered with caution. Below, the quality of the radiocarbon data will be evaluated.

The sample Siné 9, consisted of a package of more or less intact tree leaves. Fluvial transport of the material over a very short distance may have occurred. Their state of preservation renders it unlikely that they represent old reworked material. The date indicates a very high sedimentation rate for the generation 3 levees. This high sedimentation rate is probably typical for generation 3 levees. In December 1994 after inundation, a bed of 1 to 4 cm thick appeared to have been freshly deposited on the generation 3 levee near Kouna. Estimating the frequency of such an event at once every 1.5 year (section 4.4.4), this implies an (uncompacted) sedimentation rate of 7 to 27 mm/yr, which more or less confirms the high sedimentation rate obtained by radiocarbon dating.

The series of three samples from core 110 (Siné 10B/C, 10D, 10F) yielded stratigraphically consistent results. The ages indicate a fairly constant, but low sedimentation rate (table 4.3) for the dark clay bed. The radiometric evidence confirms the plausible interpretation that the strongly reduced floodbasin clay represents the early-Holocene humid period (section 4.2.4). No macroscopic organic material was identified in the samples. As a check on the accuracy of the dates from this material, of sample Siné 10D the organic residue and the alkaline-extract obtained after the standard pretreatment of the sample were separately dated. In general, the residue contains the bulk of the carbon present in a sample, while the extract contains only a small fraction of the total amount of carbon in the form of dissolved humic substances. In the standard procedure only the organic residue after pretreatment is dated. Mook & Streurman (1983, p. 51) stated that the extract generally gives a minimum age of a sample. Schoute (1984) showed that residue-ages of dark vegetation horizons may be considerably too old due to the presence of reworked organic matter in the residue, while in his case extract-ages were reliable since the extract contained in situ formed humic substances. Although extract and residue of Siné 10D yielded significantly different ages, the difference is considered to be within acceptable limits for the purpose of the present study.

The samples Siné 10B/C, 10D and 10F are characterized by a relatively high ^{13}C-content (table 4.2). High δ^{13}C-values of -6 to -19‰, are typical for desert and salt marsh plants and tropical grasses, the bulk of the plant kingdom having low δ^{13}C-values of -24 to -34‰ (Hoefs 1980, p. 127). Pessenda et al. (1996a, 1996b) showed variable δ^{13}C-values in organic matter of tropical clay-rich soils, which could be related to Holocene vegetation changes from equatorial forest to savanna. Presumably wet-tolerant savanna grasses, rich in ^{13}C, dominated the floodbasins in the Inland Delta during most of the Holocene and were the source of the dated carbon in Siné 10B/C, 10D and 10F.

The sample Siné 14 consisted of a small charcoal fragment. It is realized that this material may give erroneous dates for fluvial deposits (e.g. Blong & Gillespie 1978). In our case fluvially transported old charcoal may be older than the surrounding residual channel deposits. Thus, the date of Siné 14 probably gives a maximum age for the abandonment of the large crevasse channel in the Siné cross section.

The radiocarbon ages of the samples from underneath the generation 2 levee in the Kouna cross section (Kouna 1/2 and 5) are in agreement. The older age of Kouna 5 can be explained by its lower stratigraphic position. Since the concave base of the levee suggests scour above Kouna 5, the age of Kouna 1/2 is considered a better estimate of the start of levee deposition. Also some scour above Kouna 1/2 can not be excluded and start of levee deposition may have been later than the age of Kouna 1/2 suggests. Kouna 1/2 had a composition comparable to Siné 10B/C, 10D and 10E and also had a relatively high ^{13}C-content.

The four samples taken near the top of the buried coarse-grained terrace (Kouna 3, 4, 6 and 12) yielded strongly variable ages. Obviously inconsistent ages were obtained from Kouna 3 and 4, but also the ages of Kouna 6 and 12 seem to be stratigraphically inconsistent (figure 4.21b). Considering the composition of the samples, rejuvenation of Kouna 3, 4 and 12 is the most likely cause of the inconsistency. These samples contained very fine roots that penetrated the sediments from higher levels. The radiocarbon ages of these samples are rejected. Kouna 6 had a different composition. It consisted of a very dark-coloured clay, without macroscopically identifiable organic material. Like the other samples of this type of material (Siné 10B/C, 10D, 10F and Kouna 1/2), Kouna 6 had a relatively high ^{13}C-content. The strongly reduced appearance of the clay reminds of the Siné 10 samples and indeed its radiometric age indicates deposition in the humid early-Holocene.

Table 4.2 Radiocarbon dates from the upper Inland Niger Delta

Sample name	Laboratory nr.	^{14}C-age (yr BP)	Median cal. age [a] (yr BP)	δ^{13}C (‰)	C [b] (%)	Material
Siné 9	UtC-5606	916 ± 35	825	-29.2		leaves
Siné 10B/C	UtC-5070	6930 ± 49	7728	-17.6	0.1	dark clay [d]
Siné 10D	UtC-6191	8910 ± 60	9890	-17.2	0.1	dark clay [d] (residue)
Siné 10D	UtC-6192	8390 ± 50	9361	-19.5		dark clay [d] (extract)
Siné 10F	UtC-5071	10960 ± 60	12881 [c]	-16.9	0.2	dark clay [d]
Siné 14	UtC-5073	2736 ± 36	2843	-27.8		charcoal
Kouna 1/2	UtC-4613	3323 ± 45	3552	-19.4	0.1	dark clay [d]
Kouna 3	UtC-5068	5402 ± 46	6194	-26.3	0.1	clay with plant fragments [e]
Kouna 4	UtC-5069	4266 ± 45	4824	-27.3	0.5	sand with plant fragments [e]
Kouna 5	UtC-4614	3860 ± 60	4270	-24.2		charcoal
Kouna 6	GrA-7082	8510 ± 80	9483	-20.8	0.02	dark clay [d]
Kouna 12	UtC-5072	6040 ± 50	6897	-24.8	0.2	clay with plant fragments [e]

[a] The Groningen calibration program (version CAL20) was used (Van der Plicht 1993). The degree of smoothing of the calibration curve was based on Törnqvist & Bierkens (1994). For Siné 9 σ_s = 50 and for Siné 14 and Kouna 5, σ_s = 100 was applied. For all other samples (except Siné 10F; see [c]) σ_s = 200 was applied.
[b] Carbon content by weight.
[c] Calendar age considerably less accurate than for the other samples, as the radiocarbon age falls outside the time interval covered by the dendrochronological calibration curve (Stuiver et al. 1993).
[d] No macroscopic organic material.
[e] Including fine roots.

The remaining radiocarbon data set, after rejection of the ages of Kouna 3, 4 and 12, was used for paleogeographical reconstruction and calculation of sedimentation rates. Long-term sedimentation rates (millennia timescale) were calculated (table 4.3) on the basis of calibrated radiocarbon dates. The influence of slow long-term compaction was believed to have been restricted for two reasons. Firstly, in a semi-arid environment considerable compaction due to dehydration takes place in the dry season, rapidly after sedimentation. Secondly, peat and organic-rich deposits, usually accounting for a major part of the long-term compaction, are absent.

Table 4.3 Long-term sedimentation rates in the upper Inland Niger Delta

Sample name		Depth (cm)	Age (cal. yr BP [a])	Sedimentation rate (mm/cal. yr)
				Average
Siné 10F		326	12925	0.25
Kouna 6		514	9527	0.54
				Floodbasin
Siné 10F		326	12925	
Siné 10B/C		281	7772	
	difference:	45	5153	0.09
Siné 10F		326	12925	
Siné 10D		304	9934 [b]	
	difference:	22	2991	0.07
Siné 10D		304	9934 [b]	
Siné 10B/C		281	7772	
	difference:	23	2162	0.11
Kouna 6		514	9527	
Kouna 5		440	4314	
	difference:	74	5213	0.14
				Levee (generation 2)
Siné 10B/C		281	7772	0.36
Kouna 1/2		371	3596	1.03 [c]
Kouna 5		440	4314	> 1.02 [d]
				Levee (generation 3)
Siné 9		625	869	7.19
				Residual channel
Siné 14		340	2887	≥ 1.18 [e]

[a]   In this case: BP = before 1994.
[b]   The radiocarbon age of the residue is used.
[c]   The given rate may represent a minimum since the base of the levee may be scoured.
[d]   The given rate represents a minimum since the base of the levee is scoured.
[e]   The dated material (charcoal) gives a maximum age and therefore the sedimentation rate is a minimum rate.

The average sedimentation rates (table 4.3) show a regional difference, being lower in the Siné cross section than in the Kouna cross section. These values may be high estimates as in both cases the average is influenced by relatively high levee sedimentation rates during a substantial part of the period under consideration. On the other hand it can not be excluded that the intervals considered, include depositional hiatuses or even erosional phases (deflation, gullying) related to climatic changes. Average present sedimentation rates based on sediment budget calculations for the entire Inland Delta (Gallais 1967) are relatively low: 0.07 to 0.20 mm/yr. Strongly variable sedimentation rates in time are likely to be inherent in this fluvial system.

Differences in sedimentation rate between various fluvial environments are illustrated by the data in table 4.3. Low floodbasin sedimentation rates of 0.07 to 0.14 mm/yr were calculated. It must be noted that these values relate to early and mid-Holocene conditions. The calculated levee sedimentation rates relate to the mid- and late-Holocene. These rates show strong variation. The very high sedimentation rate of the generation 3 levees (based on Siné 14) was already discussed above. The much lower average sedimentation rates for the generation 2 levees, probably reflect periods of non-deposition. Present sedimentation rates on the generation 2 levees seem to be very slow, while locally erosion takes place. However, being inundated for 55 to 70 days every 2.0 to 2.3 years on average (see section 4.4.4), these levees can not be considered inactive presently. The data suggest that average generation 2 levee sedimentation rates upstream (Siné cross section) are significantly lower than downstream (Kouna cross section). The charcoal date from the residual channel deposits (Siné 14) indicates sedimentation rates in the order of levee sedimentation rates for this environment.

4.4.4 Bankfull discharge, stream power and flooding frequency

The Bani River undergoes marked downstream changes in bankfull discharge, stream power and flooding frequency. Parallel with the mean annual discharge (section 4.2.3), the bankfull discharge of the main channel of the Bani decreases between San and Sofara. In this study the bankfull stage was defined as the top of the generation 3 levees at the gauging stations. Usually in the study region the top of the levees is located immediately next to a break in slope indicating the channel edge. Bankfull discharge was determined for the rising and falling limb of the San and Sofara hydrographs (table 4.4). The large differences between rising and falling discharge, probably result from significant differences in gradient and from growth of dunes on the sand bed during peak discharge. Specific stream power based on these values is very low. Potential specific stream power (Van den Berg 1995) was also calculated and naturally is lower for the Sofara station, because both discharge and channel slope are lower than at the San station.

Obviously, near bankfull stage there is an important loss of water through the Souman Bani. Therefore, a decrease of bankfull discharge of the Bani main channel does not automatically imply an increase in flooding frequency. However, it appears that flooding frequency does increase downstream (table 4.5). In contrast to bankfull discharge, flooding frequency was not only determined with respect to the generation 3 levees, but also with respect to the generation 1 and 2 levees, if applicable (table 4.5). At the San gauging station for example, the generation 1 levees were never inundated during the period of the stage record, whereas the generation 3 levees experienced flooding once every two years on average. Tracing these levees down to Mopti, flooding frequency rises to once every 1.7 years at Sofara and once every 1.3 years at Mopti. A slight downstream increase in flooding frequency is also noted for the generation 2 levees between San and Sofara. This increase was corroborated by observations in the field during November 1994, when these levees just stayed dry near Siné, while they experienced several weeks of inundation near Kouna. Mean inundation periods per event and per year also increase significantly downstream to 100 and 75 days respectively at Mopti, where only the level of the generation 3 levees can be determined.

Table 4.4 Bankfull discharge and stream power of the Bani River

Gauging station	Stage	Bankfull discharge (m³/s)	Specific stream power (W/m²)	Potential specific stream power (W/m²)
San	rising	1650	2.1	3.5
	falling	1150	1.5	2.9
Sofara	rising	928	1.1	2.4
	falling	766	0.9	2.2

Table 4.5 Flooding frequency and duration along the Bani River (1952-94)

Levee	Mean return period of flooding (yr)	Mean duration of flooding per event (days)	Mean duration of flooding per year (days)
San			
Generation 1	no flooding during period of record		
Generation 2	2.5	55	20
Generation 3	2.0	65	35
Sofara			
Generation 2	2.3	70	30
Generation 3	1.7	95	55
Mopti			
Generation 3	1.3	100	75

4.5   Interpretation and discussion

4.5.1   Late-Pleistocene and Holocene geomorphological history

Previously, Gallais (1967), McIntosh (1983) and Jacobberger (1987) investigated the late-Pleistocene and Holocene paleogeography of the upper Inland Delta. Their reconstructions were mainly based on morphological and climatic considerations. Now that stratigraphic information and radiocarbon dates have become available, their reconstructions can be checked and refined. In this section I will discuss the geomorphological evolution of the upper Inland Delta per climatic period. At the end of this section the evidence for Holocene tectonic movements influencing this course of events is discussed separately. The development of the hydrographical network is illustrated by figure 4.35.

The Ogolian arid period (20,000 - 12,500 BP)
During the Ogolian period, wide-spread eolian sedimentation took place, not only in the form of large dunes, but also as wind-blown coarse silt and fine sand in floodbasin clay. The grain size composition of the relatively sandy old floodbasin deposits (figure 4.31c) is believed to reflect this process, while the more abundant oxidation testifies to the drier conditions. The age of Siné 10F (10,960 ± 60 BP), representing a level just above the top of these deposits (figure 4.19b), confirms their pre-Holocene age. Also the age of Kouna 6 (8510 ± 80 BP), is in agreement with the position of the supposed Ogolian-Holocene boundary in borehole 141 (figure 4.21b). A floodbasin sedimentation rate of 0.14 mm/yr (table 4.3) accounts for the difference in altitude and age between the Ogolian-Holocene boundary and sample Kouna 6.

In figure 4.34, the grain size compositions of these pre-Holocene floodbasin deposits and floodbasins deposits from the Netherlands are compared. Holocene floodbasin clay from the Betuwe Formation is characterized by a high silt content and a low sand content. However, Pleistocene floodbasin clay from the Kreftenheye Formation, also has a considerable sand content (mainly of the fraction 210-300 μm), which was attributed to pedogenic mixing with directly underlying fluvial sands (e.g. Van de Meene 1977) and eolian influx from nearby river dunes (e.g. Van der Woude 1983, pp. 61-62). The pre-Holocene floodbasin deposits from the Inland Delta appear to be equally heterogeneous in grain size composition, although the admixed sand fraction is less well-defined. Admixing of coarser material by bioturbation is impossible in this case, where a shallow sandy subsoil is absent. Given the climatic conditions, eolian influx seems to be most probable.

Stratigraphic evidence confirmed the view that the massive dunes of the Erg of Samayé-Djenné (section 4.4.1) are of Ogolian age. In figure 4.20b (boreholes 19 and 21) a layer of floodbasin clay covers the flank of such a dune. Laterally, next to the dune, this layer has a dark gray base and passes downward rapidly into sandy floodbasin clays. This well-developed transition is interpreted as the contact between Ogolian and early-Holocene floodbasin deposits. The massive dune is founded on pre-Holocene floodbasin deposits. Figure 4.22b (boring 24) shows a similar dune thickness and also underlying pre-Holocene floodbasin deposits.

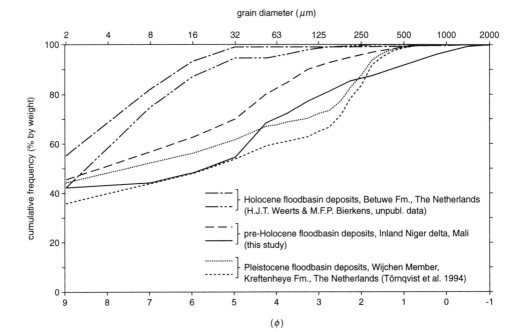

Figure 4.34   *Cumulative grain size distributions of pre-Holocene floodbasin deposits from the upper Inland Delta, and Holocene (H.J.T. Weerts & M.F.P. Bierkens, unpublished data) and Pleistocene floodbasin deposits (Törnqvist et al. 1994, fig. 6) from the Rhine-Meuse delta.*

Lack of time-control makes it impossible to tell whether all of the pre-Holocene floodbasin deposits in the cross sections are of Ogolian age or whether they pass downward into pre-Ogolian deposits. Considering the low Holocene floodbasin sedimentation rates (table 4.3) the latter seems to be likely. On the other hand, no significant lithological changes were observed in the pre-Holocene floodbasin deposits.

Absence of Ogolian dune deposits in the Siné Oualo cross section (figure 4.24b) suggests that the cordon of massive dunes has never been closed at this site. Instead of dune deposits, pre-Holocene floodbasin deposits with lenses of eolian deposits were found here. Little is known about the location of fluvial channels during the Ogolian.

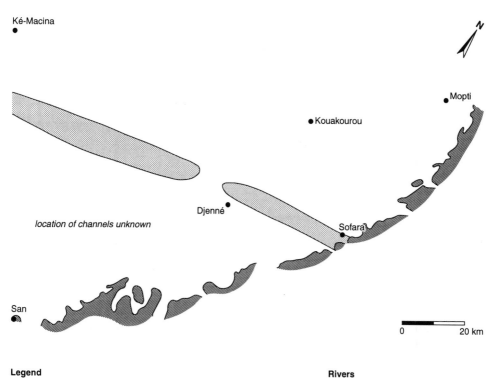

a. End of the Ogolian arid period (12,500 BP)

Ké-Macina

Mopti

Kouakourou

Djenné

location of channels unknown

Sofara

San

0   20 km

Legend

major channel

secondary or abandoned channel

presumed secondary channel (exact position uncertain)

massive dunes

fluvial burst of massive dune

longitudinal dunes

margin of the Bandiagara Plateau

tributary draining the Bandiagara Plateau

Rivers

1 = Siné Oualo

2 = Mayo Manga

3 = Konguéné

4 = Bani

5 = Souman Bani

6 = Niger

7 = Kolanguel

8 = Potékolé

Figure 4.35   The development of the hydrographical network since the late-Pleistocene. The paleogeography of the study region at: (a) the end of the Ogolian arid period, (b) the end of the early-Holocene humid period, (c) the end of the mid-Holocene arid period, (d) the end of the mid-Holocene humid period, and (e) present.

161

b. End of the early-Holocene humid period (8000 BP)

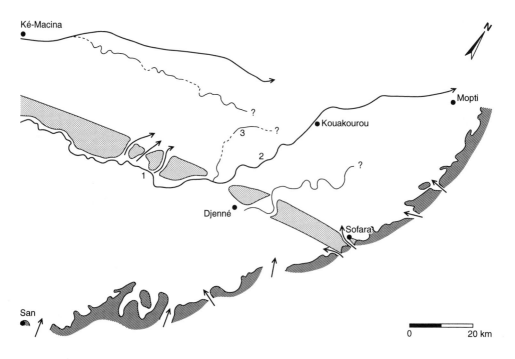

Figure 4.35 (continued; for legend see page 161)

The early-Holocene humid period (12,500 - 8000 BP)
The dark gray clay which overlies the previously described sandy Ogolian floodbasin clay, marks the onset of wetter conditions in the early Holocene. However, no positive sedimentary evidence was found for the existence of a large 'paleo Lake Débo' covering large parts of the present Inland Delta floodplain (section 4.2.4). The bed of strongly reduced clay could be lake sediment, but can equally well represent just wet floodplain conditions. Complete inundation of the upper Inland Delta requires water depths in the lower Inland Delta that seem to be in excess of the height of the blocking dunes of the Erg of Bara (figure 4.7). As mentioned above, the Erg of Samayé-Djenné was probably never closed completely near the Siné Oualo cross section and was therefore unable to cause a deep body of stagnant water south of it. In short, complete and permanent inundation of the upper Inland Delta during the early Holocene humid period can be excluded. The existence of large permanent interchannel lakes seems likely.

The low floodbasin sedimentation rates in the Siné cross section during this period (table 4.3), reflect the distal position with respect to the main channels of the river system. During these times, the Siné Oualo, with the Mayo Manga as its lower course,

162

must have been a predecessor of the Bani. Inability to cope with high discharges led to a number of breaches of the Ogolian dune cordon in the west (e.g. figure 4.16). More to the east, near Djenné, a gap was eroded in response to impeded drainage of rivers from the Bandiagara Plateau.

Judging from its morphology, the Konguéne was not an important distributary of the Siné Oualo. Indistinct abandoned channel networks in the floodbasins west of the Konguéné suggest that this channel may have been fed by distributaries of the Niger as well. Some 5 to 10 km south of the present Niger, an abandoned channel belt was identified, which probably was an important Niger distributary during these times. The upper reach of the present Niger existed already but joined the Bani further north.

In figure 4.25b (boring 3) the base of levee deposits can be seen slightly above the inferred Ogolian-Holocene boundary. This means that a channel belt became active in this area early in the Holocene. Presumably, the reach of the Niger between Kouakourou and Mopti functioned in this time as a lower course of the Siné Oualo - Mayo Manga (see also Gallais 1967, map 2).

The mid-Holocene arid period (8000 - 7000 BP)
Regular fields of longitudinal dunes (section 4.4.1) were formed during the relatively short mid-Holocene dry period. At first sight these dunes may seem to represent just a final phase of Ogolian dune formation as they are partly superimposed on the massive dunes. However, in figure 4.16 it can be seen that the massive Ogolian dune was dissected by a fluvial channel, presumably during the wet early-Holocene, prior to the formation of the smaller longitudinal dunes, which segment the channel. In the figures 4.23b (boring 11) and 4.24b (boring 28) mid-Holocene dunes are represented.

The relatively high clay content of the mid-Holocene and the Ogolian dunes (figure 4.32a) is interpreted to originate from allochthonous eolian dust derived from distal sources. Even nowadays, long-distance dispersion of clay-sized dust by Harmattan winds is an important process in West Africa (Maley 1982). A clay content of 10% was reported in freshly deposited eolian sediment in Syria (Mulders 1969, p. 94). Infiltration of eolian dust can further increase the clay content after dune formation (e.g. Winspear & Pye 1995).

From north to south the mid-Holocene longitudinal dunes show a change in orientation from ENE-WSW to NNE-SSW. This is believed to reflect the deflection of the trade winds along the southern edge of the Inland Delta, due to differential heating of the Koutiala sandstone in the south relative to the moist Inland Delta (see also section 4.2.2). Few longitudinal dunes were formed in the Pondori. The age of Sine 10B/C (table 4.2), which represents the top of a strongly reduced clay bed, indicates that probably relatively wet conditions persisted in this area. The upper part of this bed (approximately above Siné 10D) however, is less dark in colour and contains more, possibly eolian, sand than the lower part, which dates from the humid early-Holocene period.

In the Siné Oualo cross section (figure 4.24b) a large dune on top of the channel deposits can be seen. Reactivation of the massive Ogolian dunes, must have hindered the Siné Oualo which flows along them for a long distance. On the other hand, on careful observation the Siné Oualo and Mayo Manga can be seen to cut the longitudinal mid-

c. End of the mid-Holocene arid period (7000 BP)

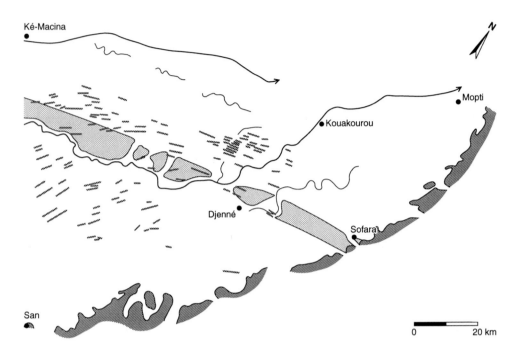

Figure 4.35 (continued; for legend see page 161)

Holocene dunes. Thus, these channels were reactivated when discharge rose again by 7000 BP, thereby (partly) evacuating invaded eolian dune sands.

The mid-Holocene humid period (7000 - 4000 BP)
The age of Siné 10B/C indicates that the Bani installed itself in the Pondori by 6900 BP. Presumably, loss of efficiency of the Siné Oualo had forced the Bani to seek a new course when discharge increased. It is hypothesized that similar blockage of Niger distributaries in the Dead Delta, caused an avulsion in an easterly direction by which the Niger took its present course between Kouakourou and Mopti.

The wide complex of avulsion belt deposits south of the Pondori basin presently constitutes the generation 1 levees of the Bani. When climate progressively became wetter, stream power increased, while the supply of sandy bed load from eolian sources was exhausted. As a result, the Bani incised the proximal avulsion belt deposits near San. Further downstream, channel belt formation had just started and generation 2 levees aggraded along the Bani and Souman Bani. The large crevasse channels, which disrupt these levees, probably also date from this mid-Holocene wet period, when discharge was highly variable in a strongly seasonal climate (section 4.2.4).

164

d. End of the mid-Holocene humid period (4000 BP)

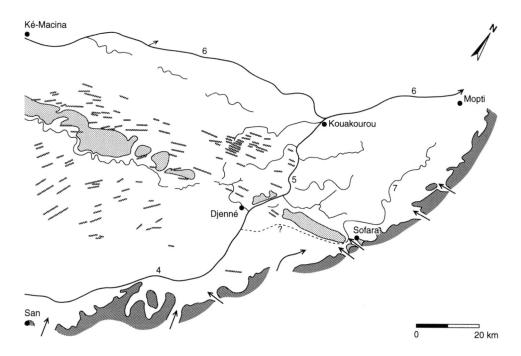

Figure 4.35 (continued; for legend see page 161)

During this time no major channels existed in the Sébéra, between Sofara and Mopti. Minor channels in this area were fed by the large crevasse channels of the Souman Bani and small streams from the Bandiagara Plateau. Probably already near the end of the mid-Holocene wet period, the Kolanguel crossed the Femaye near Sofara, fed by rivers draining the Bandiagara Plateau and perhaps by a crevasse channel of the Bani. Presently, the main channel of the Bani crosses abandoned loops of this predecessor downstream of Sofara.

The late-Holocene aridification (4000 BP - present)
In the Kouna cross section (figure 4.21b) levee deposition by the Bani main channel started by 3300 BP (age of Kouna 1/2) or perhaps even somewhat later (section 4.4.3). This major shift to the east was not an instantaneous avulsion, as the Souman Bani is still not totally abandoned today. Initially, the formation of generation 2 levees continued.

The change to a more arid climate must have invoked a fall in base-level, which was determined by the level of Lake Débo in the north of the Inland Delta (figure 4.7). While Lake Débo shrunk, incision started upstream of the lake and the sedimentation rate of the generation 2 levees decreased gradually. Some of the large crevasse channels were cut off

165

e. Present

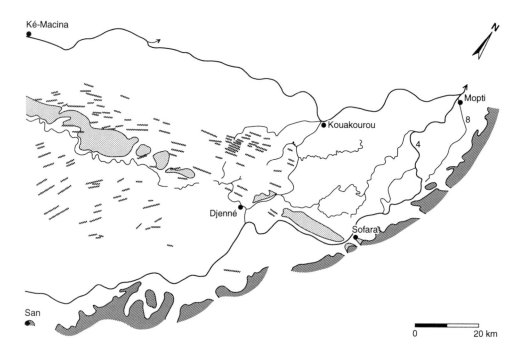

Figure 4.35 (continued; for legend see page 161)

from bed load during this process and started to fill up with suspended load. In a crevasse channel in the Siné cross section, clay sedimentation began by 2750 BP or later (age of Siné 14, table 4.2).

Meanwhile, discharge must have decreased dramatically. This is suggested by the presence of dunes founded on channel sands and (partly) buried by recent (generation 3) levees (figures 4.19b and 4.21b). A reconstruction of the formation of point bars, eolian river dunes and generation 3 levees during the late-Holocene is given in figure 4.36. The formation of eolian river dunes may have taken place during an arid phase from 2500 to 1800 BP (McIntosh 1983), when underfit streams meandered through channel sands on the bottom of oversized channels. By 2000 BP, vegetation in the Sahel changed rapidly into a more arid type (Lézine 1989a, 1989b), while soon thereafter the climate temporarily became wetter again. Together with increased human activities, especially tree-felling for iron production [metallurgy arrived in the Sahel by 2600 BP (Alimen 1987)], this led to a sharp increase in sediment supply to the rivers, causing bed aggradation. In juxtaposition to the beds, sedimentation of abundant fine sediments took place on top of sandy point bars. Vertical accretion of generation 3 levees was rapid (table 4.3). Scroll patterns suggest that a part of the generation 3 levee deposits in fact are

166

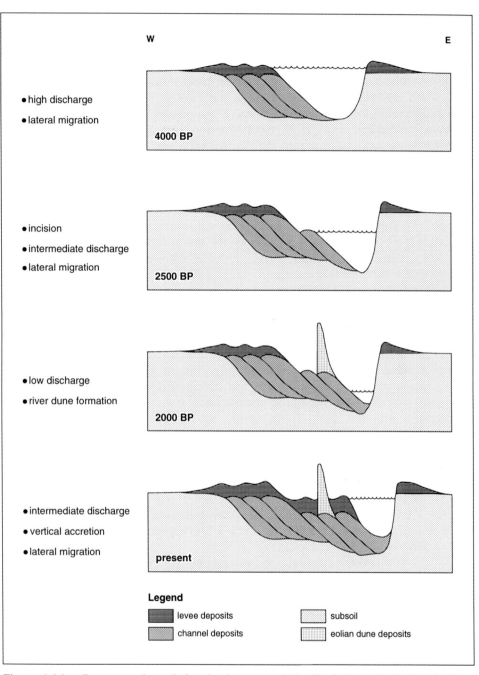

Figure 4.36   Reconstruction of the development of the Bani channel during the late-Holocene.

167

fine-grained channel deposits formed by lateral accretion of concave benches, as described by Nanson & Page (1983). Page & Nanson (1996, fig. 9) described a stratigraphy and sequential development for Riverine Plain paleochannels (southeastern Australia) that seems very similar to the stratigraphy and evolution shown in figure 4.36.

Presumably, bed aggradation was the prime cause of the most recent avulsion of the Bani, which resulted in the abandonment of the Potékolé south of Mopti. The poorly developed levees of the lower Bani River near Mopti, hosting only few sites of prehistoric and historic habitation, testify to its recent formation (Bedaux et al. 1978, p. 104). This last avulsion of the Bani is a rare shift to the west, after a long period of stepwise migration in an easterly direction.

Holocene tectonic movements

The field data strongly suggest that Holocene tectonic movements have influenced the avulsion history of the Bani River. The difference in sedimentation rates between the Siné and Kouna cross sections (table 4.3), supports the idea of Gallais (1967) of subsidence in the Mopti vicinity. The (presumed) location of faults and direction of relative movements are summarized in figure 4.37.

A first fault approximately runs along the eastern and southern edge of the Inland Delta and was already discussed in section 4.2.1. The floodplain topography however, suggests a second fault to be present to the west. This fault has a north-south orientation and probably represents the fault indicated by the DNGM (1987, fig. 3) (see section 4.2.1). The downthrown side of this fault is characterized by the deep Pondori and Yongary floodbasins and a disrupted and partly drowned Erg of Samayé-Djenné. The uplifted area to the east hosts the elevated and desiccated Korori and the Femaye, a still intact part of the Erg. The remarkably straight reach of the Bani south of Djenné might be associated with this fault. To the north, the Souman Bani roughly follows the presumed fault.

Conspicuous differences in stratigraphy on either side of the fault can be seen in figure 4.23b. To the east (boring 6), thin levee deposits are underlain by early-Holocene floodbasin clay, which soon grades into sandy Ogolian floodbasin deposits. To the west (borings 11 and 12) the Holocene-Ogolian boundary was found 2 to 2.5 m lower. Therefore, Holocene displacement rates along the fault could be 0.17 mm/yr (2500 mm/ 14,500 yr). Fault offset is thought to be maximal, halfway between the two Souman Bani cross sections (figures 4.22 and 4.23).

A third fault further to the west, was not indicated before on geological maps, but is strongly suggested by the satellite image. This inferred fault forms the western boundary of a graben structure in which the Pondori and Yongary basins and the disrupted part of the Erg of Samayé-Djenné are situated.

Given the relatively low sedimentation rates, it seems probable that tectonic movements were a driving force behind avulsions. Especially, the last major avulsion of the Bani, whereby it established its course between Sofara and Mopti, is very likely to have been mainly caused by tectonic movements. Fluvial sedimentation along the fault during the mid-Holocene humid period in combination with continued subsidence in the east, prepared a down-dip avulsion-route. A strange phenomenon which could be

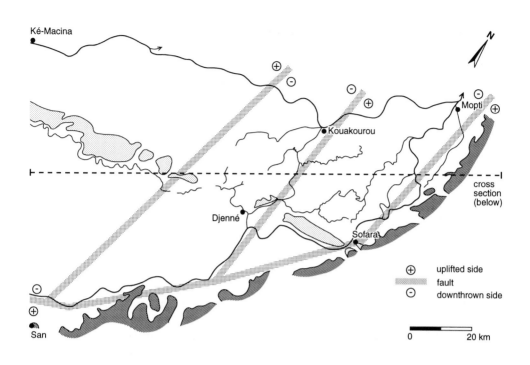

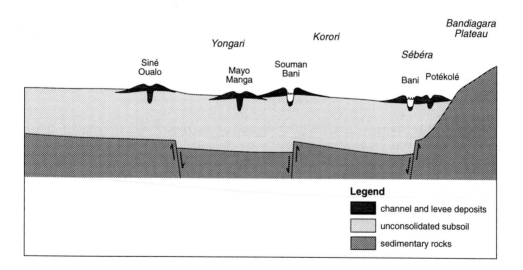

Figure 4.37   Reconstruction of the tectonic framework in the study region.

explained by tectonic tilting, is the steady lateral migration to the east of the straight reach of the Bani south of Djenné (figure 4.11). Examples of comparable phenomena in half-graben tectonic settings were described by Alexander & Leeder (1987). Down-dip avulsion following tectonic floodplain tilting was simulated in alluvial stratigraphy models (e.g. Bridge & Leeder 1979; Mackey & Bridge 1995).

4.5.2 Controlling factors of the anastomosing river system

Unlike a number of other anastomosing river systems (e.g. Smith 1973, 1983, 1986; Smith & Smith 1980), the upper Inland Delta is not subjected to a rapid rise in base-level and subsequent high floodplain sedimentation rates. Nevertheless, avulsions occurred frequently during the Holocene and led to anastomosis, due to: (1) an extremely low floodplain gradient, (2) a low channel flow capacity and (3) climate-specific avulsion-triggers.

Floodplain gradient
Even relative to other anastomosing river floodplains, the channel gradients in the upper Inland Delta are very low (compare tables 2.2 and 4.1), due to an extremely low floodplain gradient. This is due to base-level control by the Erg of Bara and to a lesser extent by the sill at Tossayé. Under such low-gradient conditions, only slight channel belt aggradation or tectonic tilting of the floodplain can easily alter the direction of the local floodplain gradient and favour avulsion. It is illustrative in this respect that short flow reversals in the Inland Delta channels are not uncommon. Niger high water usually precedes Bani high water by several weeks. As a result of the temporarily reversed water gradient, floodwaters flow upstream the Souman Bani (Gallais 1967, p. 86). Alam et al. (1985) described similar phenomena for a low-gradient stream in Australia. The Tonlé Sap River in Cambodia (figure 1.1) experiences flow reversals on a seasonal basis, controlled by the stage of the Mekong River.

Channel flow capacity
The downstream decrease in bankfull flow capacity of the river system (section 4.4.4) is a result of a low and downstream decreasing stream power (table 4.4), making the river incapable to enlarge its wet perimeter. The bankfull width/depth ratio of the Bani main channel (40-60) is relatively high (compare table 2.2) and suggests that bed aggradation might be responsible for a low channel flow capacity. A sharp increase in sediment supply since 2000 BP (section 4.5.1) contributed to this. Such a loss in flow capacity by bed aggradation, can not be compensated for by bank erosion. Although vegetation is scarce, the banks are relatively resistant. Apart from being cohesive, the bank material is indurated by strong desiccation in the dry season. In addition, precipitation of ferric oxides contributes to bank stabilisation in this tropical environment (Tricart (1959, p. 338; Gallais 1967, p. 101-102).

Avulsion-triggers

Two types of avulsion-triggers are associated with the semi-arid climate of the Inland Delta: (1) the formation of eolian dunes or just eolian supply of sediments which may choke up channels and (2) degradation of levees by gullying and deflation.

Nowadays, eolian obstruction of channels is not an active process in the upper Inland Delta. Further north however, near Timbuktu and Gao, the recent Sahelian drought and resulting increase in eolian sediment transport led to plugging of minor channels feeding lakes and invoked shallowing of the Niger River due to the formation of large bars and islands (IWACO/Delft Hydraulics 1996). Recent damming of streams by eolian landforms was also documented for other fluvial systems (e.g. Garner 1967, p. 91; Langford 1989)

In contrast, degradation of levees by gullying and deflation are presently active processes in the upper Inland Delta (section 4.4.1), accelerated by human activities, especially the grazing of cattle. Because river stages are still low during the wet season, gullies may incise deeply.

4.6 Summary

The upper Inland Niger Delta is an anastomosing river system, predominantly composed of straight channels. Lateral stability of the channels is caused by very low specific stream power (0.9 - 2.1 W/m^2) and resistant banks, due to induration of the levees by strong desiccation and precipitation of ferric oxides.

This anastomosing river system exists under relatively low floodplain sedimentation rates (0.25 - 0.54 mm/yr) in the absence of a rapid rise in base-level. In this environment, frequent avulsion which led to anastomosis can be explained by: (1) a very low floodplain gradient (3-4 cm/km), (2) a low channel flow capacity and (3) climate-specific avulsion-triggers (eolian processes and gullying). In addition, Holocene tectonic movements are likely to have influenced the avulsion history of the Bani River resulting in a stepwise migration to the east.

Major avulsions of the Bani took place by 6900 and 3300 BP. Regional base-level was controlled by Lake Débo and fell rapidly after 4000 BP, due to aridification. After a phase of incision, increased sediment supply since 2000 BP led to bed aggradation, which still continues today.

An E-W trending cordon of massive dunes, constituting the core of the Erg of Samayé-Djenné, was formed during the Ogolian. Fields of smaller longitudinal dunes in the study region date from the mid-Holocene arid period.

Deposits in the upper Inland Delta are characterized by a very low organic matter content, and peat is absent. Apart from abundant dune deposits, eolian sediments also occur as a silt/sand fraction in the Ogolian floodbasin deposits. A large part of the sandy channel deposits was formed by lateral accretion. Levee deposits are heavily bioturbated by termites.

5   Meandering and straight Holocene paleochannels of an anastomosing river system on a coastal plain (Rhine-Meuse delta, The Netherlands)

5.1   Introduction

Often, multi-channel rivers are located on coastal plains and are indicated as 'distributary systems' or just 'river deltas'. However, because of the morphological similarity with the anastomosing rivers described in the previous chapters, in this thesis such near-coastal multi-channel rivers are classified as 'anastomosing', although it may be that not all of their channels rejoin downstream. A particularly well-studied example of such an anastomosing river system is the Rhine-Meuse delta in the Netherlands (e.g. Louwe Kooijmans 1974; Berendsen 1982; Törnqvist 1993b; Weerts 1996).

Considering the morphology of the Rhine-Meuse delta on a Holocene timescale, two phenomena are apparent: (1) the number of coexisting channels varied strongly in time (figure 5.1), and (2) the channels showed marked differences in lateral stability in space and time. Hitherto, these features have been related to the rate of sea-level rise and the erodibility of the subsoil (Törnqvist 1993a). However, the influence of rapid sea-level rise, which was believed to be a prime cause of anastomosis and lateral channel stability, may have been overestimated. In the previous chapter it was demonstrated that anastomosing rivers with laterally stable channels may exist in the absence of continuous and rapid base-level rise. In addition, an important factor which has not been considered in the studies of the Rhine-Meuse delta so far, is the combined influence of slope and discharge (stream power) of the individual paleochannels.

The objective of this chapter is to re-evaluate the factors controlling the fluvial morphology in the Holocene Rhine-Meuse delta, including the influence of discharge. Case studies to reach this goal, include the detailed reconstruction of the morphology of three subrecent fluvial systems using borehole data. In this chapter, the term 'fluvial system' is applied to a paleochannel and its genetically associated deposits. Time control for the study was provided by radiocarbon dates, and at two sites information on sedimentary structures was obtained mainly by vibracoring, and by a study in a pit. Channel gradients were reconstructed by plotting the altitude of a large number of borehole data. Finally, the paleodischarge of two channels was reconstructed.

The study area is located in the central part of the Rhine-Meuse delta (figure 5.2). The westernmost and oldest of the three fluvial systems is known as the 'Schoonrewoerd' system. The two other fluvial systems were still unnamed and will be called the 'Hennisdijk' and 'Echteld' systems in the present study (figure 5.2). Locally, the studied channel deposits reach a depth of more than 12 m below the surface. The channel sands are covered by a clayey (and sometimes peaty) layer of less than one meter thickness in the eastern to three meters in the western (downstream) part of the study area.

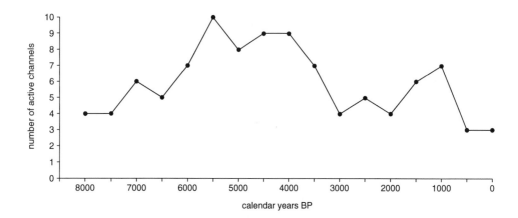

Figure 5.1   The number of coexisting Rhine-distributaries in a cross section through the central Rhine-Meuse delta, during the period 8000-0 cal yr BP (from Törnqvist 1993b).

A great deal of previous work has been done in the Holocene of the Rhine-Meuse delta. Many of the subrecent channel belts were first mapped by Vink (1926). Maps based on large numbers of (mostly shallow) borehole data became available in the 1950s and 1960s, when regional soil surveys were carried out (e.g. Pons 1957; De Boer & Pons 1960; Stichting voor Bodemkartering 1959). Since the 1970s, geological maps of the region were published (Verbraeck 1970, 1984; Berendsen 1982; Berendsen et al. 1986, 1994; Bosch & Kok 1994; Van de Meene 1977; Van de Meene et al. 1988), based on borehole data covering the entire Holocene sequence. The efforts of the Department of Physical Geography of Utrecht University in this period, resulted in a database which consists presently of around 200,000 borehole descriptions (H.J.A. Berendsen unpublished data). In addition, over 1000 radiocarbon dates from the Rhine-Meuse delta are presently available (Berendsen & Stouthamer in prep.). This extensive database enabled strategical planning of the additional fieldwork necessary for the present study.

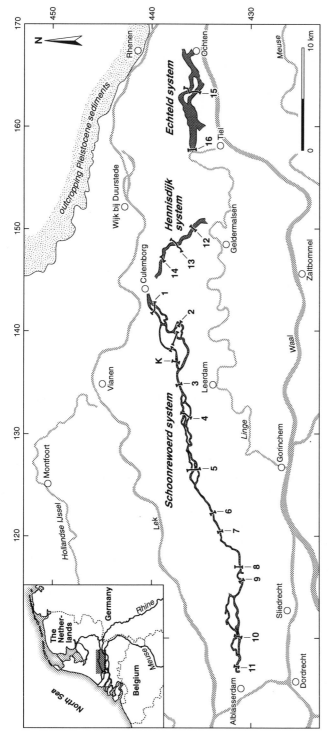

Figure 5.2   The location of the study area, the three fluvial systems and the borehole cross sections ("K" indicates the Kortgerecht cross section).

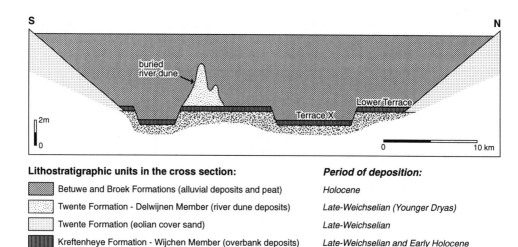

Lithostratigraphic units in the cross section:

    Betuwe and Broek Formations (alluvial deposits and peat)

    Twente Formation - Delwijnen Member (river dune deposits)

    Twente Formation (eolian cover sand)

    Kreftenheye Formation - Wijchen Member (overbank deposits)

    Kreftenheye Formation (channel deposits)

Period of deposition:

Holocene

Late-Weichselian (Younger Dryas)

Late-Weichselian

Late-Weichselian and Early Holocene

Weichselian and Early Holocene

Figure 5.3   *Schematic cross section through the central part of the Rhine-Meuse delta showing the structure of the Late-Weichselian subsoil.*

5.2   General background

5.2.1   Late-Weichselian and Holocene fluvial geomorphology of the Rhine-Meuse delta

In this section I will introduce the Holocene evolution of the fluvial geomorphology in the Rhine-Meuse delta with a special focus on the west-central part and the distribution of channel types in space and time. Since the Pleistocene subsoil is one of the controlling factors, a brief introduction about its origin will also be given. In figure 5.3 its structure is shown schematically. For a general description of the lithostratigraphic units of the Late-Weichselian and Holocene Rhine-Meuse delta, the reader is referred to Berendsen (1982, pp. 91-112) and Weerts (1996, pp. 25-56).

During the Late-Pleniglacial, the central part of the present Rhine-Meuse delta consisted of a braidplain upon which large amounts of gravelly sand were deposited. This braidplain had a relatively steep gradient [29 cm/km on average (Verbraeck 1984, p. 100)] and was called the 'Lower Terrace' (e.g. Pons 1957). Higher grounds of eolian cover sands flanked the braidplain on both sides. The effects of climatic warming during the Bølling-Allerød interstadial induced a change in river pattern from braided to meandering (e.g. Berendsen et al. 1995; Makaske & Nap 1995). During this period the 'Lower Terrace' became covered by a characteristic bed of sandy clay, which is considered as an overbank deposit of incipient meandering rivers (e.g. Törnqvist et al. 1994). Subsequently, a switch to a braided channel pattern accompanied by incision during the Younger Dryas stadial led to the formation of a new braidplain at a lower elevation, which was called 'Terrace X' (Pons 1957). The difference in altitude between the two terraces is in the order of one meter in the central part of the present delta, but decreases from east to west (e.g. Törnqvist 1998). Also dating from the Younger Dryas are many river dunes (e.g. Verbraeck et al. 1974), which formed preferentially on the 'Lower Terrace'. During the Preboreal, climatic warming again induced a change in river pattern from braided to meandering and Terrace X became also covered by a bed of sandy clay. As early-Holocene meandering rivers incised, the flooding frequency of Terrace X was very low, resulting in low sedimentation rates.

It is likely that sedimentation never ceased completely in the western part of the present delta (Törnqvist et al. 1994, p. 257). A vegetation horizon developed near the surface, while consolidation of the clay took place. The rapid relative rise in sea-level during the early Holocene (e.g. Jelgersma 1980), caused a reduction of the river gradients, leading to backfilling of the valleys in the Terrace X. In the early-Atlantic [around 7500 BP (Bosch & Kok 1994; Van der Woude 1983)], rapid sedimentation of mainly clay and organic material began on top of the vegetation horizon in the western part of the present study area. Onset of rapid sedimentation progressively took place further to the east and by the end of the Atlantic period (5000 BP) the onlap already reached east of the present study area (e.g. Verbraeck 1984, fig. 71).

Channel belts in the early-Atlantic were relatively wide and river channels are interpreted to have been meandering (Törnqvist 1993a; Bosch & Kok 1994). Floodbasin fines were the bulk of the deposited sediments. Later in the Atlantic, networks of narrow and deep channels developed in the west-central part of the Rhine-Meuse delta in a permanently wet, 'fluvio-lagoonal' environment (Van der Woude 1983). The presence of straight channels in this period is suggested by the low width/thickness ratio of the channel sand bodies, typically 8 to 15 (Törnqvist 1993a). In time, these networks of straight channels occurred further eastward at the expense of the wider channel belts. The narrow channels were termed 'anastomosing channels' by Törnqvist (1993a). According to the classification used in this thesis (section 2.2.4) they would more properly be described as 'straight channels', albeit that they were part of an anastomosing system. Anyway, by 4000 BP the complex of straight channels, reached its maximum eastward extent near Geldermalsen (Törnqvist 1993a) (see figure 5.2 for location of towns). Abundant crevasse-splays developed in the floodbasins between the straight channels in the west. These wetlands were dominated by clay sedimentation in the marshes, gyttja and clay sedimentation in the lakes, and development of peat in mires. Sand deposition was restricted to channel beds, while sedimentation of sandy and silty clay occurred on the levees and crevasse splays. Weerts & Bierkens (1993) clearly illustrated the extreme lateral facies variability which is associated with this sedimentary environment.

Upstream of Geldermalsen, wider channel belts of more or less meandering rivers existed during this period. Laterally, sedimentary environments were much less variable than downstream: lakes, mires and crevasse splays were much less abundant and floodbasins were better drained. Also along the margins of the Rhine-Meuse delta, meandering instead of straight channels existed (Berendsen 1982; Weerts & Berendsen

1995). The above-sketched distribution of channel types in the Holocene Rhine-Meuse delta was summarized in a time-space model by Törnqvist (1993a) (figure 5.4).

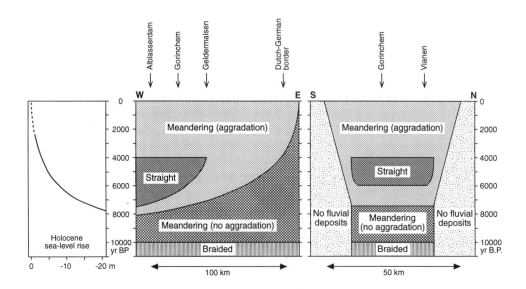

Figure 5.4   *Relative sea-level rise in the Rhine-Meuse delta (Van de Plassche 1982) and a time-space model showing the Holocene development of channel types in the Rhine-Meuse delta (adapted from Törnqvist 1993a). The term 'anastomosing' in the original figure of Törnqvist has been replaced by 'straight', in accordance with the terminology used in this thesis (section 2.2.4).*

Törnqvist (1993a) attributed the observed distribution to two factors: the rate of sea-level rise and the subsoil erodibility. Straight channels were supposed to have formed exclusively when floodplain sedimentation rates (due to sea-level rise) were high, and where the cohesive Holocene cover was thick. These conditions were met in the west-central part of the delta in the mid-Holocene, when the cohesive Holocene cover was thick enough some time after the onset of rapid Holocene sedimentation. At the northern and southern margin of the fluvial plain, easily erodible Pleistocene eolian cover sands were at shallow depth resulting in meandering channels. Upstream, sedimentation rates dropped below some critical value (Törnqvist et al. 1993), while the sandy Pleistocene subsoil occurs at shallower depth. Törnqvist suggested a switch from straight back to meandering channels by 4000 BP, which was attributed to a decreasing rate of sea-level rise. However, no causal mechanism between the rate of sea-level rise and lateral channel stability was discussed. Törnqvist et al. (1993) stated that a floodplain sedimentation rate of at least 1.5 mm/yr was required for laterally stable channels to develop. This value was based on longitudinal analysis of a 22-km reach of the Schaik paleochannel (figure 5.5a). However, the supposed downstream decrease in lateral migration of this paleochannel can equally well be explained by: (a) the downstream loss of discharge in abundant crevasses (the paleochannel probably terminated and never reached the coast) and (b) the possible downstream decrease in period of activity (Törnqvist et al 1993, p. 215).

Obviously an important change took place in the west-central delta around 4000 BP. Almost the complete network of straight channels in this area became abandoned and widespread peat-growth replaced clastic sedimentation. This development was accompanied by a change in coastal evolution from a retrograding 'open coast' with many tidal inlets to a prograding 'closed coast' with a massive series of beach barriers (Beets et al. 1992). Around 2000 BP peat-growth was interrupted by clastic sedimentation again, when four major Rhine-channels became active in this area. Of these channels the Lek and the Waal are still active today, while the Hollandse IJssel and Linge were both dammed by man around 1300 AD (Berendsen 1982, p. 186; Verbraeck 1984, p. 229-230) (see figure 5.5a for location of the channel belts).

Törnqvist (1993a) simply classified all these recent channels as 'meandering'. Considering the criteria mentioned in section 2.2.4, only the Waal and the upper reach of the Linge are truly meandering. In general, the sinuosity indexes of the recent channels are fairly low, although in places some restricted lateral migration of the channels is apparent. Presently, the Waal channel has a very low sinuosity index of just below 1.0. However, this is due to (man-induced) concave-bank bench accretion and artificial straightening of the river since embankment (Middelkoop 1997). In the late Middle Ages the lower reach of the Waal (downstream of Tiel) was more or less meandering with probably a sinuosity index of around 1.3. The sinuosity index of the Linge decreases downstream from 1.4 to below 1.3. The Hollandse IJssel and the lower reach of the Lek however, are typified by little or almost zero lateral channel migration (sinuosity indexes 1.0 to 1.1). For the upper reach of the Lek, sinuosity indexes of between 1.2 and 1.3 prior to human interference were estimated. Nevertheless, the recent channel network in the area clearly differs in two respects from its mid-Holocene counterpart: (1) the recent channel belts are wider on average and (2) substantially less crevasses are connected to the recent channels. The decrease in the number of crevasses can not be attributed to river embankments, since these took place long after the formation of the channels in question (around 1200 AD).

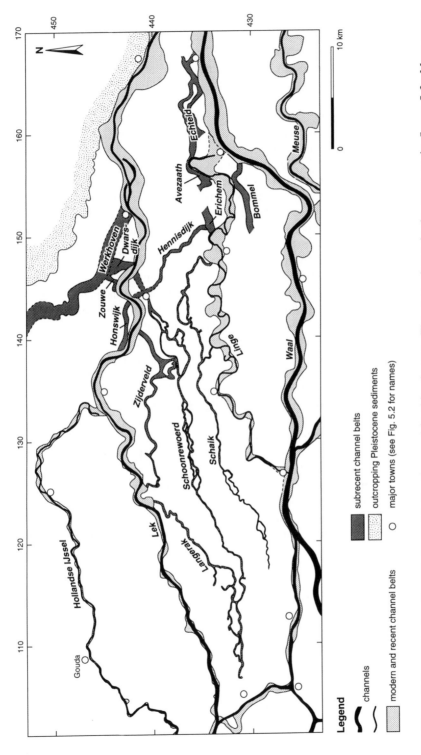

Figure 5.5a   The location of channel belts discussed in this chapter. The area shown is the same as in figure 5.2. Many more channel belts exist in the area but these have been omitted for clarity. For the same reason, some of the older channel belts mentioned in the text (Middelkoop, Achthoven, Tienhoven and Ochten) are not shown. Based on geological maps of Verbraeck (1970, 1984), Berendsen (1982), Törnqvist et al. (1993), Berendsen et al. (1994), Bosch & Kok (1994), Berendsen et al. (1995), and data from the borehole database of the Department of Physical Geography of Utrecht University (H.J.A. Berendsen unpublished data).

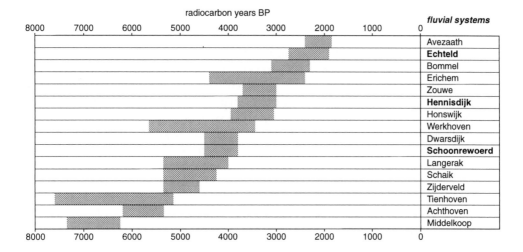

Figure 5.5b   *The periods of activity of the subrecent channel belts shown in figure 5.5a and some older channel belts mentioned in the text. Based on Berendsen (1982), Törnqvist (1993b), Berendsen & Stouthamer (in prep.) and data from this study.*

An important factor, not included in the model of Törnqvist, is the role of the magnitude of the discharge of paleochannels, through its influence on stream power. Studies of modern environments show a strong relationship between stream power and lateral channel stability (section 2.3.3). However, the magnitude of paleodischarge is hard to estimate from the size of abandoned channel belts, due to lateral and vertical accretion. It is remarkable that during the mid-Holocene when the Rhine distributed over many channels (figure 5.1), lateral stability of the channels seems to have been greater than during the late-Holocene when the number of coexisting channels had decreased. It also can not be excluded that the mid-Holocene straight channels in the west-central Rhine-Meuse delta effectively were nothing more than large crevasses of the bigger meandering channels that existed at that time along the margins of the delta. In this picture, the lateral stability of the straight paleochannels is explained by their low discharge and stream power instead of the effect of rapid sea level rise.

In conclusion, the model of Törnqvist (1993a) leaves room for alternative explanations, which will be explored in this chapter.

5.2.2   Previous work on the studied fluvial systems

The three fluvial systems selected for the present study are all located in the central part of the Rhine-Meuse delta. In this area relatively thick, and mostly cohesive, Holocene

181

deposits occur, that are underlain by the predominantly sandy and gravelly Late-Weichselian Kreftenheye Formation. Initially, the three fluvial systems were believed to have been active at the same time and were taken to represent the upper, middle and lower reaches of one long system as suggested by Verbraeck (1984, pp. 173, 213 and maps). Radiocarbon dates indicating the period of activity, were absent for the upper and middle reaches of this presumed system. In the course of the present study, radiocarbon dates unambiguously indicated that we were dealing with three different fluvial systems, with no overlap in their periods of activity (see also section 5.4.4).

While little is known about the Echteld and Hennisdijk systems, a great deal of work has been done on the Schoonrewoerd system. The Schoonrewoerd channel belt can be traced over a long distance (45 km), and has all the characteristics of the mid-Holocene channel belts, such as many bifurcations, a low width/thickness ratio of the channel-belt sand bodies and abundant associated crevasse deposits.

Remarkably, the Schoonrewoerd system seems to have survived much longer than its mid-Holocene neighbours, the Zijderveld and the Schaik systems (Törnqvist 1993b, p. 143-144). Various authors claimed that the period of activity of the Schoonrewoerd system can be subdivided into two phases, separated by a phase of reduced activity (De Boer & Pons 1960, p. 26; Verbraeck 1970, p. 87; Louwe Kooijmans 1974, p. 98). According to Törnqvist (1993b, p. 143) the Schoonrewoerd system was active between 5350 and 3600 BP, with a phase of reduced activity between 4700 and 4500 BP. Louwe Kooijmans (1974, p. 99) supposed that in the second 'wild' phase the stream was connected to the sea, while in the first 'quiet' phase it ended up branching into numerous small crevasse channels in the swamps. The detailed landscape reconstructions of Van der Woude (1983) confirmed that the well-defined Schoonrewoerd paleochannel dates from the second phase, while the first phase was dominated by fine clastic deposition, probably through a network of many small channels. During most of both phases of activity, the floodbasins were dominated by an open-water environment interrupted by a phase of dense swamp forest between 4600 and 4100 BP. The term 'fluviolagoon' was introduced (Van der Woude 1984) to indicate the back-barrier open fresh-water environment dissected by fluvial channels.

The marine influence on fluvial sedimentation in this environment has been a matter of debate for a long time (Hageman 1969, 1972; Van der Woude 1979, 1983; Berendsen 1982, 1984a). An important related question is whether the mid-Holocene channels in this area really had an open connection to the sea, in this case the former Meuse-estuary south of Rotterdam (e.g. De Groot & De Gans 1996). Hageman (1972) published a map of the western part of the present study area, depicting mid-Holocene westward bifurcating channels which were replaced to the west by eastward bifurcating channels. Few connections between the two channel networks seemed to exist. Later it appeared that only the eastern network was of mid-Holocene age, while the western network was much younger (e.g. Bosch & Kok 1994, p. 82). The narrow mid-Holocene paleochannels in this area are difficult to trace westward, since they occur at increasing depth below the surface and are frequently eroded by younger channels. Furthermore, mapping to the west is hindered by extensive urban areas. Some authors suggested that the channels indeed ended up in the fluviolagoon without ever reaching the sea (e.g. Bosch & Kok 1994, pp. 82-83; De Groot & De Gans 1996, fig. 8c).

5.3   Methods

In spite of the large number of data already available, additional fieldwork proved to be necessary. This was carried out in 1992, 1993 and 1995. Meanwhile, the three fluvial systems were mapped using the field data and the extensive borehole database set up at the Department of Physical Geography by H.J.A. Berendsen (Utrecht University). The available geological and soil maps were used in addition. Approximately 9000 boreholes from the database were used for mapping, with a borehole density of about 60 /km^2.

Sixteen cross sections were made for detailed reconstruction of the channel belts and to detect longitudinal trends in geometry. The cross sections were more or less evenly spaced along the fluvial systems at distances of five km on average. For construction of the cross sections, around 370 borings were used, of which 320 were carried out for this study, while another 50 borehole descriptions were taken from the database. In principle, borings reached to the Pleistocene subsoil and/or the base of the channel belt deposits. A maximum boring depth of 14.8 m was reached. Maximum borehole spacing was generally around 40 m based on guidelines provided by Weerts & Bierkens (1993). However on the narrow Schoonrewoerd channel belt, borings were often carried out only 10 to 20 m apart. The equipment used included an Edelman-auger and a gouge for clay, silt and peat, as well as a Van der Staay suction-corer (Van de Meene et al. 1979) for saturated sand below the groundwater table. Sediment properties were described every 10 cm, following Berendsen (1982, pp. 17-22).

In order to sample sedimentary structures, vibracoring was carried out in two cross sections. Weerts (1996, p. 162-163) gives a description of the vibracorer, which was later adapted for coring depths of 10 m needed for the present study. A total of 15 vibracores was collected of the Hennisdijk and Schoonrewoerd channel deposits. Penetration depths ranged from 7.2 to 10.2 m below the surface. The core diameter was 7 cm. The recovery of most cores was around 70%, but at three locations the recovery was only near 35%. At these locations new cores were collected using a mechanical bailer drilling unit (Oele et al. 1983, fig. 5). In a casing, undisturbed cores were collected by hammering of a one meter long sampler. This equipment was developed by the Netherlands Geological Survey. Penetration depths were approximately 12 m below the surface, with a core diameter of 10 cm and a recovery averaging 73%.

All cores, which were collected in PVC tubes placed within the steel sampler, were drained and split lengthwise. Subsequently, laquer peels were made, the cores were photographed and grain size samples were taken. Grain size analysis was done with a Fritsch 'Laser Particle Sizer' A22 of which the accuracy was investigated by Konert & Vandenberghe (1997). All boreholes were levelled relative to an absolute datum to enable reconstruction of gradient lines.

An additional opportunity to study sedimentary structures was offered by the presence of a pit (area ± 200 x 75 m), 100 m upstream of the mechanically cored cross section, exposing the uppermost 1,5 m of the Hennisdijk channel deposits.

Eleven samples of humic clay and peat collected in the cross sections were radiocarbon- dated. Eight samples were taken from auger boreholes to date the periods of activity of the three studied fluvial systems and an older fluvial system. For sampling, a 6 cm diameter gouge or a Dachnovsky-sampler (a hand-operated cylindrical sampler which can be opened at the appropriate depth) was applied. The sampling strategy will be explained in section 5.4.4. Three samples of reworked organic material were taken for identification of the base of the Hennisdijk channel belt deposits (see section 5.4.3). These samples were collected from two bailer cores and a Van der Staay core.

From all samples terrestrial macrofossils were selected for dating. This procedure yields more accurate results than the dating of bulk sediment samples (Törnqvist et al. 1992). After sampling in the field, the samples of humic clay and peat were cut into 1 cm thick slices, which were treated with 5 % KOH for 12 hours at room temperature prior to sieving over a 150 μm screen. Subsequently terrestrial macrofossils (such as fruits and nuts) were identified using a binocular microscope, and suitable macrofossils were picked for dating. All radiocarbon samples received an AAA (acid-alkaline-acid) chemical pretreatment comparable to the standard procedure described by Mook & Streurman (1983). The ^{14}C-dating was carried out at the Robert J. van de Graaff Laboratory (Utrecht University).

5.4   Results

5.4.1 Geological maps

For geological mapping of the fluvial systems, the borehole descriptions were genetically interpreted. Although many borehole descriptions are needed for detailed mapping of the planform of the fluvial systems, their channel belts can often easily be traced by their morphological expression in the present landscape. Especially in the western part of the Rhine-Meuse delta compaction of thick peat beds caused the channel sand bodies to stand out as alluvial ridges (figure 5.6). Geological maps of the three fluvial systems are briefly described below.

The Schoonrewoerd channel belt has an average width of about 100 m, but in many places a system of multiple connected channel belts is present (figure 5.7). Equally narrow in planform are the natural levee deposits flanking the channel deposits. The channel belts show irregular bends, alternating with long straight reaches. Residual channel deposits are rarely found. Laterally, peat is abundant and freakish networks of crevasse deposits dissect the floodbasin deposits.

Figure 5.6   *The Schoonrewoerd alluvial ridge near the Bleskensgraaf cross section (appendix 3, cross section 10). Bumps in the road mark the places where it crosses the two Schoonrewoerd sand bodies. The oncoming cars on the road (background) are on top of the southernmost ridge.*

The Hennisdijk channel belt is wider ($\pm$ 300 m) and fringed by wider areas with natural levee deposits (figure 5.8). Fragments of a residual channel could be mapped, which suggest a sinuosity index of around 1.2 for the final stage of the paleochannel. Northwest of the Hennisdijk channel belt, crevasse deposits are fingershaped in planform and occur isolated. To the southwest, crevasse deposits are more abundant and have the appearance of interconnected stringers. Clayey floodbasin deposits dominate. Only in the western part, substantial amounts of peat were mapped.

The Echteld channel belt is the widest (up to 1 km) but its width is also variable (figure 5.9). It has at least one important bifurcation. Mapped residual channel deposits enabled estimation of a sinuosity index of around 1.3 for the final stage of the paleochannel. Natural levee deposits are virtually absent along some reaches of the channels belts, while elsewhere being restricted to a relatively narrow band. Laterally, clayey floodbasin deposits dominate, whereas crevasse splay deposits are rare and peat is absent.

In summary, the three fluvial systems show marked differences in planform. In the next section the cross-sectional architecture of three fluvial systems is examined in detail.

185

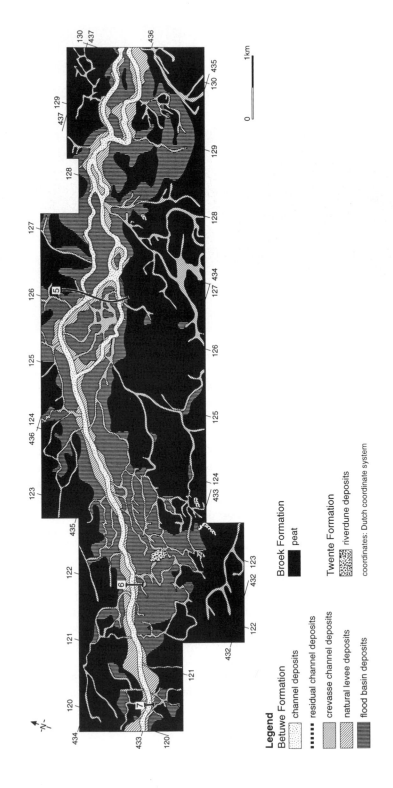

Figure 5.7   Geological map of the Schoonrewoerd system around the cross sections 5, 6 and 7. See figure 5.2 for the location of the cross sections.

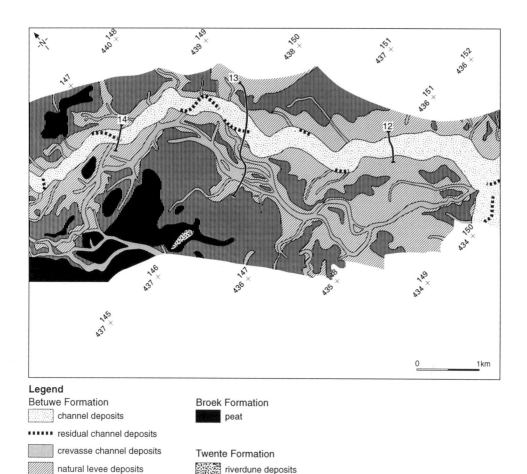

Legend

Betuwe Formation

[channel deposits pattern] channel deposits

■■■■■ residual channel deposits

[crevasse channel deposits pattern] crevasse channel deposits

[natural levee deposits pattern] natural levee deposits

[flood basin deposits pattern] flood basin deposits

Broek Formation

[peat pattern] peat

Twente Formation

[riverdune deposits pattern] riverdune deposits

coordinates: Dutch coordinate system

Figure 5.8   Geological map of the Hennisdijk system.

5.4.2   Description of the borehole cross sections

A series of borehole cross sections (appendices 3 and 4), more or less gives a three-dimensional picture of the depositional architecture of the three fluvial systems. Generally, Holocene fluvial systems in the Rhine-Meuse delta roughly have a cross-sectional appearance as sketched in figure 5.10, with the sand body being interpreted as channel deposits, the 'wings' of silty and sandy clay taken as levee deposits, while the wedges of clay are considered as floodbasin deposits. Isolated lenses of sandy and silty clay and small sand bodies are usually interpreted as crevasse splay and crevasse channel deposits and small clay or peat plugs on top of the sand bodies have been described as

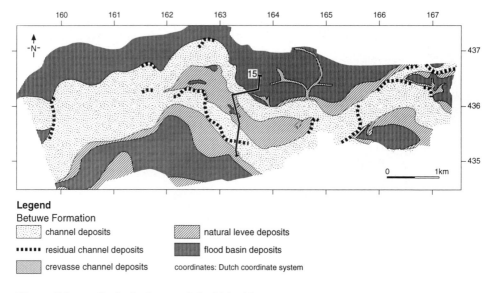

Figure 5.9   Geological map of the Echteld system.

residual channel deposits (e.g. Berendsen 1982; Törnqvist 1993b; Weerts 1996). Ideally, the fluvial systems are separated by peat.

The cross sections in the appendices 3 and 4 depict the sediment textures as described in the field. Additionally, distinction is made between four formations. Most of the sediments represented in the cross sections belong to the Betuwe Formation as defined by Berendsen (1982, 1984b). the Betuwe formation is Holocene in age and includes all clastic deposits genetically related to the investigated paleochannels. The Holocene peat in the study area is included in the Broek Formation following Berendsen (1982, 1984b). The lower part of the cross sections consists of sand and clay of the Kreftenheye Formation which was defined by Doppert et al. (1975). The upper part of the Kreftenheye Formation consists of a sheet of gravelly sand capped by a bed of strongly consolidated sandy clay. The top of the Kreftenheye Formation is Weichselian to early-Holocene in age. Late-Weichselian terraces dominate the morphology of the top of the Kreftenheye Formation. The stiff sandy clay directly on top of these terraces (section 5.2.1) was defined as the Wijchen Member by Törnqvist et al. (1994) and represents the uppermost member of the Kreftenheye Formation. An unconformity separates the Kreftenheye and Betuwe Formations. At places where channel sands of the Betuwe Formation erosively overlie sands of the Kreftenheye Formation, the boundary between both formations is hard to distinguish from borehole data. In the lower part of some cross sections, eolian sands of the Twente Formation are present. These are river dune deposits of Younger Dryas age which rest on top of the fluvial deposits of the Kreftenheye Formation. Törnqvist et al. (1994) defined similar river dune deposits as the Delwijnen Member of the Twente Formation.

188

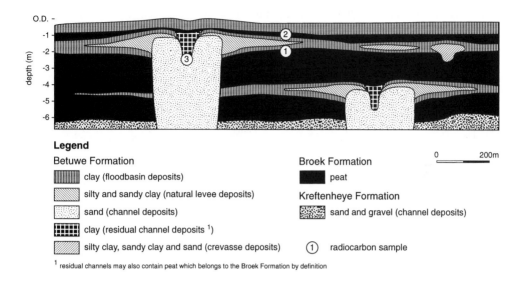

Figure 5.10   *Idealized cross section of two fluvial systems in the Rhine-Meuse delta. The positions of various types of radiocarbon samples for establishing the age of fluvial systems are also indicated (adapted from Berendsen 1996).*

The cross sections of each fluvial system will be described going downstream, to start with the oldest fluvial system. The numbers of the cross sections correspond to those in appendices 3 and 4, figure 5.2 and table 5.1. Paleoflow through all cross sections is away from the observer. The dimensions of the major fluvial sand bodies as determined from the cross sections, are listed in table 5.1. The radiocarbon samples, indicated in the cross sections, will be discussed in section 5.4.4. The periods of activity of fluvial systems mentioned are given in figure 5.5b. For clarity of description, characters in the cross sections indicate features discussed in the text. Interpretation of the described phenomena will follow in the sections 5.5.1 and 5.5.2.

The Schoonrewoerd system

The *Culemborg cross section (1)* of the Schoonrewoerd system is located just west of the town of Culemborg, where the Schoonrewoerd alluvial ridge emerges from under the built-up area. In this cross section the deposits of the Schoonrewoerd system appear as an up to 5 m thick wedge of sandy and silty clay almost fully encasing two sand bodies (**a** and **b**) both having a relatively high width/thickness-ratio of around 40. The clastic wedge is underlain by a one to two metres thick bed of peat directly resting on the Kreftenheye Formation. A small clay plug (**c**) is present on top of sand body **b**.

Table 5.1 Dimensions of the sand bodies in the borehole cross sections

Cross section			Distance [a] (km)	Width [b] (m)	Thickness [c] (m)	W/T [d] (-)
Schoonrewoerd system						
(1)	Culemborg	(east)	1.7	140	3.55	39
		(west)	2.0	195	4.50	43
(2)	Diefdijk	(southeast)	5.4	180	6.90	26
		(middle)	6.0	80	≥8.25 [e]	≤9
		(northwest)	6.4	70	4.75	15
(3)	Schoonrewoerd		11.6	125	5.60	22
(4)	Leerbroek	(south)	15.3	130	5.60	23
		(north)	14.8	95	5.20	18
(5)	Noordeloos	(south)	21.5	60	7.35	8
		(north)	21.5	90	≥7.30	≤12
(6)	Goudriaan		26.5	95	8.05	12
(7)	Ottoland		28.4	80	9.00	9
(8)	Molenaarsgraaf I		32.8	65	8.75	7
(9)	Molenaarsgraaf II		34.6	50	10.50	5
(10)	Bleskensgraaf	(south)	40.6	65	≥7.55	≤9
		(north)	40.6	50	≥8.50	≤6
(11)	Alblasserdam		43.8	120	≥11.15 [f]	≤11
Hennisdijk system						
(12)	Buren		1.8	360	9.90 [g]	36
(13)	Asch		4.6	380	≥4.55	≤84
(14)	De Bosjes		7.0	200	≥3.90	≤51
Echteld system						
(15)	Echteld	(south)	4.8	370	≥3.85	≤96
		(north)	5.3	190	≥2.75	≤69
(16)	Tiel		10.8	440	6.55	67

[a] Measured along the main sand body from its most upstream occurrence as apparent from geological maps. Presumed upstream connections were left out of consideration.

[b] May be smaller than in the cross sections if these are not perpendicular to the sand body orientation. The margins of the sand body were assumed to be located halfway between bounding boreholes.

[c] When the sand body rests on the sand of the Kreftenheye Formation and the base of the sand body could not be distinguished, the top of the sand of the Kreftenheye Formation was taken as a substitute for the lower boundary of the sand body. In those cases only a minimum sand body thickness is given.

[d] Width/thickness.

[e] Minimum thickness based on identification of the boundary between the sand body and the sand of the Kreftenheye Formation in one of the boreholes.

[f] Thickness based on lithofacies analysis (section 5.4.2).

[g] Thickness is established by detailed lithofacies analysis and radiocarbon dating of reworked wood (section 5.4.3).

Only 4 km downstream, the deposits of the Schoonrewoerd system already have a very different architecture. In the *Diefdijk cross section (2)* the sand bodies are much narrower and thicker, each having its own lateral wings of silty and sandy clay. Sand body **a** is relatively fine-textured and has a width/thickness ratio of 26. Sand body **b** is rich in coarse sand and obviously crosscuts various peat and clay layers. This sand body rests on sand of the Kreftenheye Formation. A maximum width/thickness ratio of 9 is calculated for sand body **b**. It has wings of sandy and silty clay that extend laterally for 50 to 150 m. The sheets of clay (**S**) extend much further, but are split by thin but extensive layers of peat. Sand body **c** is small and fine-textured. It crosscuts several beds of peat and clay as well as a clastic package (**M/Z**) that seems to belong to the Middelkoop and Zijderveld systems (location of Zijderveld channel belt shown in figure 5.5a). Sand body **c** is fully surrounded by Betuwe Formation sediments and has a fairly low width/thickness-ratio of 15.

Only one major sand body was mapped a little west of the town of Schoonrewoerd. In the *Schoonrewoerd cross section (3)* the sand body (**a**) rests on the stiff sandy clay of the Kreftenheye Formation, which is exceptionally thick at this location. It is capped by sandy and silty clay which tapers out laterally rapidly into clay. Another, much smaller sand body (**b**) is present to the north. It shares a silty and sandy clay wedge with the sand body **a**. A layer of peat (0.1 - 0.5 m thick) underlies the clastic wedges, but is cut by sand bodies **a** and **b**. Another small sand body (**c**), which was partly eroded on its southern flank, occurs to the north just below this peat layer. This sand body and the clay package **M** belong to the older Middelkoop system of which the channel belt occurs a few hundred meters to the south (Verbraeck 1970; Van der Woude 1983, fig. 10). Compared to the Diefdijk cross section, the main sand body of the Schoonrewoerd system appears relatively small in the Schoonrewoerd cross section. However, it is likely that smaller sand bodies of the Schoonrewoerd system existed outside of the cross section (e.g. Van der Woude 1983, fig. 10).

Further downstream, in the *Leerbroek cross section (4)*, the Schoonrewoerd system comprises two major sand bodies having a width/thickness-ratio of around 20. Sand body **a** has a core of coarse sand and a plug (**b**) of clay and peat above its southwestern flank. Sand body **a** is almost fully encased in clastic sediments, but near its base it cuts two layers of peat which seems to mark the base of its lateral clastic wedge. A few hundred meters to the northeast this thick package of clay (**S**) is sandwiched between two major layers of peat. Sand body **c** is bordered over its full depth by a thick but laterally very restricted package (**d**) of predominantly sandy clay, which seems to cut a 0.5 m thick layer of peat. This layer of peat marks the base of the lateral clay wedge (**S**). Sand body **c** also has wings of silty and sandy clay which taper out in the clay wedge. Under the peat layer, near the base of the cross section, the top of a relatively wide sand body (**e**) can be identified. This sand body belongs to the Achthoven system (Berendsen 1982, p. 145), which was mapped by Verbraeck (1970). Its clastic wedge (**A**) rests directly on the Kreftenheye Formation. A deep channel occurs in the top of the Kreftenheye Formation.

Downstream of the Leerbroek cross section, the thickness of the Schoonrewoerd sand bodies significantly increases. Along with a decrease in width, this leads to a width/thickness-ratio of around 10 in the *Noordeloos cross section (5)*. This cross section is based on a cross section published by Törnqvist (1993a, fig. 6c; 1993b, enclosure). For the present study, the earlier cross section was refined with new boreholes. In the southern part of the cross section a Schoonrewoerd sand body (a) just cuts the top of the stiff bed of Kreftenheye Formation clay (Wijchen Member), while being flanked by a considerably wider sand body **b** which rests on the Kreftenheye Formation sand. Sand body **b** belongs to the Middelkoop system (e.g. Törnqvist 1993b, p. 143). Sand body **a** cuts the clastic wedge (**M**) of the Middelkoop system and the continuous peat layer (around 4 m below O.D.) that covers the system. The Schoonrewoerd clastic wedge **S** is relatively thick and encloses a small sand body (**c**). Sand body **c** cuts the thinner clastic bed **Z**, which probably belongs to the Zijderveld system (this will be further explained in section 5.5.1). A discontinuous peat layer separates the beds **Z** and **S**. In the northern part of the cross section another Schoonrewoerd sand body (**d**) cuts the Middelkoop clay wedge (**M**) and the clastic bed **Z**. The Schoonrewoerd clastic wedge tapers out to the north. It encloses two bodies of silty and sandy clay and sand (**e** and **f**) that seem to cut the clastic bed **Z**. Both Schoonrewoerd sand bodies (**a** and **d**) have restricted (up to 50 m wide) wings of silty and sandy clay.

A little more than 1 km west of the Noordeloos cross section, the Schoonrewoerd sand bodies rejoin and for approximately 10 km the Schoonrewoerd system comprises only one major sand body, which is rather straight in planform. The thickness of the sand body increases steadily in a westerly direction as can be seen in the *Goudriaan and Ottoland cross sections (6 and 7)*. The width/thickness ratio remains about 10 in these cross sections. In the Goudriaan cross section, sand bodies (**b** and **c**) of presumably the Middelkoop system can be seen on both sides of the Schoonrewoerd sand body (**a**). Around 5 m below O.D., a peat layer covers this fluvial system. Wings of silty and sandy clay are attached to the top of the Schoonrewoerd sand body and seem to taper out in its clay wedge **S**. Lower in the section, clastic bed **Z** seems to be cut by the Schoonrewoerd sand body. In the Ottoland cross section, located a few kilometres downstream, a roughly comparable depositional architecture can be seen.

An exceptionally thick clastic wedge was found adjacent to the Schoonrewoerd sand body in the *Molenaarsgraaf I cross section (8)*. The Schoonrewoerd sand body (**a**) is underlain by peat and has a width/thickness ratio of only 7. A peat plug occurs in the silty and sandy clay on top of the sand body. Laterally, thick peat layers dominate the sequence. Apart from the clay at the surface, three clastic beds are obvious. The Schoonrewoerd clastic wedge (**S**) contains lenses of silty and sandy clay, while the other clastic beds (**M** and **Z**) consist predominantly of clay. Clastic bed **M** is presumed to belong to the Middelkoop system, while clastic bed **Z** probably belongs to the Zijderveld system (section 5.5.1). Close to the sand body the Schoonrewoerd clastic wedge seems to merge with clastic bed **Z**, resulting in a complex architecture.

The geological map (Bosch & Kok, 1994) indicates an important bifurcation of the Schoonrewoerd sand body 0.5 km west of the Molenaarsgraaf I cross section. Excellent detailed mapping of Van der Woude (1983) in this particular area however, showed no major bifurcation of the Schoonrewoerd sand body up to the *Molenaarsgraaf II cross section (9)*. In this cross section the sand body (**a**) has an extremely low width/thickness ratio of 5. Due to a considerable increase in thickness with respect to the Molenaarsgraaf

I cross section, the base of the sand body cuts the sands of the Kreftenheye Formation at this location. Remarkable is also the relatively low position of the Schoonrewoerd clastic wedge. While the sand body rests on firm subsoil, a thick peat layer at 8 to 9 m below O.D. has undergone considerable compaction, causing the lateral wedges to subside relative to the sand body. Clastic bed **Z** is relatively thin and is separated from the Schoonrewoerd clastics (**S**) by a thin peat layer.

West of the Molenaarsgraaf II cross section, the geological map (Bosch & Kok 1994) shows increasing complexity of the Schoonrewoerd system. Down to the *Bleskensgraaf cross section (10)* there is a number of bifurcations, with some minor sand bodies branching off. On the other hand, the available maps (Stichting voor Bodemkartering 1959; Bosch & Kok 1994) show another sand body coming in from the northeast, that joins the Schoonrewoerd system in this area (figure 5.5a). This system is called the Langerak system (Berendsen & Stouthamer, in prep.) and may have been connected to the upstream Zijderveld system. The top of the Langerak sand body occurs about one meter deeper below the surface than the Schoonrewoerd sand body. In the Bleskensgraaf cross section the Schoonrewoerd sand bodies (**a** and **b**) are totally covered by peat. Sand body **a** rests on top of an unnamed and unmapped Betuwe Formation sand body (**c**), which may be connected to the Middelkoop system. A maximum width/thickness ratio of 9 can be calculated for sand body **a**. The lateral wedges of clay and silty clay seem to taper out over a short distance into the surrounding peat. Sand body **b** has a slightly lower position and rests on sand of the Kreftenheye Formation. It cuts the clay wedge of the older fluvial system. The width/thickness ratio of sand body **b** is low with a maximum value of only 6. Its clastic wedges are dominated by silty clay and have their base at roughly the same level as the southern sand body.

The two sand bodies found in the Bleskensgraaf cross section rejoin about 2 km downstream. Further west, a relatively wide sand body (**a**) resting on the sand of the Kreftenheye Formation was found in the *Alblasserdam cross section (11)*. On its southern flank the sand body grades into a thick sequence of silty and sandy clay (**b**), which also erosively overlies the top of the Kreftenheye Formation. In the core of the sand body, were penetration was deepest, a rhythmic bedded sequence (figure 5.11) was cored below -11 m (relative to O.D). A similar sequence was nowhere found in other cross sections upstream. The individual beds are approximately 25 cm thick and each possesses a grading from medium sand at the base to silty or sandy clay at the top. Organic debris is abundant throughout these beds and often occurs as fine particles in thin horizontal laminae. Since this heterolithic facies extends from the sand body down to two meters below the top of the Kreftenheye Formation, the thickness of the sand body is estimated to be at least 11.15 m, leading to a maximum width/thickness ratio of around 11. The lateral clastic wedges have their base at around 7 m below O.D. and seem to taper out rapidly into the surrounding peat. Somewhat lower, a complex facies of interlayered clay and silty clay (often laminated, calcareous and slightly humic) and peat occurs on top of the Kreftenheye Formation. A small plug of humic clay was found on top of the sand body (see adjacent detailed cross section).

Figure 5.11   *Core of a rhythmic bedded sequence around 12 m below O.D. in the central part of the sand body in the Alblasserdam cross section (appendix 3, cross section 11). The sandy bases of the beds appear wider on the photograph, due to flow of the water-saturated sediment.*

The Hennisdijk system

The *Buren cross section (12)* of the Hennisdijk system reveals a fairly symmetrical architecture of the sand body. It consists of a core of coarse sand (**a**), with occasional gravel lenses, which is mantled by fine and medium sand. Laterally, the sand grades into predominantly sandy clay (**b**). A plug of (humic) clay (**c**) was found on top of the central part of the sand body. The base of the lateral clastic wedge is marked on both sides of the sand body by a thin peat layer. The Hennisdijk sand body cuts deeply into the Kreftenheye Formation. Analysis of sedimentary structures and radiocarbon dates of reworked wood in the sand body (section 5.4.3) suggest a sand body thickness of 9.90 m, implying a width/thickness ratio of 36. The sand body dissects a thick package of Betuwe Formation clay and silty clay as well as a thick layer of consolidated clayey deposits of the Kreftenheye Formation (the Wijchen Member).

The *Asch cross section (13)* reveals more about the architecture of the lateral clastic wedges of the Hennisdijk system. To the southwest the clastic wedge encases a sand sheet (**a**) with a very high width/thickness ratio of around 350. The sheet-like body has a small clay-filled depression (**b**) on top of it. The location of this part of the Asch cross section is identical to that of a cross section published by Verbraeck (1970, fig. 57a), in which the sand sheet is unjustly presented as a thick sand body resting on the Kreftenheye Formation. In fact, the thick and laterally extensive peat layer that underlies the clastic wedge is only cut by the much bigger Hennisdijk sand body. The architecture of the Hennisdijk sand body is almost similar to that in the Buren cross section, having a core of coarse sand (**c**) grading into a thick package of sandy and silty clay (**d**) along its flank, and a clay plug (**e**) on its top. Since the thickness of the sand body is unknown, only a maximum width/thickness ratio of 84 can be calculated. Northeast of the Hennisdijk sand body, the Hennisdijk clastic wedge (**H**) consists primarily of clay, while the underlying

194

peat is thinner. A thick layer of sandy and silty clay and clay (**T**), resting directly on the Kreftenheye Formation probably belongs to the Tienhoven system of which the main sand body is located about 1 km northeast of the Hennisdijk sand body, outside of the cross section (Berendsen 1982, Verbraeck 1984). The Tienhoven clastic wedge thins to the southwest and is cut by the Hennisdijk sand body. It comprises two small sand bodies (**f** and **g**).

Only a few kilometres downstream, in the *De Bosjes cross section (14)*, the Hennisdijk sand body (**a**) is narrower and a core of coarse sand is lacking. It has a maximum width/thickness ratio of 51. Phenomena consistent with the preceding cross sections are the clay and peat plug on top (**b**) as well as the lateral grading into sandy clay (**c**) along the flanks of the sand body. On the eastern side, the sand body cuts a lower sand body (**d**) of presumably the Tienhoven system. The Hennisdijk clastic wedge directly overlies the Tienhoven system. Likewise on the western side, the Tienhoven and Hennisdijk clastic wedges merge into a single thick clayey package separated from the Kreftenheye Formation by a thin peat layer.

The Echteld system

A major bifurcation characterizes the Echteld system. A little more than 5 km downstream from the place were the Echteld system emerges from under the modern Waal River channel belt, two predominantly coarse-grained sand bodies can be recognized in the *Echteld cross section (15)*. Both sand bodies rest on sand of the Kreftenheye Formation, but their exact thickness is unknown. The lower part of the sand body, depicted as belonging to the Betuwe Formation, might actually belong to the Kreftenheye Formation. Sand body **a** has a clay plug (**b**) on its top. The width/thickness ratio of sand body **a** is ≤96. Sand body **c** has an irregular top and a width/thickness ratio ≤69. Both sand bodies are capped by a package of silty and sandy clay extending laterally as wings. The base of the Echteld clay wedge (**E**) is hard to delimit precisely since it merges with the underlying clay wedge (**O**) of the older Ochten system (Berendsen & Stouthamer in prep.). Sand body **c** probably belongs to the Ochten system as well as to the Echteld system, as indicated by its the double wings of silty and sandy clay. A thin and laterally restricted peat lens (location of radiocarbon sample 3) seems to split the Ochten and Echteld clastic wedges locally. To the south the wings of silty and sandy clay of the Echteld system, obviously overlie a small sand body (**d**) of presumably the Ochten system.

The Echteld sand body (**a**) in the *Tiel cross section (16)* only just cuts the top of the Kreftenheye sands. Its width/thickness ratio is 67. Being dominated by medium sand, it includes pockets of coarse sand and occasional gravel lenses. A thick clay plug (**b**) occurs on top of the sand body. Laterally, thick packages of silty and sandy clay (**E**) were found.

5.4.3 Description of the sand body lithofacies

In the Molenaarsgraaf I and the Buren cross sections a more detailed lithofacies analysis of the Schoonrewoerd and Hennisdijk sand bodies was carried out, mainly using mechanically drilled undisturbed cores. Sedimentological logging of the cores helped to identify a number of distinct facies in both cross sections. The boundaries between these facies are gradual. The orientation of the described section of the cores is parallel to the trend of the sand body. Dip angles of cross strata cited below, represent angles as measured from these sections and may therefore be smaller than the true dip angles. The main facies characteristics are summarized in table 5.2. The interpretation of the lithofacies described below is given in the sections 5.5.1 and 5.5.2.

Molenaarsgraaf I cross section

The Schoonrewoerd sand body in the Molenaarsgraaf I cross section (cross section 8 in Appendix 3) consists of three different facies (figure 5.12a). The bulk of the sand body can be classified as *facies 1*. Facies 1 is composed of clean sand, which is predominantly medium textured and moderately well sorted according to the scale of Folk & Ward (1957). Only near the erosive base of the sand body, facies 1 consists of coarse sand and may be very poorly sorted, while the top meter is dominated by fine sand (figure 5.12b). Granules, mud clasts and organic litter do occur, but are minor components. The same holds for mud drapes of which only a few were recorded in facies 1. The most typical sedimentary structure is cross bedding, occurring in sets, up to 50 cm thick, that are stacked into fairly homogeneous sequences (figure 5.12c). These sequences, which occur in the centre of the sand body (cores 12-14) show only a poorly developed fining upward trend in grain size (figure 5.12b) and hardly any trend in the scale of sedimentary structures. Most cross beds are planar and have dip angles up to 30°. Reactivation surfaces are common. Smaller scaled structures occur in facies 1 along the margins of the sand body. Along the northern flank (core 15), sets of tabular and trough cross lamination of a few centimetres thick, organized into cosets (decimeters thick), alternate with cross-bedded sets over the full thickness of the sand body (figure 5.12c). In the southern part of the sand body (cores 10 and 11), where facies 1 overlies facies 3, thick cross-bedded sets are lacking. Instead, dominant horizontal lamination and bedding alternates with thin (around 2 cm thick) tabular and trough cross-laminated sets. Cross lamination occurs in cosets of decimeters thick.

Figure 5.12   *(facing page) (a) Distribution of facies 1, 2 and 3 in the sand body of the Molenaarsgraaf I cross section. (b) Vertical trend in median grain size in core 13. (c) Samples of the analyzed cores showing observed sedimentary structures and sedimentological logs.*

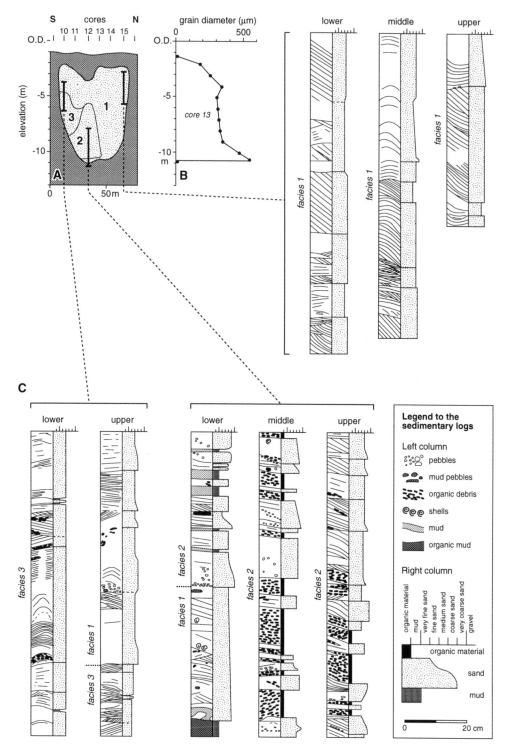

197

Facies 2 is characterized by a heterogeneous lithological composition. Abundant reworked organic material is the prime feature of facies 2. The organic litter consists primarily of wood and occurs as up to 15 cm thick beds, overlain and underlain by coarse and medium sand (figure 5.12c). The sand is predominantly planar cross-bedded with typical set thickness ranging from 5 to 15 cm. The cross beds frequently contain fine organic material, granules and shell fragments. Sets of horizontal lamination and planar cross lamination (up to a few centimetres thick), constitute a less important component of facies 2. Near the base of the sand body (in core 12) facies 2 consists of a heterolithic package (50 cm thick) of interbedded sand and mud (figure 5.12c). The mud drapes vary in thickness between 0.1 and 3 cm.

Facies 3 consists of mud and fine sand. The dominant sedimentary structure is horizontal and subhorizontal fine lamination (figure 5.12c). Thin cross-laminated sets (1 to 2 cm thick) occur as well. Fine reworked organic material and many thin mud laminae are incorporated in the sedimentary structures. Near the base of the sand body (in core 10) facies 3 includes some relatively thick sets (up to 20 cm) of cross bedding and lamination in fine sand. The cross beds and laminae have steep dip angles up to 30°.

Buren cross section

The Hennisdijk sand body in the Buren cross section (cross section 12 in Appendix 4) rests on the sand of the Kreftenheye Formation. Consequently its base is hard to delimit. Three radiocarbon samples of reworked organic material within the sand yielded a Holocene age and therefore indicated a minimum depth of the base of the Hennisdijk sand body. This information and interpretation of the sedimentary logs led to reconstruction of the erosive base as sketched in figure 5.13a. The top of the sand body could be much better studied than in the Molenaarsgraaf I cross section, thanks to the presence of a large pit nearby. The Hennisdijk sand body is composed of three facies, which are different from the ones described above.

Facies 4 is mostly found near the base of the sand body and consists of very coarse sand, gravelly sand and gravel which is moderately well to poorly sorted. In some cores, facies 4 is absent, while in other cores it is several meters thick. The largest clasts of facies 4 are pebble-sized, but much larger logs and lumps of clay and peat were observed (figure 5.13c). Facies 4 is mostly massive or faintly cross-bedded in structure.

Figure 5.13   *(facing page) (a) Distribution of facies 4, 5 and 6 in the sand body of the Buren cross section. (b) Vertical trend in median grain size in core 5. (c) Samples of the analyzed cores showing observed sedimentary structures and sedimentological logs.*

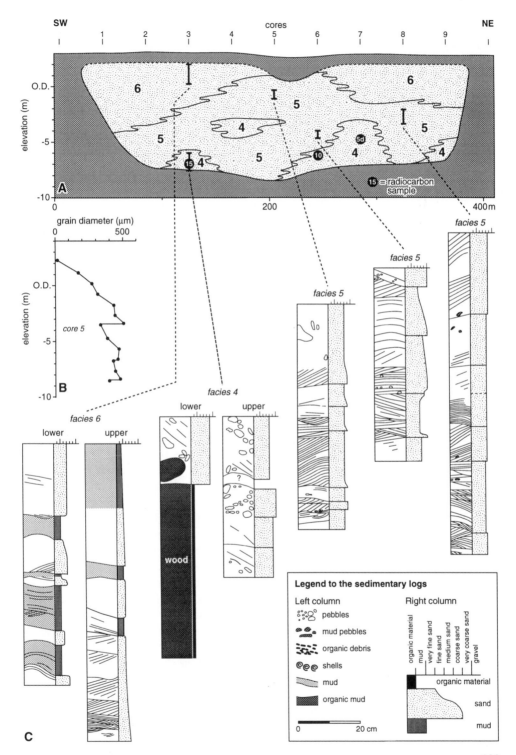

199

Table 5.2 The main characteristics of the six facies

	Texture	Structure	Remarks
Facies 1	medium sand	cross bedding	homogeneous sequence
Facies 2	organic litter, coarse sand, medium sand, and mud	cross bedding	thick (≤ 15 cm) beds of pure reworked wood, sand-mud interbeds near base
Facies 3	fine sand and mud	fine horizontal and subhorizontal lamination	
Facies 4	gravel, gravelly sand and very coarse sand	cross bedding and massive	large logs and lumps of clay and peat
Facies 5	coarse sand and medium sand	cross lamination/bedding, horizontal lamination/bedding, subhorizontal lamination/bedding	multiple fining upward cycles, poorly developed overall fining upward
Facies 6	fine sand and mud	IHS [a], horizontal lamination and subhorizontal lamination	dip angle IHS is 6.5°

[a] Inclined heterolithic stratification

Facies 5 generally overlies facies 4 and represents the bulk of the sand body. Its texture is medium to coarse sand which is moderately well sorted. Near the base of sets, the sand may contain abundant granules. Mud clasts occur occasionally, while reworked organic matter is rare. Although there is a general fining upward trend through facies 4, it is poorly developed and it is composed of multiple shorter fining upward sequences (figure 5.13b). Sedimentary structures in facies 5 are strongly variable in type and scale, and from the cores there hardly appears to be a preferred order or sequence. The assemblage of structures comprises cross lamination and cross bedding, horizontal and subhorizontal cross bedding and lamination (figure 5.13c). Cross beds and laminae have variable dip angles and may be planar as well as trough-shaped. Set thickness ranges from 1 cm in the case of cross lamination to around 40 cm in the case of cross bedding.

Facies 6 overlies facies 5 and is thickest near the margins of the sand body. Facies 6 consists predominantly of mud and fine sand (figure 5.13c). Medium sand also occurs interlayered with mud. The most important structure of facies 6 is inclined heterolithic stratification (IHS) (figure 5.14), which could be studied in a nearby pit down to 2.0 m below the surface. The individual inclined heterolithic strata are convex-up and laterally stacked. In the cross sections studied, the strata dip fairly uniform in a northerly direction, which is towards the centre of the sand body. The sand-mud couplets range in thickness from approximately 2 to 30 cm, with the sand layer usually being slightly thicker than the mud layer. Sand-mud contacts can be sharp as well as gradational and may be wavy (figure 5.15). Thinner mud laminae are discontinuous, but thicker mud beds (up to 20 cm thick) extend laterally for tens of meters. Occasionally the mud contains fine reworked organic matter. The dip angle of the lower (and steeper) part of the inclined strata is 6.5° on average (31 measurements). Internally, the inclined strata often appear rather structureless and are rooted and bioturbated near the top of facies 6. Sedimentary structures observed in the cores, are dominant horizontal and subhorizontal lamination and subordinate trough and planar cross lamination (sets up to 5 cm thick).

Figure 5.14   *Inclined heterolithic stratification in an excavation near the Buren cross section (appendix 4, cross section 12). Capping clay has been stripped of the surface of the point bar complex. The scale staff measures 3.0 m.*

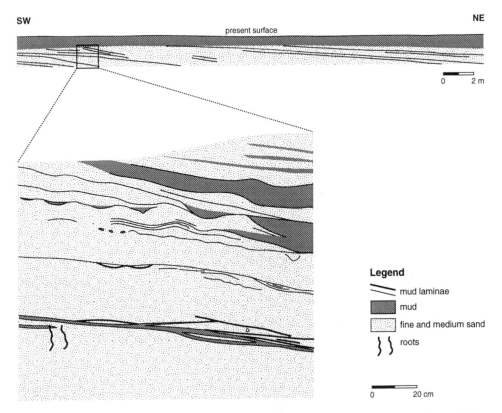

SW   NE

present surface

0   2 m

Legend

mud laminae

mud

fine and medium sand

roots

0   20 cm

*Figure 5.15   Close up of the inclined heterolithic strata, showing strongly variable
thickness of the fine members and occasional wavy appearance.*

5.4.4   Radiocarbon dates and the chronology of the fluvial systems

The radiocarbon dates from the cross sections are listed in table 5.3. In this table,
mention is made of various types of samples, which are schematically depicted in figure
5.10. Samples from just below the clastic wedge (type 1 samples) are suitable for dating
the beginning of activity of a fluvial system, while samples from just above the clastic
wedge (type 2 samples) and samples from the base of a clay/peat plug (type 3 samples)
are suitable for dating the end of fluvial activity (e.g. Berendsen 1982, pp. 114-118).
Type 3 samples are preferred to type 2 samples, since there is often a hiatus at the clastic-
organic transition below type 2 samples (Törnqvist & van Dijk 1993, p. 143). The
samples 5d, 10 and 15 (table 5.3) do not belong to any of these three types. These
samples were taken of reworked organic material in the sand body to help in the
identification of the erosive base (section 5.4.3).

202

Table 5.3 Radiocarbon dates from the studied fluvial systems

Sample	Laboratory nr.	^{14}C-age (yr BP)	Depth below surface (cm)	Coordinates [a] and elevation of core location relative to Dutch Ordnance Datum (m)	Material	Sample type
1	UtC-4639	1901 ± 35	198-200	163.095/435.370/+5.5	5 *Scirpus lacustris* nuts	3
3	UtC-4640	2770 ± 90	161-163	163.460/436.565/+4.7	10 *Rumex maritimus* fruits	1
5d	UtC-4641	4640 ± 60	810-815	150.030/435.900/+3.2	33 *Typha* fruits, 4 *Alisma plantago-aquatica* fruits, 6 *Carex rostrata* nuts	
6	UtC-4642	2975 ± 35	375-376	147.015/438.905/+2.6	5 *Oenanthe aquatica* mericarps, 4 *Alisma plantago-aquatica* fruits, 2 *Mentha aquatica* mericarps, 1 *Scirpus lacustris* nut, 2 *Carex* sp. nuts, 1 *Ranunculus acris* fruit	3
7	UtC-4643	3818 ± 42	226-228	148.865/437.940/+2.5	4 *Scirpus lacustris* nuts	1
8	UtC-4644	5170 ± 110	324-325	148.865/437.940/+2.5	1 *Solanum dulcamara* seed, 1 *Typha* fruit, 3 *Urtica dioica* fruits, 8 *Alisma plantago-aquatica* fruits	2
9	UtC-4645	6220 ± 70	570-571	148.865/437.940/+2.5	4 *Alnus glutinosa* nuts, 2 *Oenanthe aquatica* mericarps	1/2
10	UtC-4646	6150 ± 50	920-935	150.030/435.855/+3.1	wood and roots	
12	UtC-4647	3823 ± 40	347-350	107.155/431.473/−0.8	1 *Alnus glutinosa* cone	3
14	UtC-4648	5120 ± 70	536-537	110.080/431.193/−1.6	2 *Cornus sanguinea* endocarps	1
15	UtC-4649	4180 ± 50	1035	149.935/435.800/+3.2	wood	

[a] According to the Dutch coordinate system.

The period of activity of the Schoonrewoerd system was already established by a large number of radiocarbon dates (summarized by Törnqvist & Van Dijk 1993). However, all previous radiocarbon samples originated from locations upstream of cross section 9. For the present study two new radiocarbon samples were collected more to the west.

In cross section 10 (appendix 3) a type 1 sample was taken just below the base of the clastic wedge. The age of sample 14 indicates a beginning of fluvial activity around 5100 BP. This is slightly later than previous dates from upstream locations, which point to a start of fluvial activity around 5350 BP (Törnqvist & Van Dijk 1993). In section 5.5.1 it is shown that actually none of these dates relates to the start of fluvial activity of Schoonrewoerd system, and it is demonstrated that this system came into existence much later, by 4500 BP.

Further downstream, in cross section 11 (appendix 3) a type 3 sample was taken from the base of a humic clay plug. The age of sample 12 implies that fluvial activity of the Schoonrewoerd system ended by 3800 BP. Previous research at upstream locations suggested that fluvial activity ceased by 3600 BP (Törnqvist & Van Dijk 1993, p. 136). This age however was entirely based on type 2 samples that generally yield ages that are too young, due to the common occurrence of depositional hiatuses on top of the clay wedge (Törnqvist & Van Dijk 1993).

The period of activity of the Hennisdijk system was only poorly established previously. Verbraeck (1984, fig. 57a) dated the top of the thick peat layer that underlies the Hennisdijk clastic wedge in cross section 13 (appendix 4). One sample yielded an age of 3895 ± 40 BP (GrN-6229; sample V in cross section 13), whereas another yielded 3945 ± 35 BP (GrN-6230; outside the cross section). Verbraeck accepted these dates as representing the beginning of activity of a presumed fluvial system, solely represented by the overlying sand sheet. He supposed the much bigger Hennisdijk sand body to belong to the Schoonrewoerd system and therefore to be much older (Verbraeck 1984, p. 173). For the present study, a new type 1 sample (sample 7) was taken in cross section 13 northeast of the Hennisdijk sand body from the humic clay representing the transition between the peat and the Hennisdijk clastic wedge. The age of this sample (3818 ± 42 BP) agrees well with the dates published by Verbraeck and suggests beginning of Hennisdijk fluvial activity around 3850 BP. From the radiocarbon dates and the stratigraphy in cross section 13 it is obvious that both the sand sheet and the big Hennisdijk sand body belong to the same fluvial system. The age of beginning of activity of the Hennisdijk system indicates that Schoonrewoerd activity must have ceased earlier than 3600 BP, the date suggested by Törnqvist & Van Dijk (1993), since the younger Hennisdijk system crosscuts the Schoonrewoerd system under the town of Culemborg (figure 5.5a). The age of sample 12 (3823 ± 40 BP) from cross section 11 (appendix 3) seems to be a better approximation for the end of activity of the Schoonrewoerd system.

In cross section 13 also the base of the peat layer that underlies the Hennisdijk clastic wedge was sampled (sample 8). The peat layer covers a clastic layer that probably belongs to the Tienhoven system. The age of sample 8 suggests an end of Tienhoven clastic deposition prior to 5200 BP. This is in agreement with findings of Berendsen (1982, p. 148), who assumed an end of activity of the Tienhoven system around 5350

BP, based on relative dating, palynological data and ^{14}C dating of the Benschop system which is the downstream continuation of the Tienhoven system (Berendsen 1982, p. 157). Recent unpublished radiocarbon dates of the Tienhoven system are in close agreement (Berendsen & Stouthamer pers. comm.). A phase of reduced clastic deposition around 6200 BP is suggested by the age of sample 9, that represents a minor peat layer within the Tienhoven clastic wedge.

The end of activity of the Hennisdijk system was not established before. In cross section 14 (appendix 4), presence of a thick peat and clay plug (representing the residual channel) enabled extraction of a type 3 radiocarbon sample. The age of sample 6 indicates that the activity of the Hennisdijk system ceased around 3000 BP.

Previously, no absolute dates were available for the period of activity of the Echteld system. Based on relative dating of fluvial systems, palynological data and archeological finds on the alluvial ridge, Verbraeck (1984, p. 213) supposed a period of activity from the late-Atlantic to the early-Subatlantic for the Echteld system. He also suggested that the Echteld system initially fed the Schoonrewoerd and Zijderveld systems. However, radiocarbon dates carried out for the present study, show that at least the beginning of activity of the Echteld system took place much later. A type 1 radiocarbon sample (sample 3) from a peat lens underlying the Echteld clay wedge in cross section 15 (appendix 4) yielded an age of 2770 ± 90 BP, which approximately represents the beginning of activity of the Echteld system (see also section 5.4.2 for a description of the Echteld clastic wedge in cross section 15). A type 3 sample to date the end of activity of the Echteld system was taken more to the south. The clay plug on top of the southern sand body is poorly developed in the cross section, but much richer in organic material 200 m downstream (see inset with location of radiocarbon sample 1). The age of sample 1 indicates that the activity of the Echteld system came to an end by 1900 BP.

In short, the radiocarbon dates demonstrate that the Schoonrewoerd, the Hennisdijk and the Echteld fluvial systems roughly succeed each other in time with virtually no overlap in their periods of activity (figure 5.5b). Therefore the inclusion of these three systems into one system, as suggested by Verbraeck (1984), is erroneous.

5.4.5 Gradient lines

As a first step in the reconstruction of the channel gradients of the three fluvial systems (needed for calculation of paleodischarge), sand body gradients were established. This was previously done by Berendsen (1982, pp. 124-133) for a great number of different fluvial systems in the Rhine-Meuse delta. He described the general procedure for the reconstruction of sand body gradient lines. In this section I basically follow his approach. When accepting sand body gradient lines as representative for river channel gradients, a longitudinally constant difference between the upper level of sand deposition and the river water level at a certain discharge is assumed. However, longitudinal changes in channel pattern and channel dimensions as well as tectonic deformation may cause divergence.

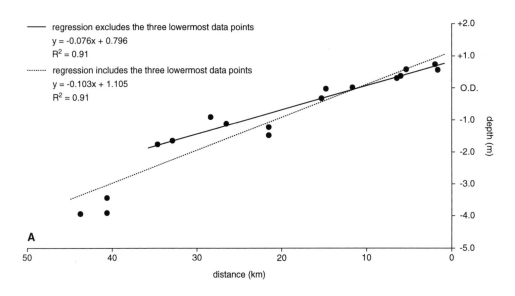

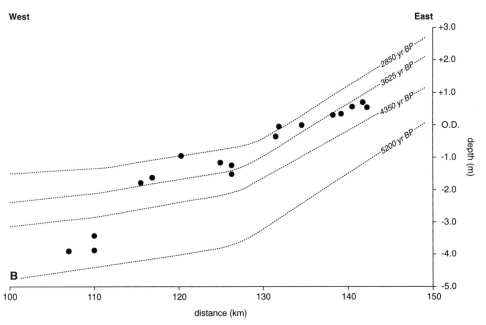

Figure 5.16 (a) *The gradient of the Schoonrewoerd sand body. On the X-axis is the distance along the axis of the main sand body. See text for details on regression lines.* (b) *Groundwater gradient lines (Van Dijk et al. 1991) and data points for the top of the Schoonrewoerd sand body in the cross sections. On the X-axis is the downvalley distance in X-coordinates of the Dutch coordinate system.*

An independent check on the accuracy of river gradients reconstructed from sand body gradients is provided by groundwater gradient lines. In general, the groundwater gradient of a near-coastal river floodplain in a humid climate may be expected to approximate the floodplain gradient, which on its turn represents a maximum channel gradient (if sinuosity is 1.0 and the channel follows the maximum slope). Van Dijk et al. (1991) reconstructed groundwater gradient lines for the Holocene Rhine-Meuse delta. These gradient lines were obtained by constructing time-depth graphs indicating the rate of groundwater level rise at various sites along an east-west section through the Rhine-Meuse delta. The time-depth graphs each resulted from a series of compaction-free basal peat samples taken at various elevations on the flank of late-Pleistocene river dunes that are covered by Holocene peat formed near the groundwater table.

For the Schoonrewoerd system the highest occurrence of sand in each sand body was selected from every cross section. These values were plotted against the distance measured along the axis of the main sand body (in case of multiple sand bodies). Linear regression on these data points yields a sand body gradient of 10.3 cm/km (figure 5.16a). This value however is strongly influenced by the very low position of the three westernmost data points. The exact reason for this phenomenon is unknown, but it can be excluded that the paleochannel gradient strongly increased (to about 25 cm/km) in the lower reach. Berendsen (1982, p. 131) attributed apparently 'too steep' sand body gradient lines to tidal influence. Exclusion of the three westernmost points from the regression yields a significantly lower gradient of only 7.6 cm/km (figure 5.16a). Remarkably, the groundwater gradient line has a concave shape with a marked knickpoint which is not reflected by the sand body data (figure 5.16b). Poor correspondence between the sand body gradient and the groundwater gradient line may be partly explained by differential compaction, since the Schoonrewoerd sand body is underlain by Holocene peat in many cross sections. Compaction can not explain the very low position of the three westernmost data points (appendix 3).

A detailed reconstruction of groundwater gradient lines downstream of the knickpoint by Verbruggen (1992, fig. 5) yielded gradients of 4.0 to 3.0 cm/km (3200 and 2200 BC respectively) for the reach between the cross sections 7 and 10. Strong deviation of the paleochannel gradient from these values is highly unlikely and they are considered to represent the most accurate approximations of the energy gradient needed for calculation of paleodischarge through cross section 8 (section 5.4.6).

Of the Hennisdijk system only three cross sections are available, therefore a slightly different procedure was followed to obtain more data points for establishing the sand body gradient. The Hennisdijk sand body was divided into nineteen segments of 0.5 km long. For each segment the highest occurrence of sand was selected from borehole descriptions present in the database of the Department of Physical Geography (Utrecht University) including the cross-sectional data from the present study. Around 320 boreholes were used in the analysis. The altitudes of the highest occurrences of sand were plotted for each segment and linear regression on these data points yielded a gradient of 14.3 cm/km (figure 5.17). This value is in reasonable agreement with the groundwater gradients obtained by Van Dijk et al. (1991, p. 323). Their reconstruction indicates a groundwater gradient of 16 cm/km in this area around BP.

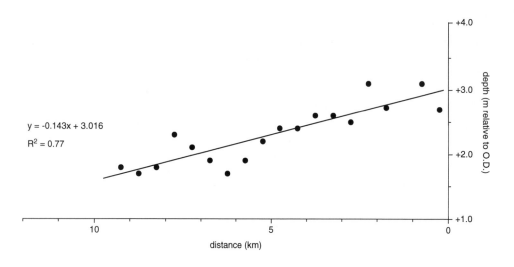

Figure 5.17   *The gradient of the Hennisdijk sand body. On the X-axis is the distance along the axis of the main sand body. The data points represent the highest occurrence of sand in segments of 0.5 km long. Regression line based on the data points is also shown.*

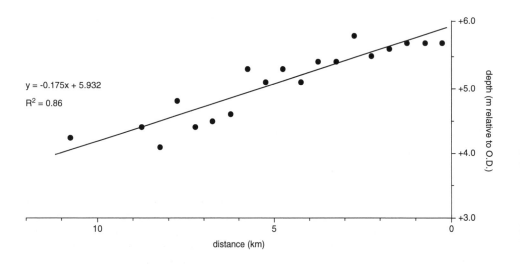

Figure 5.18   *The gradient of the Echteld sand body. On the X-axis is the distance along the axis of the main sand body. The data points represent the highest occurrence of sand in segments of 0.5 km long. Regression line based on the data points is also shown.*

The same procedure as for the Hennisdijk system was used to establish the sand body gradient of the Echteld system (figure 5.18). Around 285 boreholes were used in the analysis. The resulting gradient of 17.5 cm/km seems slightly too steep with respect to the groundwater gradient of 16 cm/km given by Van Dijk et al. (1991). It should be realized however that especially in this area, gradients are influenced by neotectonic activity along the northwest-southeast trending Peel Boundary Fault which crosses the Echteld system (Verbraeck 1984, fig. 18), with the downthrown block located on the downstream side. Törnqvist et al. (1998) showed that reconstructed groundwater gradient lines for the first half of the Holocene in this area are offset by 45 cm, which seems to be due to neotectonic movements. Although such discontinuities are not obvious from data covering the younger Holocene, it can safely be concluded that reconstructed former river gradients in this area are prone to errors due to differential tectonic movements. The present sand body gradient of 17.5 cm/km is probably somewhat higher than the former channel gradient of the Echteld system.

5.4.6 Paleodischarge

To gain insight into the relative importance of the Schoonrewoerd and Hennisdijk systems, two cross sections were selected for reconstruction of paleodischarge. It was tried to estimate the bankfull discharge of the systems in their mature state, when the paleochannels had reached their maximum size. This paleodischarge was estimated by application of the Chézy equation:

$$Q_p = CA \sqrt{(RS)}$$

in which:

Q_p	=	paleodischarge (m^3/s)	
C	=	Chézy-coefficient (m$^{0.5}$/s)	
A	=	flow area (m^2)	
R	=	hydraulic radius (m)	
S	=	energy gradient (-)	

The cross sections were selected to provide optimum conditions for proper establishment of the channel dimensions (A and R) based on lithofacies interpretation, and of the channel slope (S) based on sand body (and groundwater) gradient lines. The flow resistance (C) remained an important unknown factor. Several independent methods exist to estimate its order of magnitude. Firstly, Brownlie's (1983) equation (section 3.4.5) can be solved for Q_p as well as C, since all the other variables are known. A second way is to calculate the roughness height (k_s) of former bed forms of which the (minimum) height can be estimated from sedimentary structures. Application of C = 18log(12R/k_s) then yields flow resistance. A third method is to apply the Chézy-coefficients derived for a modern analogue having comparable dimensions, morphology, slope and sedimentary characteristics.

The paleodischarge of the Echteld system was not reconstructed, because a meaningful estimate of the channel gradient of the Echteld system was difficult to make and opportunities were lacking for estimating the flow area of the paleochannel in a reliable way.

The Schoonrewoerd system

The Molenaarsgraaf I cross section (cross section 8 in Appendix 3) was chosen for reconstructing the paleodischarge of the Schoonrewoerd system. In this reach of the Schoonrewoerd system, detailed reconstructions of groundwater gradients (Verbruggen 1992, fig. 5) are available to approximate the former channel gradient. The sand body in the cross section is taken to represent the channel deposits of the Schoonrewoerd system as indicated by its concave, scoured base and its sedimentary structures revealed by vibracoring (section 5.4.3). In this reach the Schoonrewoerd system comprises only one sand body, which is fully encased in peat and clayey sediments and therefore can be sharply delimited. Furthermore, the sand body has a very low width/thickness ratio, which makes lateral migration and accretion of the paleochannel unlikely (figure 2.11). Its width/thickness ratio of 7 is comparable to the lowest width/depth ratios reported for laterally stable modern fluvial channels (e.g. table 3.2) and is equal to the width/thickness ratio of a sandy channel-fill of a nearly abandoned, laterally stable Columbia River channel (channel 4; section 3.4.2). In view of this, the width of the sand body was assumed to represent the width (w) of the paleochannel.

Although lateral erosion and accretion can be excluded, vertical accretion of the fluvial system has to be taken into account (figure 2.11). Therefore two alternative flow areas were determined. The minimum flow area (A_{min}) is taken to be the cross-sectional area of the sand body up to the level of the base of the levees. In the Molenaarsgraaf I cross section this level was taken at the top of the peat split which occurs around 5 m below O.D. (appendix 3, cross section 8) (in fact this level must have been located higher originally, since compaction of peat has lowered the levees with respect to the sand body). The clastic wedge above this level represent the overbank deposits of the Schoonrewoerd system (section 5.4.2). The presumed first phase of the Schoonrewoerd system, represented by clastic bed Z, will not be considered (see section 5.5.1). A maximum flow area (A_{max}) is represented by the cross-sectional area of the sand body up to the top of the sandy and silty clay covering the sand body. This level is taken to approximate the bankfull level of the paleochannel during its final stage of activity. The true flow area of the paleochannel during most of its period of activity must have been between A_{min} and A_{max}, with an aggrading sandy bed as well as still aggrading levees.

On the basis of these two alternative flow areas, also two alternative values of the hydraulic radius (R_{min} and R_{max}) were determined. A channel gradient (S) of 4.0 cm/km [using the 3200 BC groundwater gradient line of Verbruggen (1992, fig. 5)] is assumed to belong to the case of minimum flow area and hydraulic radius. This could represent the situation just after channel formation around 4500 BP. Likewise, a channel gradient of 3.0 cm/km [using the 2200 BC groundwater gradient line of Verbruggen (1992, fig. 5)] was accepted to be representative for the case of maximum flow area and hydraulic radius, that could only have occurred shortly before the end of activity around 3800 BP.

210

Table 5.4 Estimates of paleodischarge using Brownlie's method

Cross section		A (m²)	R (m)	S (cm/km)	w (m)	d_{50} (μm)	σ_s (μm)	C (m^0.5/s)	Q_p (m³/s)
Molenaarsgraaf I	*min*	360	5.2	4.0	65	340	1.50	51.0	265
	max	546	7.3	3.0	65	340	1.50	49.3	398
Buren	*min*	350	4.7	11.9	72	432	1.53	45.9	380
	max	827	6.1	11.9	133	432	1.53	47.0	1047

A = flow area
R = hydraulic radius
S = channel slope
w = bankfull channel width
d_{50} = grain size in a distribution for which 50 percent, by weight, is finer.
σ_s = 1/2 (d_{50}/d_{16} + d_{84}/d_{50}) representing the gradation of the bed material (d_{16} and d_{84} represent grain sizes in a distribution for which 16 and 84 percent, by weight, respectively are finer).
C = Chézy-coefficient
Q_p = paleodischarge

The paleodischarge (Q_p) was calculated with the Brownlie equation for the two scenarios (one applying A_{min}, R_{min}, and S = 4.0 cm/km and another applying A_{max}, R_{max} and S = 3.0 cm/km). In both scenarios the sedimentary characteristics (d_{50} and σ_s) and the channel width (w) are supposed to have been constant. The grain size distribution of ten samples from the sand body was used to determine a mean d_{50}, and a mean σ_s. In table 5.4 the resulting estimates of the paleodischarge are given as well as the input data. The associated Chézy-coefficients (C), determined from C = $Q_p/[A(RS)^{0.5}]$, are also given.

An independent estimate of the Chézy-coefficient can be based on the thickness of the planar cross-bedded sets observed in facies 1 (section 5.4.3). These steeply dipping beds can be interpreted as being produced by slipface migration of large ripples. A maximum set thickness of 0.5 m can be considered as indicative for a minimum bedform height (the top is commonly eroded). Taking $k_s \approx$ ½ bedform height (= 0.25 m) yields C = 43.2 m^0.5/s (applying R_{min}) and C = 45.8 m^0.5/s (applying R_{max}). Although being somewhat lower than the values in table 5.4, these C-values are in the same order of magnitude. In these considerations of flow resistance however, the influence of vegetation and channel morphology is not explicitly taken into account. The data for the Columbia river main channel, which has roughly the same hydraulic, sedimentary and morphological characteristics, also suggest somewhat lower C-values (table 3.8).

211

Table 5.5 Minimum and maximum estimated paleodischarge

Cross section		C (m$^{0.5}$/s)	A (m^2)	R (m)	S (cm/km)	Q$_p$ (m^3/s)
Molenaarsgraaf I	*min*	35.0	360	5.2	3.0	157
	max	55.0	546	7.3	4.0	513
Buren	*min*	35.0	350	4.7	11.0	279
	max	55.0	827	6.1	13.0	1281

C = Chézy-coefficient
A = flow area
R = hydraulic radius
S = channel slope
Q$_p$ = paleodischarge

In addition to the two more or less probable scenarios, it was attempted to quantify the range of error in the determination of the paleodischarge. This was done by assuming relatively low and high estimates for C, together with A$_{min}$, A$_{max}$, R$_{min}$, R$_{max}$ and the two estimates of S, in extreme combinations as an input for Q$_p$ = CA $\sqrt{(RS)}$ (table 5.5). The bankfull discharge of the Schoonrewoerd system during its mature stage almost certainly fell within the given range and may well have been around 350 m^3/s. Of course, during an early phase of channel scour as well as during the final phase of infilling, bankfull discharge has been lower than the minimum calculated. On the other hand it is very unlikely that the Schoonrewoerd system, throughout its period of activity, has experienced discharges higher than the calculated maximum.

The Hennisdijk system
The procedure followed for calculation of the paleodischarge of the Hennisdijk system was roughly comparable to that outlined above for the Schoonrewoerd system. Nevertheless delimiting the flow area of the paleochannel was less straightforward in the case of the Hennisdijk system for various reasons.

Firstly, since the Hennisdijk sand body rests on the sand of the Kreftenheye Formation, the base of the sand body had to be determined by detailed lithofacies analysis of undisturbed cores in combination with radiocarbon dating of reworked organics (section 5.4.3). In the Buren cross section (cross section 12 in Appendix 4), the base of the sand body was found at 7.5 m below O.D. on average.

Secondly, the Hennisdijk sand body is interpreted to be the result of lateral erosion and accretion, causing the sand body to be much wider than the paleochannel (figure 2.11). This interpretation is based on its relatively high width/thickness ratio of around 36, and the identification of inclined heterolithic stratification (IHS) in facies 6 (section 5.4.3) which can be interpreted as lateral accretion surfaces left by migration of a paleochannel. The observed average dip angle of 6.5° (range 2 to 12°) is fairly close to the angle of 8-9° reported by Bierkens & Weerts (1994) for the lateral accretion surfaces from a point bar of the modern Waal River (the present main branch of the Rhine) near Zaltbommel (figure 5.2). The dip angle of lateral accretion surfaces obviously decreases with increasing channel size (e.g. Leeder 1973, fig. 4). Makaske & Nap (1995) for example, found relatively steep angles averaging 18° for the lateral accretion surfaces of a small Late-Weichselian channel (depth 1-2 m) in the central Netherlands. Within the maximum dip-value range of 0-29° for fluvial IHS deposits mentioned by Thomas et al. (1987), the dip angles measured for the Hennisdijk system can be considered as relatively low. The measured dip angles will be used for the reconstruction of the flow area of the paleochannel.

At some stage, the Hennisdijk paleochannel must have reached a depth of around 8.5 m, as indicated by the difference in elevation between the base of the levee deposits (1 m above O.D.) and the base of the sand body [average 7.5 m below O.D. (appendix 4, cross section 12)]. The IHS dip-angles measured in facies 1 probably stem from a later, infilling stage of the paleochannel. Makaske & Nap (1995) illustrated that deeper scour of the subsoil is associated with steeper lateral accretion surfaces. Therefore lateral accretion surfaces during the earlier scour phase of the Hennisdijk paleochannel are supposed to have dip angles near the upper end of the measured range, rather than near the average value. Schematizing one of the banks of the paleochannel as a straight plane with a constant slope (α) of 10°, reaching down to a depth (d) of 8.5 m, the total width (w) of the paleochannel can be estimated with the relationship $w = 1.5d/\tan\alpha$ (Leeder 1973). Application of this relationship yields a paleochannel width (w_{min}) of 72 m. A field example of an actively eroding bank of a modern fluvial channel of comparable depth was used to complete the reconstruction of channel perimeter. A bankfull flow area A_{min} of 350 m^2 with an hydraulic radius R_{min} of 4.7 m was calculated. To approximate of the paleochannel gradient, the sand body gradient was divided by the sinuosity index. The sinuosity index was estimated at 1.2, based on mapped fragments of the residual channel and channel belt morphology (section 5.4.1). Sedimentary characteristics (mean d_{50} and mean σ_s) were based on the grain size distributions of 21 samples from the sand body. The Brownlie equation was applied to calculate the paleodischarge (Q_p) for the above-sketched scenario. In table 5.4 the results and the input data are given.

A second possible scenario relates to the case of fully aggraded levees, with the paleochannel base still near the present base of the sand body. In this case, paleochannel depth could have been 10.1 m. Following the same procedure as outlined above, a w_{max} of 133 m, an A_{max} of 827 m^2 and a R_{max} of 6.1 m can be calculated. Now $\alpha = 6.5°$ is applicable, since this mean value was determined for the upper part of the sand body. The sedimentary characteristics are presumed to have remained unchanged.

The Chézy-coefficients for both scenarios (table 5.4), are roughly in the middle of the common range for fluvial channels. Sedimentary structures from the Buren cross section provide few clues to check their accuracy by reconstruction of bedform heights. Thick sets of steeply dipping foresets are not a consistent phenomenon of the Hennisdijk lithofacies. Bedforms are more likely to have been composite forms of which the height is hard to figure out. Hydraulic roughness and flow resistance remain poorly controlled factors in the calculation of paleodischarge.

In a similar way as was done for the Schoonrewoerd system, two additional 'best case' and 'worst case' paleodischarge scenarios were considered, especially to take into account a possible variability in flow resistance (table 5.5). Channel gradient values were varied from 11.0 cm/km (to account for a relatively high sinuosity index of 1.3) to 13.0 cm/km (for a low sinuosity index of 1.1).

Calculations for the Hennisdijk system yield a much wider range of paleodischarges than for the Schoonrewoerd system. This is largely due to paleochannel geometry of the Hennisdijk system, which causes width and flow area to vary strongly with the estimated depth. Despite the wide possible range of flow areas and paleodischarges, the most likely case remains the intermediate situation of a paleochannel with a discharge of around 750 m^3/s. This discharge could have occurred in a situation of maximum scour contemporaneously with moderately developed levees.

Although the paleodischarge ranges of both fluvial systems show considerable overlap (table 5.5), the more probable scenarios indicate that the Hennisdijk system was more important than the Schoonrewoerd system. Bankfull discharge of the Schoonrewoerd system may have decreased longitudinally due to the numerous crevasse channels (figure 5.7) carrying water into the floodbasins.

5.5   Interpretation and discussion

5.5.1   The Schoonrewoerd system

Revised period of activity
In a number of cross sections the clay wedge of the Schoonrewoerd system is split by a laterally continuous peat layer. By various authors this peat split was interpreted as representing a period of reduced activity of the Schoonrewoerd system (section 5.2.2). Temporarily decreased overbank deposition from the Schoonrewoerd channels would have enabled peat growth in the period 4700-4500 BP (Törnqvist & Van Dijk 1993). Careful analysis of the available cross sections, leads to objections against this view.

Firstly, the double wedges of overbank deposits are not obvious in all cross sections. Secondly, if two beds of overbank deposits are present near the sand body, the lower bed is often humic, discontinuous and relatively thin (sometimes a few decimeters only). This is quite different from what one would expect from overbank deposits in the proximity of a channel belt with a period of activity of approximately 700 cal. yr. Thirdly, in many cross sections the channel sand bodies seem to cut the peat layer that separates the two beds of overbank deposits. This implies preservation of peat on top of the levees during reactivation of a channel belt, which is a highly unlikely situation. Finally, it can be observed that the lower bed of overbank deposits often does not thicken towards the Schoonrewoerd channel belt. This suggests later scour of Schoonrewoerd channels through the peat into the lower bed of overbank deposits. In that case the lower overbank deposits have to be associated with a different fluvial system.

214

In the cross sections the above-mentioned features are obvious. In the cross section 1 (appendix 3) for example, the deposits of the Schoonrewoerd system clearly consist of a single massive layer. The same holds for the southeastern part of cross section 2. In the other parts of cross section 2, thin peat splits can be identified in the distal overbank deposits, but (as will be explained below) chronostratigraphic correlation with the presumed first phase of the Schoonrewoerd system fails. Further downstream, in the cross section 3, only one thick layer of overbank deposits can be identified. Correlation with a nearby cross section (< 1 km upstream) of Van der Woude (1983, figure 10) shows that the underlying clastics (below 3.5 m below O.D.) belong to the Middelkoop system. In cross section 4, the lower bed (occurring between the two sand bodies at approximately 3.0 m below O.D.) is very thin and discontinuous compared to the upper bed. A similar situation is shown in a nearby cross section published by Törnqvist & Van Dijk (1993, fig. 3). In this section the radiocarbon-dated lower bed and the overlying peat are clearly cut by the Schoonrewoerd channel sand body, which seems to be genetically unrelated to it. Also in the cross section 5 the lower bed (Z) is relatively thin, while the northern sand body cuts the overlying peat layer. Further downstream, Törnqvist & Van Dijk (1993, fig. 4) found a relatively thin and discontinuous radiocarbon-dated lower bed at around 6.0 m below O.D. near the cross section 7. On the other hand, several kilometres downstream in the cross section 8, the lower bed (Z) is very thick and its basal geometry suggests scour next to the sand body. In the short cross sections 6, 7 and 9, the Schoonrewoerd sand body obviously cuts a thin peat layer overlying the lower bed (Z).

Because of these features it is concluded that the lower bed was not deposited by the Schoonrewoerd channel belt, but instead by a more remote channel belt. Fluvial systems active in the area during the period considered were the Schaik and Zijderveld systems (figure 5.5a). In cross section 2 (appendix 3) a clastic wedge, that seems to belong to the neighbouring Zijderveld system, occurs between 1.0 and 3.5 below O.D, under the Schoonrewoerd overbank deposits. The wedge is cut by a small channel sand body of the Schoonrewoerd system and thickens in a west-northwesterly direction. In this area, the Schoonrewoerd channel belt approaches the Zijderveld channel belt within a few hundred meters. On the other hand, the wedge could equally well belong to the older Middelkoop/Tienhoven system that underlies the Zijderveld system in this area (Verbraeck 1984). Since the wedge is fairly thick, a third possibility is that the lower part of the wedge belongs to the Middelkoop/Tienhoven system, while the upper part belongs to the Zijderveld system. A clear split within the wedge is absent.

A new cross section (figure 5.19) was augered, to clarify the stratigraphic relationship between the Zijderveld and Schoonrewoerd systems. In this cross section, located between cross section 2 and cross section 3 (figure 5.2), the Middelkoop and the Zijderveld channel belts appear separated. Like in cross section 2, in figure 5.19 the Schoonrewoerd system comprises a single wedge of overbank deposits underlain by peat resting on top of the Zijderveld overbank deposits. De Jong (1970-1971) obtained an age of 4620 ± 60 BP from the base of residual channel deposits of the Zijderveld system about 2 km upstream, which is an approximation of the age of the top of the Zijderveld overbank deposits in figure 5.19. Törnqvist (1993b, p. 144) dated the base of the Zijderveld overbank deposits 10 km downstream at 5345 ± 40 BP.

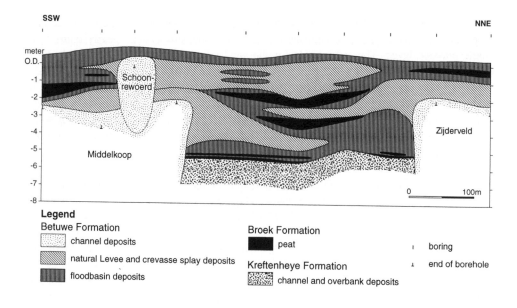

Figure 5.19   Kortgerecht cross section (for location see figure 5.2).

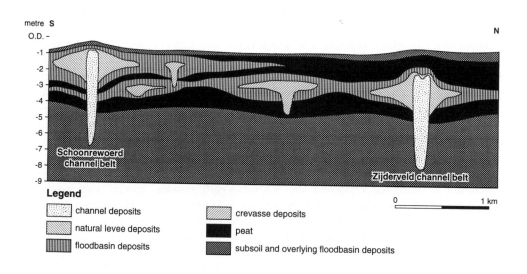

Figure 5.20   Schematic cross section showing the stratigraphic relationship of the Schoonrewoerd and Zijderveld systems.

216

Remarkably, the period of activity of the Zijderveld system matches very well with the presumed first phase of activity of the Schoonrewoerd system (5350-4700 BP). Because of this and the above outlined phenomena, it has to be concluded that the overbank deposits attributed to the first phase of the Schoonrewoerd system in fact belong to the Zijderveld system. Both systems are known to have a similar fluvial architecture of narrow channel belt deposits and complex overbank deposits, characterized by abundant crevasse splay deposits. Especially the networks of crevasse channels are difficult to map in detail and it is conceivable that crevasse channels from the Zijderveld system routed overbank sediments into the area later followed by the Schoonrewoerd channel belt. The Zijderveld channel belt more or less parallels the Schoonrewoerd channel belt, being located at maximum 4 km to the north (figure 5.5a). In a long cross section through the area (Törnqvist 1993b, enclosure), large bodies of crevasse splay deposits can be observed at the relevant stratigraphic level between the Zijderveld and Schoonrewoerd channel belts. At some places, the Schoonrewoerd system may have reactivated reaches of abandoned Zijderveld crevasse channels. In figure 5.20 the stratigraphic relationship of the Zijderveld and Schoonrewoerd systems is shown schematically.

With regard to the beginning of activity of the Schoonrewoerd system, the available radiocarbon dates unambiguously point to an age of 4500 BP (Törnqvist & Van Dijk 1993, fig. 10a). A suitable date of this event is GrN-10886: 4520 ± 60 BP (Törnqvist pers. comm.). Concerning the end of activity, the radiocarbon evidence is less clear. Törnqvist (1993b, p. 143) accepted a date of 3570 ± 70 BP (GrN-10108) as being the most accurate. An older date was obtained in the present study [sample 12: 3823 ± 40 BP (table 5.3)]. The latter date more accurately approximates the end of activity of the Schoonrewoerd system since the Hennisdijk system, of which the start of activity was dated unambiguously at around 3850 BP, crosscuts the upper reach of the Schoonrewoerd system (see also section 5.4.4).

Excluding this lower reach, the revised period of activity of the Schoonrewoerd system (4500-3800 BP) spans 950 cal. yr instead of the 2270 cal. yr previously assumed. The former value is much closer to the typical value of approximately 1000 cal. yr for fluvial systems in the Rhine-Meuse delta reported by Törnqvist (1993b, p. 158).

Longitudinal change
The Schoonrewoerd system displays a steady downstream change in sand body geometry. A spectacular drop in width/thickness ratio takes place between cross section 1 and cross section 2, while further downstream width/thickness ratios decrease more gradually (figure 5.21a). In the westernmost cross sections, width/thickness ratios seem to become greater again. In this reach however, only maximum values could be determined, while a different period of activity and the influence of the Langerak system also may disturb the observed trend. Therefore this reach will not be discussed here.

A similar trend was described for the Schaik system by Törnqvist et al. (1993). They supposed a downstream decreasing rate of lateral accretion of the Schaik paleochannel, mainly as a result of a downstream increasing rate of groundwater-level rise. However, the described downstream increase in groundwater-level rise was so subtle (range 1.25-1.55 mm/yr) that its decisive influence can seriously be questioned. Moreover, no mechanism was presented through which rapid groundwater-level rise suppresses the process of lateral channel migration. Hence there must exist different and more important causes for a longitudinal trend in sand body geometry as observed for the Schoonrewoerd system.

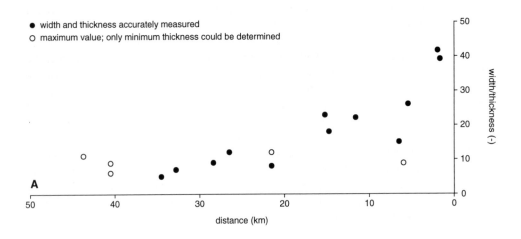

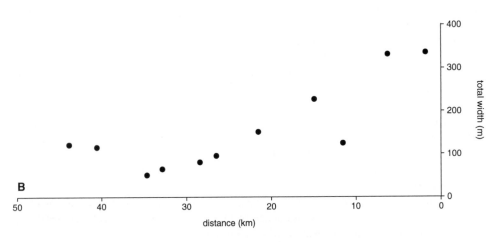

Figure 5.21   (a) *The width/thickness ratio of the Schoonrewoerd sand body versus the distance along the axis of the main sand body.*
(b) *The total width of the Schoonrewoerd sand bodies (summed in case of various parallel sand bodies) versus the distance along the axis of the main sand body.*

It seems reasonable to accept a strong relationship between channel geometry and subsoil erodibility. In the cross sections it can be observed that the composition of the subsoil was fairly uniform along the system. The least erodible facies includes the transition between the Betuwe and Kreftenheye Formations. The stiff, consolidated clay of the Wijchen Member is usually overlain by strongly compacted early-Holocene basal peat. The channels of the Schoonrewoerd system usually were able to erode the softer Holocene peat and clay but were unable to erode the compact basal peat and Wijchen Member clay, which in most cross sections directly underlies the channel sand body. Since the Pleistocene subsoil occurs at progressively greater depths to the west, paleochannel depth and consequently sand body thickness also steadily increased westward (table 5.1). For reasons of flow continuity, this increase in depth is naturally followed by a decrease in width (figure 5.21b). Subsoil strongly influenced sand body geometry in cross section 1 (appendix 3). Here the peat underlying the Schoonrewoerd clastic wedge is extremely compact over its full thickness of one to two meters. The sand bodies hardly cut the peat and are exceptionally shallow and wide. The peat layer seems to have collapsed and compacted under the weight of thick overlying clastics prior to channel scour and sand body formation.

Nevertheless, the influence of subsoil erodibility only offers a partial explanation of the observed trend in sand body geometry. From table 5.1 it appears that the total width of the Schoonrewoerd channel sand bodies decreases by a factor 6.7 while their thickness increases by a factor 2.6 between cross section 1 and 9. Consequently, the total cross-sectional area of the sand bodies decreases downstream. This may indicate a decrease in paleochannel flow capacity. This would be a logical phenomenon since numerous crevasse channels were connected to the Schoonrewoerd channels (e.g. figure 5.7), which routed water to the floodbasins. In a westerly direction the Rhine-Meuse floodplain widens and therefore storage capacity of the floodbasins increased. As a result, floodbasin water was not forced back into the river channels as would be the case in a more confined setting like the Columbia Valley (chapter 3).

In addition, the strong decrease in total width of the Schoonrewoerd sand bodies (figure 5.21b) may also indicate a decrease in lateral migration of the paleochannel. The well-established relationship between lateral channel stability and stream power (section 2.3.3) then would suggest a downstream decrease in (paleo) stream power. This must indeed have been the case since stream power is a function of discharge and channel slope, and both decreased downstream (see also figure 5.16b).

Lithofacies interpretation
The three facies in the Molenaarsgraaf I cross section (section 5.4.3), reveal details about the infilling process of the Schoonrewoerd paleochannel. Noteworthy is the absence of a well-developed coarse channel-lag, which is indicative for low flow competence and/or the depletion of coarse material. During infilling of the channel, flow strength remained highest in the northern part of the channel (figure 5.12a), as testified by the thick sets of cross bedding in facies 1. These were interpreted to have been formed by migrating megaripples. Abundant reactivation surfaces indicate strongly variable flow strength. Near the northern margin of the channel, smaller-scaled ripple cross lamination indicates lower

flow strength in shallower water. In the southern part of the channel, preservation of up to 3 cm thick mud beds in facies 2, suggests lower flow strength in this part of the channel. Interbedding of the mud with coarse sand, again indicates variable flow strength. The supposed distribution of flow strength and the capture of abundant reworked organic material in facies 2 was probably associated with its position on the inner side of a slight bend in the paleochannel (e.g. geological maps of Van der Woude 1983 and Bosch & Kok 1994). Structure and texture of facies 3 reflect low-energy conditions along the margin of the channel.

Facies geometries suggest that facies 2 attained a bar-like form, more or less shading a slough channel of which the fill is represented by facies 3. Inferred current directions in facies 2 are generally concordant with the westerly paleoflow direction. In facies 3 however, small ripple foresets show no preferred orientation, while some have mud-draped foresets. This could point to the existence of temporary eddies causing reverse flow in the slough channel. The extreme content of organic litter in facies 2 could be well explained by capture and rapid burial associated with eddy accretion. However, the mechanism behind eddy generation and its exact relation to channel bend morphology remains unknown. It could well be a local phenomenon caused by stuck logs or irregularities in bank morphology due to slumps. In some cross sections of the Schoonrewoerd system (e.g. appendix 3, cross sections 4 and 11), thick sequences of fine-grained channel deposits resemble facies 3.

Poorly developed fining upward in facies 1, in combination with the inferred vertical mode of in-channel accretion, imply that flow remained relatively strong, until fairly sudden complete abandonment of the channel. A similar style of infilling was observed in one of the Columbia River channels (channel 4, section 3.4.2). The fact that facies 1 overlies facies 2 and 3 near the top of the channel fill, suggests lateral expansion of a slightly more energetic regime in the final stage of channel infilling. Apparently, significant discharge was still imposed from upstream, prior to complete abandonment.

Marine influence on the process of channel infilling cannot be excluded. Indicators of flow variability, such as reactivation surfaces, and mud drapes are present throughout the sand body, although the latter are not abundant and do not occur in a rhythmic pattern. A strong majority of the steep ripple foresets in facies 1 dip in the main flow direction. Most of the documented flow variability was probably caused by variations in discharge imposed from upstream. Marine influence at the Molenaarsgraaf I cross section was restricted. More downstream the situation was different. The rhythmic bedded sequence (figure 5.11) in the Alblasserdam cross section, indicates pulsating flow conditions. This typical facies was not found upstream, which suggests a downstream control of this phenomenon. This control was probably damming of river flow by sea-level set up, due to storms or spring tides.

The origin of the Schoonrewoerd system
Built-up areas and erosion by younger channel belts hampered detailed mapping of the Schoonrewoerd system upstream from cross section 1. The available evidence suggests that the Schoonrewoerd system originated from the Werkhoven system (figure 5.5a) which was investigated in detail by Berendsen (1982). This system was a major Rhine

distributary, with an up to 1 km wide channel belt that was active between 5600 and 3400 BP (Berendsen 1982, p. 161). The revised period of activity of the Schoonrewoerd system almost covers the second half of this time interval.

North of the modern Lek River there seem to be two alternatives for the connection of the Schoonrewoerd system to the Werkhoven system. The Zouwe system is an erosional remnant of only 1 km long. The top of the sand body is at 2.4 m above O.D. (Berendsen 1982, p. 171) and the sand body rests on the sand of the Kreftenheye Formation. The relatively high position of the sand body and its lateral clastic wedges, renders its connection to the Schoonrewoerd system unlikely. A better candidate is the Dwarsdijk system about 1 km to the east, of which the sand body reaches to 2.0 m above O.D. (Berendsen 1982, p. 149). The Dwarsdijk sand body probably does not rest on the sand of the Kreftenheye Formation. The altitude of the top of this sand body is strongly variable, a feature it also shares with the Schoonrewoerd sand body in cross section 1 (appendix 3).

Around 4500 BP, during the early stages of the avulsion which ultimately led to establishment of the Schoonrewoerd system, large amounts of clastics must have been introduced into the floodbasins south of the Werkhoven channel belt. According to the avulsion model of Smith et al. (1989), scour of channels through these splays into the subsoil is a next stage in the avulsion process. In the case of the Schoonrewoerd system it seems as if this never happened in the proximal reach. In the cross section 1 (appendix 3), channel sand bodies remained shallow and almost fully encased in the thick wedge of splay deposits. Further downstream, clastic wedges are finer textured and thinner, while channel sand bodies gradually reach down deeper into the peaty subsoil.

There may have been two reasons for the apparent lack of channel scour in the upper reach of the Schoonrewoerd system: (1) the initial rapid deposition of the thick clastic wedge in the proximal avulsion belt led to strong compaction of the underlying peat, making it erosion-resistant, and (2) the continued supply of sand from the bigger Werkhoven system into the proximal reach of the Schoonrewoerd system counteracted scour. Storage of this material in the proximal clastic wedge led to depletion of bed load downstream, which was conducive to scour. Both hypotheses relate to the low stream power of the Schoonrewoerd system (section 5.5.3).

In general, the downstream trend in the facies geometries of the Schoonrewoerd system seems to agree fairly well with the avulsion model of Smith et al. (1989). A major difference however is the finer texture of the sediments. Sand sheets for example, representing the proximal stage I crevasse splays in the avulsion model were not found in the Schoonrewoerd system and rarely occur in the Holocene sequence of the Rhine-Meuse delta. Splay texture in the Rhine-Meuse delta corresponds better to the example described by Smith & Pérez-Arlucea (1994). Interpreting the cross sections in terms of the avulsion model (figure 5.22a and b), the thick clastic wedge in cross section 1 represents the distal part of a stage I splay. Characteristic for this type of splay is the architecture of a single thick wedge that encases several channel sand bodies (figure 5.22b). Cross section 1 is located around 7.5 km downstream of the supposed avulsion node. The next reach of the Schoonrewoerd system, down to the cross section 5, can be described as a stage II splay complex. The main characteristic of this type of splay is the anastomosed pattern of the

221

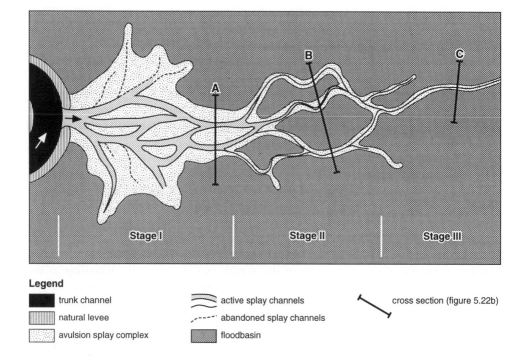

Figure 5.22a   Interpretive summary sketch of the planform patterns associated with the Schoonrewoerd avulsion. Interpretation of splay stages based on Smith et al. (1989).

sand bodies which represent relatively stable channels that have scoured into the peaty subsoil. The sandy and silty wedges now appear detached in the cross sections, while the remainder of the splay body consists of clay (figure 5.22b). The reach further downstream, down to cross section 9, can be typified as a stage III splay, which is an isolated ribbon of sand, that cuts deeply into the peaty subsoil. The sand body has restricted lateral wings of silty and sandy clay encased in a more extensive clay wedge (figure 5.22b). Downstream of the cross section 9, the connection with the Langerak system blurs the observed longitudinal trend in facies geometry.

Smith et al. (1989), supposed that usually a fluvial system after initial avulsion, passes through several stages to end up as a mature channel belt, which should be characterized by a single channel occupying only a limited portion of the avulsion belt. They supposed that scour of such a dominant channel would start upstream and progress gradually downstream. Apparently, this process never took place in the Schoonrewoerd system, which instead seems to have come to a dead stop halfway in the avulsion cycle. One can only speculate about the reason for this. It may well have been a lack of gradient advantage. At first sight this seems obvious, since the sand body gradient (measured 2along the meandering residual channel) of the Werkhoven system was 14.2 cm/km

222

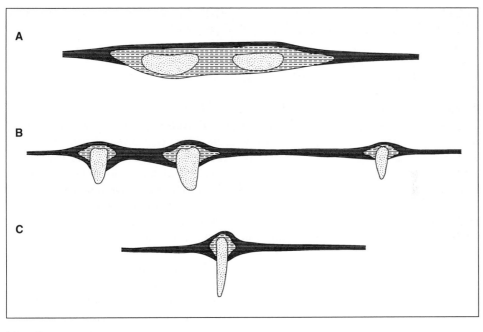

Figure 5.22b   Cross-sectional view of the depositional architecture of the three splay stages shown in figure 5.22a, after abandonment.

(Berendsen 1982, p. 128), against 7.6 cm/km for the Schoonrewoerd sand body (section 5.3.5). However, this comparison does not account for concavity of the Schoonrewoerd sand body gradient line and does not include data from upstream of Culemborg. Therefore the balance at the avulsion node may have been different. What may then be the reason for the 'failed' avulsion?

The Werkhoven channel belt scoured deeply into easily erodible sandy subsoil of Pleistocene eolian cover sands (Twente Formation), occurring at shallow depth along the margin of the Rhine-Meuse delta (e.g. Berendsen 1982, fig. 8.4). The subsoil of the Schoonrewoerd channel belt, which flowed towards the central part of the delta, consists of a much thicker cover of Holocene peat. Supposing a similar stream power for both systems, the Werkhoven system had a much easier job in enlarging and maintaining channel capacity by scour than the Schoonrewoerd system. If this hypothesis is correct, there should be a tendency for fluvial systems to concentrate along the margins of the Holocene fluvial district. This indeed seems to be the case: important Rhine distributaries

223

(including the Werkhoven system) persisted along the northern margin of the delta floodplain for some 4500 years (Berendsen 1982, pp. 188-191).

5.5.2 The Hennisdijk and Echteld systems

Periods of activity and connections to other fluvial systems
Geological maps suggest that the Hennisdijk system avulsed from the Erichem system, presently an only 2 km long erosional remnant. The beginning of activity of the Hennisdijk system [dated at 3818 ± 42 BP (section 5.4.4)] was later than that of the Erichem system, which was estimated from indirect evidence at around 4400 BP (Berendsen & Stouthamer, in prep.). The end of activity of the Hennisdijk system [dated at 2975 ± 35 BP (section 5.4.4)] is significantly earlier than the end of activity of the Erichem system: a type 3 sample from the Erichem residual channel yielded 2420 ± 140 BP [UtC-4638 (Berendsen & Stouthamer, in prep.)]. Thus, the available evidence is in agreement with the supposed connection.

At its downstream end, the Hennisdijk system disappears under the built-up areas of Culemborg. The Schoonrewoerd system passes this same area. During the early stages of its formation, the Hennisdijk channel crosscut the Schoonrewoerd channel belt, which was just abandoned by that time [3823 ± 40 BP (section 5.4.4)]. The presently available chronological evidence suggests that a connection existed between the Hennisdijk and the Honswijk system (figure 5.5a and b). The Honswijk system parallels the modern Lek River to the north, just west of Culemborg (Berendsen 1982, p. 170). No direct dates of the beginning of activity of the Honswijk system are available. Its end of activity was established by dating of two type 3 samples (Berendsen 1982, p. 170). Berendsen considered GrN-8714 (3050 ± 30 BP) to be most representative for the end of activity. This date matches very well with the age for the end of activity of the Hennisdijk system [2975 ± 35 BP (section 5.4.4)]. Additionally, the sand body elevation of the Honswijk system [top of the sand body between 1.7 m (upstream) and 0.6 m (downstream) above O.D. (Berendsen 1982, p. 170)] connects well to that of the Hennisdijk system.

The upper reach of the Echteld channel belt (upstream of Ochten) seems to have been almost totally eroded by the wide channel belt of the modern Waal River (fig. 5.5a). The geological map (Verbraeck 1984) suggests the presence of some erosional remnants of the system further upstream, north of the Waal River. No important channel belt of the same age as the Echteld system is known from the area south of the Waal River. (Berendsen et al. 1995). At its downstream end, the channel belt seems to have been almost fully eroded by the Linge system. Berendsen & Stouthamer (in prep.) preliminary mention the Avezaath and Bommel systems (figure 5.5a) as the most probable downstream continuations, but more research in this area is needed to establish these links with certainty.

The periods of activity of the Hennisdijk and Echteld systems, span 1070 and 1060 cal. yr respectively. Like the period of activity of the Schoonrewoerd system, also these values are close to the typical period of about 1000 cal. yr for fluvial systems in the Rhine-Meuse delta mentioned by Törnqvist (1993b, p. 158).

224

Lithofacies interpretation

The field data indicate that the paleochannel characteristics of the Hennisdijk and Echteld systems, were notably different from those of the Schoonrewoerd system. Width/thickness ratios of both the Hennisdijk and Echteld sand bodies are considerably higher than those of the Schoonrewoerd sand body. Sinuosity of the residual channels with respect to the sand body trend, and ridge and swale patterns also indicated lateral migration of the paleochannels. Lateral accretion surfaces, (indicated by IHS) in the Hennisdijk channel belt, provided further supporting evidence.

Although both the Hennisdijk and the Echteld channel belts are interpreted to have been formed by lateral accretion, the channel belt deposits of the Hennisdijk system abundantly comprise a facies which seems to be absent in the Echteld channel belt. The facies in question consists of sandy and silty clay and fine sand and occurs consistently along the margins of the Hennisdijk sand body [cross sections 12-14 (appendix 4)]. It grades into the coarser sand facies occurring in the central part of the channel belt, while having sharp lateral contacts with the finer facies outside of the channel belt. Because of its fine texture this facies was included in facies 6 (section 5.4.3).

In the classic meandering river lithofacies model (Allen 1970), channel deposits were considered to consist entirely of sand, with a gravelly channel lag, finer deposits being interpreted as overbank deposits; for example the levee deposits draping the point bars. Later it was shown that substantial quantities of mud can be deposited within the channel (e.g. Nanson 1980, Jackson 1981). Essentially, mud deposition in laterally migrating channels occurs in two subenvironments. (1) Mud will drape the point bar when current velocities in the channel strongly decline at high flow stage, for instance due to tidal effects (Smith 1987). Preservation of these mud drapes, between sand beds, result in IHS, which is usually best developed near the top of the point bar sequence (Thomas et al. 1987) (2) Under a wider range of flow conditions, mud may also be deposited near the downstream tail of a point bar, especially if flow separation occurs (Nanson 1980). This locus of mud deposition may extend along the concave bank of the next channel bend and in that case the resulting depositional form is termed 'concave-bank bench' (Hickin 1979; Page & Nanson 1982; Nanson & Page 1983; Page 1983). This type of fine-grained channel deposits may reach 5 m in thickness (Page & Nanson 1982).

Facies 6 is interpreted to contain upper point bar deposits (including IHS) as well as concave-bank bench deposits. Hickin (1986, p. 119) drew attention to the fact that in borehole logs upper concave-bank bench and upper point bar deposits are effectively indistinguishable. Both usually consist of flood cyclothems, known as IHS from upper point bar deposits. Lower in the section however, textural differences between point bar and the concave-bank bench deposits become apparent, the concave-bank bench deposits being much finer than the point bar deposits. According to Hickin (1986, p. 120) the contrasting facies interfinger in a transition zone.

Facies 4 is interpreted to represent the lower point bar and channel-lag deposits, while facies 5 is considered as lower and middle point bar deposits. Noteworthy is the coarse texture of channel-lag deposits as opposed to the near-absence of a channel lag in the Schoonrewoerd paleochannel. The bulk of the Hennisdijk sand body (facies 5) displays a much richer variety in sedimentary structures than the main part of the

Schoonrewoerd sand body (facies 1), while orientation of cross lamination and bedding is much more variable. The directional variability and the presence of small sets of ripple cross lamination between the larger-scaled structures indicate the presence of secondary currents in the paleochannel. Multiple fining upward cycles in facies 5 (figure 5.13b) reflect the growth of large composite bedforms, welding with the accretionary bank.

The consistent occurrence of thick sequences of facies 6 along the Hennisdijk sand body can be interpreted as the result of principally downstream migration of channel bends, as suggested by Nanson & Page (1983, p. 141-142). They stated that strips of fine-grained concave-bank bench deposits typically occur along the channel belts of confined meandering rivers (figure 5.23). The channel belt of such rivers is bounded by relatively resistant material, inhibiting further lateral migration. Therefore, bends are forced to migrate downstream, with continued fine-grained concave-bank bench deposition taking place in the upstream limbs of the outer bends along the margins of the channel belt. Airphoto study of many cases in western Canada revealed that confined meanders with systematic concave-bank bench development is most pronounced when the ratio of valley width to channel width is between 3 and 5 (Hickin 1986, p. 112). Substituting sand body width (table 5.1) for valley width and applying the reconstructed channel widths (table 5.4), this ratio can be estimated to have been between 2.7 and 5.0 for the Hennisdijk system. Meandering of the Hennisdijk system was confined because of relatively low stream power (section 5.5.3) in relation to laterally contiguous cohesive overbank sediments.

In the Echteld channel deposits a similar fine-grained facies was not identified in the borehole cross sections. Probably the Echteld paleochannels meandered more freely, which is also suggested by the higher width/thickness ratio of the channel sand body in the Tiel cross section (table 5.1). In contrast, the laterally more restricted Hennisdijk paleochannel is likely to represent a transitional form between straight and fully meandering channels.

5.5.3   Stream power, subsoil erodibility and lateral channel stability

In the previous sections, major differences in lateral stability of the paleochannels were inferred from plan views, cross-sectional facies geometries and lithofacies. Differences in stream power may have been partly responsible for the observed differences. The reconstructed paleodischarges for the Schoonrewoerd and Hennisdijk systems, enable an assessment of the validity of this hypothesis.

In table 5.6 estimates of stream power in the paleochannels are given, based on the estimates of channel and valley gradients and reconstructions of channel width and paleodischarge (sections 5.4.6 and 5.4.5). The equations used can be found in the sections 2.3.3 and 3.4.5. From the data presented in table 5.6 it is obvious that at bankfull discharge specific stream power in the Schoonrewoerd and Hennisdijk paleochannels must have differed substantially. Even accepting the widest conceivable ranges in specific stream power, no overlap between both ranges exists.

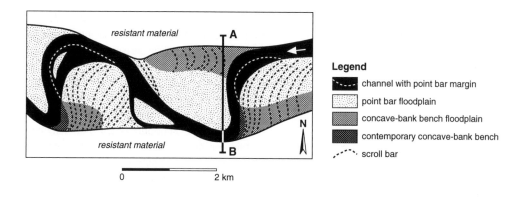

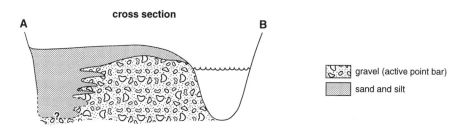

Figure 5.23 *Map of downstream migrating confined meanders, leaving behind strips of concave-bank bench deposits along the margins of the channel belt (from Page & Nanson 1982) and cross section along the line A-B (from Hickin 1986).*

Table 5.6 Estimates of stream power in the paleochannels

Cross section		ω_B (W/m²)	ω_m (W/m²)	ω_p (W/m²)
Molenaarsgraaf I	*min*	1.6	0.7	0.8
	max	1.8	3.1	1.9
Buren	*min*	6.2	4.2	5.0
	max	9.2	12.3	10.8

ω_B = specific stream power based on values for channel slope and paleodischarge from table 5.4 (Brownlie's method).

ω_m = specific stream power based on values for slope and paleodischarge from table 5.5 (minimum and maximum estimated paleodischarge).

ω_p = potential specific stream power (Van den Berg 1995), using S_v = 16.0 (cm/km) (Van Dijk et al. 1991) and estimates of paleodischarge from table 5.5.

Differences in specific stream power therefore seem to be a major cause of the inferred differences in lateral stability of the paleochannels, given the now widely accepted relationship between lateral channel stability and specific stream power (section 2.3.3). Naturally, bank material composition remains another crucial factor for lateral channel stability. The potential specific stream power (ω_p) estimated for the Schoonrewoerd paleochannel is extremely low with respect to the reference data for braided and meandering channels published by Van den Berg (1995). Furthermore, the estimates of specific stream power (ω_B and ω_m) for the Schoonrewoerd paleochannel (range 0.7 - 3.1 W/m^2) correspond closely to that for the modern Columbia River main channel [range 1.5 - 2.6 W/m^2 (table 5.6)]. The low specific stream power was accepted to be the prime cause of the observed lateral stability of the Columbia River main channel (section 3.5). Likewise, the inferred lateral stability of the Schoonrewoerd paleochannel is attributed to a similar low specific stream power. Törnqvist (1993a) attributed the apparent lateral stability of the Schoonrewoerd and neighbouring mid-Holocene paleochannels (apart from the cohesive subsoil) to rapid vertical aggradation caused by sea-level rise.

The abundant evidence for lateral migration of the Hennisdijk paleochannel corresponds well to its higher stream power. The estimates of potential specific stream power for the Hennisdijk paleochannel group among the data for other low-energy meandering channels given by Van den Berg (1995, fig. 3a). Ferguson (1981, p. 118) stated that actively meandering rivers in Britain range in power between 5 and 350 W/m^2, with a median of about 30 W/m^2. Its position near the lower end of this range, explains why the Hennisdijk channel belt deposits possess an architecture that reminds of confined meandering rivers. A different explanation was suggested by Törnqvist (1993a). According to his model, lateral migration of the Hennisdijk paleochannel was mainly allowed by a decreased rate of aggradation.

Data on the paleohydraulics of the Echteld paleochannel are lacking. The thin, around 2 m thick, cohesive subsoil may have favoured active meandering of the paleochannel, even at relatively low stream power.

Now having completed the analysis of the paleochannels, it can be concluded that differences in stream power and subsoil erodibility satisfactorily explain the inferred differences in morphology of the paleochannels. The case studies strongly suggest that there is no need to suppose that aggradation rate really had a direct influence on lateral channel stability in the Holocene Rhine-Meuse delta. In section 5.2.1, I outlined the major objections against the direct coupling of floodplain sedimentation rates and lateral channel stability, most importantly the lack of a theoretical basis in the form of a conceptual causal mechanism. Obviously, a revision of the factors controlling channel patterns in the Holocene Rhine-Meuse delta is needed. The present study suggests 'stream power' and 'subsoil erodibility' as the main explanatory factors, instead of 'sea-level rise' and 'subsoil erodibility' suggested previously (Törnqvist 1993a). Of course, stream power is not totally independent of sea-level rise, since the latter for example influences river gradients. Sea-level rise is clearly not a direct control of lateral channel stability, but rather one of the factors influencing stream power.

Another linking mechanism between the rate of sea-level rise and stream power needs to be evaluated. Starting from a positive relationship between base-level rise, aggradation rate and avulsion frequency, it is reasonable to suppose that rapid sea-level rise makes the number of coexistent delta distributaries increase by frequent avulsion (section 2.3.2). Since the same amount of water has to be distributed over an increasing number of channels, stream power for the individual channels will inevitably decrease, resulting in an increase in lateral channel stability.

This course of events seems to be consistent with the data from the Holocene of the Rhine-Meuse delta (Törnqvist 1993a, 1993b). Many Rhine distributaries existed during the mid-Holocene period of rapid sea-level rise. A substantial number of these paleochannels was laterally stable. For example, the Schoonreweord system, with its relatively low paleodischarge, was only one out of the many Rhine distributaries active during that time (figure 5.1). During the late-Holocene, the rate of sea-level rise strongly decreased, the number of distributaries decreased, and lateral channel stability generally seemed to decrease as well. For instance, during the period of activity of the Hennisdijk system, the number of coexisting Rhine distributaries [in the cross section studied by Törnqvist (1993b)] dropped from nine to four (figure 5.1).

In the early-Holocene, apparently relatively few avulsions took place (Törnqvist 1993b, p. 153), in spite of the rapid sea-level rise. This may be related to the influence of the still shallow sandy Pleistocene subsoil. In the sandy erodible subsoil the existing channels probably could easily maintain their flow capacity, thereby reducing the chance for avulsion. It is also believed that initially, cross-levee gradients to the floodbasins were too gentle to favour avulsion. The mechanisms and external controls of avulsion in the Holocene Rhine-Meuse delta are presently the subject of ongoing research (Stouthamer & Berendsen 1997).

5.6 Summary

Three different Holocene paleochannels within the anastomosing river system of the Rhine-Meuse delta were investigated. In this study, the paleochannels and their genetically associated deposits were termed 'fluvial systems'. The three fluvial systems show major differences in depositional architecture and it was attempted to establish the causes of these differences through detailed facies mapping and subsequent reconstruction of paleochannel morphology, slope and discharge.

The Schoonreweord system is the oldest of the three systems, having been active from 4500 to 3800 BP in the central part of the Rhine-Meuse delta. Overbank deposits representing the previously presumed first phase of activity of the Schoonreweord system (5350-4700 BP), seem to belong to the neighbouring Zijderveld system. A spectacular downstream decrease in channel sand body width/thickness ratio from around 40 to 5, characterizes the Schoonreweord system. This is the result of changing paleochannel dimensions and a decrease in lateral migration. Controlling factors were a downstream dip in the erosion-resistant subsoil, a loss of discharge through crevasse channels, and a decrease of the gradient. The average Schoonreweord sand body gradient is 7.6 cm/km for the principal reach. The sand body lithofacies of the Schoonrewoerd system mainly consists of homogeneous sequences of planar cross-bedded sets. The dominant texture is medium sand, showing a poorly developed upward fining. Organic litter may be very abundant, and locally thick laminated muddy sequences occur as well. The facies generally indicate strong flow variability, but obvious marine influence is only evident in the most downstream reach studied. The signs of marine influence show that the system does not end up in the fluviolagoon as was suggested by some authors. The Schoonrewoerd system is interpreted to represent a frustrated avulsion. Originating from the Werkhoven system, the Schoonrewoerd system shows a downstream succession of three stages in channel belt evolution. Paleohydraulic reconstructions near Molenaarsgraaf indicate that Schoonrewoerd paleodischarge was probably between 265 and 400 m^3/s, for the case of bankfull discharge in the paleochannel at its maximum capacity. Specific stream power is estimated to have been extremely low, with a maximum range of 0.7 to 3.1 W/m^2. This was the prime cause of the lateral stability of the Schoonrewoerd paleochannel.

The Hennisdijk system is located upstream of the Schoonrewoerd system and was active from 3800 to 3000 BP. The channel sand body width/thickness ratio of around 35, on average is greater than that of the Schoonrewoerd system, while the gradient of the sand body is 14.3 cm/km. Sand body geometry as well as lithofacies indicate substantial lateral migration of the paleochannel. The most typical lithofacies characteristic is the presence of IHS in the top of the sand body, which represents lateral accretion surfaces. Thick sequences of a fine-textured facies (fine sand and mud) seem to occur systematically along the margins of the sand body, laterally interfingering with the coarser sand body facies. These fine-grained deposits were interpreted as concave-bank bench deposits. Other lithofacies differences with the Schoonrewoerd sand body are the much higher variability in orientation, scale and type of sedimentary structures as well as the occurrence of a gravelly facies, representing channel lag and lower point bar deposits. Reconstructions suggest that, even when considering only the most probable cases, the paleodischarge of the mature Hennisdijk paleochannel may have been in the wide range of 380 to 1050 m^3/s. Specific stream power was significantly higher than that of the Schoonrewoerd system, but in general it can still be considered relatively low (maximum range 5.0 to 10.8 W/m^2). Meandering of the Hennisdijk paleochannel seems to have been confined, as a result of the relatively low stream power in combination with the cohesive bank material.

The Echteld system is located upstream of the Hennisdijk system and was active from 2800 to 1900 BP. The channel sand body width/thickness ratio (around 65) is higher than that of the Hennisdijk system. The gradient of the sand body is 17.5 cm/km, but is likely to have been influenced by neotectonic movements. Probably the Echteld paleochannel was fully meandering, partly as a result of the relatively shallow sandy Pleistocene subsoil.

	Schoonrewoerd system	Hennisdijk system	Echteld system
Sand body:		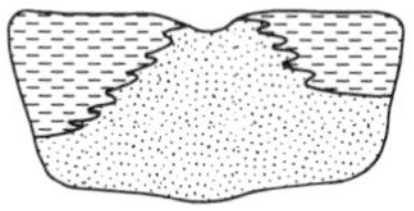	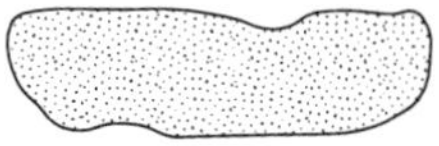
Width/thickness:	typically < 15 (downstream decrease)	± 35	± 65
Channel deposits:	- medium sand	- medium and coarse sand - fine sand, sandy and silty clay	- medium and coarse sand
Stream power:	1 - 3 W/m^2	4 - 12 W/m^2	?
Subsoil:	- peat and clay	- thick clay and peat - base scoured into gravelly sand	- thin clay and peat - base scoured into gravelly sand
Paleochannel interpretation:	straight	confined meandering	meandering

Figure 5.24   Summary of the main characteristics of the three channel belts studied.

In figure 5.24 the main results from the three case studies are summarized. The case studies show that the paleochannel morphology can be satisfactorily explained by the factors 'stream power' and 'subsoil erodibility'. It appears superfluous to suppose a direct influence of aggradation rate (due to sea-level rise) on channel morphology in the Rhine-Meuse delta. However, an indirect negative coupling between rate of sea-level rise and stream power may exist.

6   Synthesis and conclusions

6.1   Comparison of the studied anastomosing river systems

A superficial comparison of the three river systems described in the previous chapters, shows that the anastomosing rivers constitute a very diverse group of rivers (table 6.1). Obviously, an important part of this diversity is associated with differences in climatic and geological setting. However, a closer inspection also reveals important similarities that throw light on the origin of anastomosing rivers. The major differences and similarities can be grouped into five themes that will be discussed below. The main elements of the three studied systems are summarized in block diagrams to enable quick comparison (figures 6.1, 6.2 and 6.3). In general, the case studies confirmed the assumptions put forward in section 2.5.

Organic material and bank stability
Variability of the vegetation cover, and variability in the preservation of organic material in the sedimentary record, represent prime differences between the three studied systems. In the Columbia Valley, a temperate humid climate promotes the development of a dense vegetation cover. The vegetation has a strong influence on the development of the fluvial morphology, through the occurrence of log jams and through bank stabilization by root networks. Presumably, the same holds for the Holocene Rhine-Meuse delta, having a roughly comparable climatic setting. A major difference concerns the development of peat. In the proximal montane setting of the upper Columbia Valley, peat-growth is limited due to a large input of clastic material, whereas peat-growth was widespread in the Holocene Rhine-Meuse delta. In addition to root networks, (compacted) peat layers enhanced bank stability in this environment.

In the upper Inland Niger Delta a very different situation exists. Due to aridity, the vegetation cover is much more limited and very little organic material is preserved, peat being absent. Vegetation and peat contribute very little to bank stability in this environment, but their role is taken over by strong desiccation of the bank material and cementation due to precipitation of ferric oxides.

Apparently, the influence of vegetation and organic material on the morphology of anastomosing rivers (e.g. Smith 1976; Harwood & Brown 1993) is of local importance only, and is not a universal feature of anastomosing river systems.

Base-level control and floodplain sedimentation rate
The nature of base-level control in the studied systems is variable and strongly related to their geological setting. The associated floodplain sedimentation rates cover a wide range. Cross-valley alluvial fans obstruct the upper Columbia River in its narrow montane valley and provide local base-levels. Fan aggradation facilitates rapid sedimentation on the floodplain, averaging at 1.7 mm/yr since around 4500 cal. yr BP. In the Rhine-Meuse delta base-level rise (= sea-level rise) resulted in average floodplain sedimentation rates

ranging from 1.55 to 0.4 mm/yr in the period of 5200-2000 cal. yr BP (i.e. the time span covered by the present study). In contrast, complex base-level movements occur in the upper Inland Niger Delta. Here, a local base-level is formed by a lake that formed behind cordons of eolian dunes. Lake-levels oscillated in response to climatic variations and dune reactivation. Long-term slow tectonic subsidence of the Inland Delta is superimposed on the lake-level variations. Average Holocene floodplain sedimentation rates are relatively low, varying regionally between 0.25 to 0.55 mm/yr.

Table 6.1 Comparison of the studied anastomosing river systems.[a]

	Upper Columbia R.	Upper Inland Niger Delta	Rhine-Meuse delta
Climate	temperate humid	tropical semi-arid	temperate humid
Geological setting	montane valley	intracratonic basin	coastal plain
Base-level control	cross-valley alluvial fans	slow tectonic movements, damming eolian dunes	sea-level
Floodplain sedimentation rate (mm/cal. yr)	1.7	0.25 - 0.55	0.4 - 1.0[b]
Mean annual discharge (m³/s)	108[c]	1330 (Niger)[d] 400 (Bani)[e]	2200 (Rhine)[f] 230 (Meuse)[g]
Valley gradient (cm/km)	9	3 - 4	3 - 16[h]
Specific stream power (W/m²)	2.6	0.9 - 2.1	0.7 - 12.3
Channel morphology and w/d[i]	straight, 6 - 10	straight, 10 - 60	straight, ≥ 5; confined meandering, 8-13; meandering, w/d ?
Cause of bank stability	cohesive sediments, dense vegetation and root networks	indurated and strongly consolidated cohesive sediments (scattered vegetation)	cohesive sediments, peat (dense vegetation and root networks likely[j])
Avulsion triggers	log jams	in-channel eolian dune formation	unknown (log and ice jams likely, marine influence?)

Table 6.1 (continued)

	Upper Columbia R.	Upper Inland Niger Delta	Rhine-Meuse delta
Levees	narrow and prominent; consist mainly of silty and sandy clay with very high silt content; often sandy avulsion-splay deposits near the base	wide, floodbasinward margins sharp to gradual; relatively fine-textured, consist mainly of clay and silty clay with high silt content	morphology unknown (sedimentary evidence suggests variable morphology); consist mainly of silty and sandy clay
Crevasse splays	abundant, fan-shaped, consist mainly of of sand	common, finger-shaped; relatively fine-textured, consist mainly of clay and silty clay	rare to abundant, stringer-shaped; consist mainly of silty and sandy clay
Floodbasins	abundant but small-sized; deposition of clay, minor peat-formation	extensive; deposition of clay (may be sandy due to eolian influx)	extensive; deposition of clay and wide-spread formation of peat
Lakes	abundant and permanent	abundant but seasonal	abundant (permanent on lower delta plain [k])
Faunal activity	beaver dams and drag trails, bioturbation in floodbasins by waterfowl and moose [l]	intense bioturbation of levees by termites	unknown (beaver activity likely)

[a] Data from the present study unless otherwise specified.
[b] Based on groundwater gradient lines for the central Rhine-Meuse delta for the period 5200-2000 cal. yr BP as reconstructed by Van Dijk et al. (1991). Contrary to the other figures, these figures are sedimentation rates prior to compaction.
[c] Data for Nicholson gauging station (figure 3.2) (Water Survey of Canada 1991a).
[d] Data for Koulikoro gauging station (figure 4.1) (Direction Nationale de l'Hydraulique et de l'Energie, Bamako, Mali, unpubl. data).
[e] Data for San gauging station (figure 4.1) (Direction Nationale de l'Hydraulique et de l'Energie, Bamako, Mali, unpubl. data).
[f] Present mean annual discharge of the Rhine River near the Dutch-German border (figure 5.2) (Rijkswaterstaat 1996).
[g] Present mean annual discharge of the Meuse River near the Dutch-Belgian border (figure 5.2) (Rijkswaterstaat 1996).
[h] Based on groundwater gradient lines for the central Rhine-Meuse delta for the period 5200-2000 cal. yr BP as reconstructed by Van Dijk et al. (1991).
[i] Width/depth ratio.
[j] According to landscape reconstructions by Van der Woude (1983).
[k] Van der Woude (1984)
[l] Smith (1983)

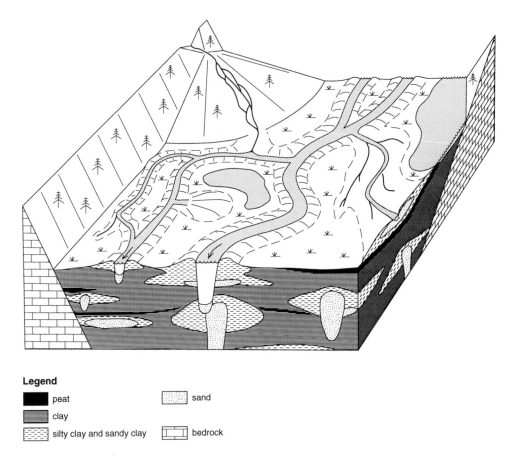

Legend

⬛	peat	▦	sand
▨	clay	▦	bedrock
▨	silty clay and sandy clay		

Figure 6.1   *Schematic diagram showing geological setting, surface morphology and subsurface of the upper Columbia River. Area shown measures ~ 2 km in width. Vertical scale strongly exaggerated; thickness shown ~ 10 m.*

Although the above-mentioned values for anastomosing river floodplain sedimentation rates cover a wide range, even more extreme values were reported for anastomosing river floodplains in literature. The lowest sedimentation rates are 0.04 mm/yr for the Cooper Creek floodplain which is located in a fairly stable intracratonic basin in Australia (Knighton & Nanson 1993). The Magdalena River floodplain experiences the highest sedimentation rate of 3.8 mm/yr, which is associated with its setting in a rapidly subsiding foreland basin in front of the Andes Mountains (Smith 1986).

It can be concluded that anastomosing rivers are not necessarily associated with a rapid rise in base-level and high floodplain sedimentation rates.

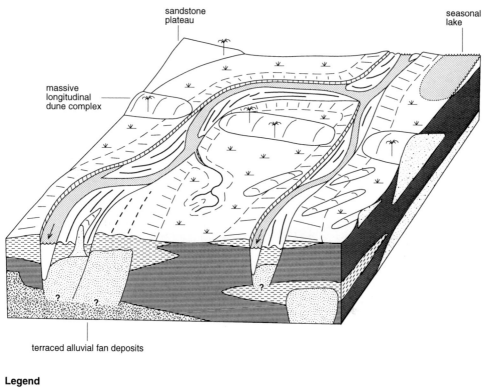

sandstone
plateau

seasonal
lake

massive
longitudinal
dune complex

terraced alluvial fan deposits

Legend

Fluvial deposits

▨ clay

▨ silty clay and sandy clay

☐ sand

▨ gravelly sand

Eolian deposits

▨ sand

Figure 6.2   *Schematic diagram showing surface morphology and subsurface of the*
upper Inland Niger delta. Area shown measures ~ 40 km in width.
Channel belts are oversized for clarity. Vertical scale strongly exaggerated;
thickness shown ~ 10 m.

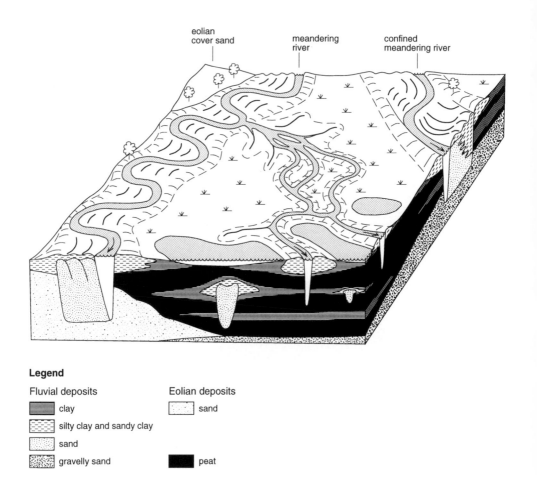

eolian
cover sand

meandering
river

confined
meandering river

Legend

Fluvial deposits

░ clay

░ silty clay and sandy clay

░ sand

░ gravelly sand

Eolian deposits

░ sand

█ peat

*Figure 6.3   Schematic diagram showing surface morphology and subsurface of the mid-
to late-Holocene Rhine-Meuse delta. Area shown measures ∼ 25 km in
width. Channel belts are oversized for clarity. Vertical scale strongly
exaggerated; thickness shown ∼ 10 m.*

Channel morphology and stream power

The individual channels within the studied anastomosing river systems, show marked
differences in morphology. The upper Columbia River channels can all be classified as
'straight', with lateral erosion and accretion being almost totally absent. Mature channels
in the system have a low width/depth ratio: between 6 and 10. In contrast, the major Bani
channel in the upper Inland Niger Delta has a much higher width/depth ratio, which is
typically between 40 and 60, with a minimum of 20 recorded. Smaller channels in the
Inland Delta have a width/depth ratio close to the Columbia River channels. Considering

238

their sinuosity index, the Inland Delta channels can also be called 'straight', but restricted lateral scroll topography is common. This predominantly reflects subrecent lateral fill of channels in response to reduced discharge. Presently, the channels are laterally quite stable. The studied paleochannels in the Rhine-Meuse delta were of various types ranging from 'straight', through 'confined meandering' to 'meandering'. Reconstructed channel width/depth ratios for the 'straight' and 'confined meandering' channels were relatively low (table 6.1).

In the previous chapters, channel morphology has already been related to specific stream power and bank material. Van den Berg (1995) introduced 'potential specific stream power' as a predictive parameter (section 3.4.5). Plotting the potential specific stream power of a large number of channels of known morphology against the median grain size of their bed material, he was able to discriminate between meandering and braided channels. He was unable to discriminate between straight and meandering channels, mainly due to a lack of good descriptive data for his set of low-sinuosity channels (P ≤ 1.3), which included laterally very active as well as laterally stable channels. The present study yielded the necessary data for a number of straight, laterally stable, channels and enables comparison with the meandering and braided river data set of Van den Berg (1995).

For adequate comparison, the new channels should be reclassified according to the criteria used by Van den Berg. For practical reasons Van den Berg used sinuosity (P) instead of the sinuosity index ($P_{ind.}$) [the latter parameter is favoured in this study (section 2.2.4)], to define straight and meandering channels. Straight channels were defined by P ≤ 1.3 and meandering channels by P > 1.3. All channels from the present study, except for the Hennisdijk paleochannel (P ≈ 1.6) can be classified as straight according to this criterion.

In figure 6.4 the data points for the straight channels of this study cluster below meandering channel data points. It should be noted that certain high-sinuosity channels (P > 1.3) , classified as 'meandering' by Van den Berg, are in fact laterally stable. The sinuosity of these channels is not the result of lateral migration. An example is the Barwon River (Taylor & Woodyer 1978), which plots near the straight channels from this study in figure 6.4. The Hennisdijk paleochannel plots among the meandering channel data, as expected. Confined lateral migration and concave-bank bench accretion was documented for the Hennisdijk paleochannel. It is interesting to note that data points representing the Murrumbidgee River (Schumm 1968) plot near the vertical bar of the Hennisdijk paleochannel (figure 6.4). Like the Hennisdijk paleochannel, the Murrumbidgee River is characterized by concave-bank bench accretion and confined lateral migration (Page & Nanson 1982; Nanson & Page 1983). A preliminary separation line is drawn between the populations of the 'meandering' and the 'straight' channels. Many more straight channel data points are needed to establish the separation line with reasonable confidence. Furthermore, the population of 'meandering channels' (P > 1.3) as presented by Van den Berg, should actually be screened on lateral stability.

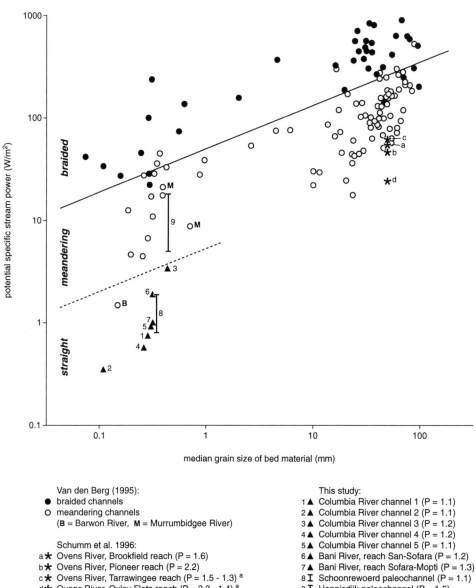

Van den Berg (1995):
- ● braided channels
- ○ meandering channels
  (B = Barwon River, M = Murrumbidgee River)

Schumm et al. 1996:
- a ★ Ovens River, Brookfield reach (P = 1.6)
- b ★ Ovens River, Pioneer reach (P = 2.2)
- c ★ Ovens River, Tarrawingee reach (P = 1.5 - 1.3) [a]
- d ★ Ovens River, Oxley Flats reach (P = 2.3 - 1.4) [a]

[a] P is lowered due to human intervention

This study:
- 1 ▲ Columbia River channel 1 (P = 1.1)
- 2 ▲ Columbia River channel 2 (P = 1.1)
- 3 ▲ Columbia River channel 3 (P = 1.2)
- 4 ▲ Columbia River channel 4 (P = 1.2)
- 5 ▲ Columbia River channel 5 (P = 1.1)
- 6 ▲ Bani River, reach San-Sofara (P = 1.2)
- 7 ▲ Bani River, reach Sofara-Mopti (P = 1.3)
- 8 I Schoonrewoerd paleochannel (P = 1.1)
- 9 I Hennisdijk paleochannel (P ≈ 1.6)

Figure 6.4   *Stability diagram of channel type in relation to grain size and potential specific stream power (defined in section 3.4.5). Data from the present study are plotted together with the data set on braided and meandering channels presented by Van den Berg (1995). Some data from Schumm et al. (1996) are also plotted.*

It must be stated clearly that the preliminary line does not separate 'anastomosing channels' from 'meandering channels'. Although most anastomosing channels investigated in the present study can be classified as 'straight' and plot below the separation line, anastomosing channels may have higher P and $P_{ind.}$ values and plot among meandering channels. One example is the Hennisdijk paleochannel. Lack of paleodischarge data prevented plotting of interpreted meandering paleochannels from the Rhine-Meuse delta in figure 6.4. Schumm et al. (1996) described meandering channels in the Ovens River anastomosing system (Australia). These high-sinuosity gravel-bed anastomosing channels show active lateral migration and neatly plot among the meandering river data in figure 6.4.

In short, anastomosing channels are variable in morphology. The described straight, confined meandering and meandering channels generally have a relatively low width/depth ratio although more moderate values occur as well. Many anastomosing channels can be classified as 'straight'. In contrast to meandering channels, straight channels are characterized by very restricted to zero lateral migration. These channels have a typical combination of stream power and bed material, different from that of meandering and braided channels.

Channel-fill succession

It is impossible to give a standard succession for anastomosing channel deposits, since the nature of the channel deposits depends on individual channel morphology and flow energy, rather than on the fact that an infilling channel is part of an anastomosing network or not. In figure 6.5 typical examples of sedimentary successions from the studied anastomosing channels are given and will be briefly discussed below.

The straight Columbia River channels are dominated by vertical accretion. Abandoned channels often fill up with sand completely, until flow becomes sufficiently shallow for vegetation to colonize the bed and trap fine suspended load. This results in a sand body with a poorly developed upward fining and an abrupt top. The straight Schoonrewoerd paleochannel has a very similar homogeneous channel-fill succession. Due to its distal setting, a gravelly channel lag is absent. Thick cross-bedded sets occur up to near the top. Bedforms of a similar height were observed in a nearly completely infilled Columbia River channel.

The straight channels in the upper Inland Niger Delta show lateral as well as vertical accretion. The depth of the base of the coarse lateral accretion deposits is unknown, but the top of the sandy deposits is abrupt. The onset of rapid vertical accretion of a thick muddy succession is likely to be a complex response to a change in climate, vegetation and human activities. These fine-grained deposits can be considered as levee deposits, covering bars within an old oversized channel. Where the package of fines is very thick and contains organic material, the lower part probably represents channel deposits which are akin to laterally accreted concave-bank bench deposits.

Essentially two types of sedimentary successions developed in meandering and confined meandering paleochannels in the Rhine-Meuse delta. A typical point bar lateral accretion succession (cf. Allen 1970) was found in the core of the Hennisdijk channel belt. This succession is characterized by upward fining and a gravelly channel lag. Major

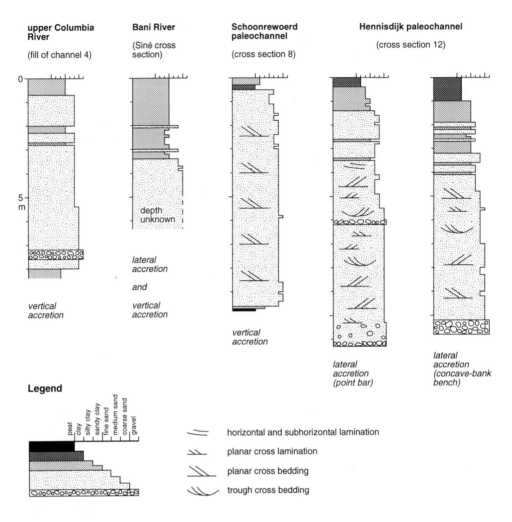

Figure 6.5 Typical sedimentary successions from studied anastomosing channels.

scour surfaces may be present within the succession. Near the top, the sand passes gradually into the muddy levee deposits. Thin mud drapes mark the lateral accretion surfaces in the upper part of the sand facies. Variability of scale and orientation of sedimentary structures is caused by the variable influence of relatively weak secondary currents in the paleochannel. A second type of sedimentary succession only occurs along the margins of confined meandering channel belts and is formed by concave-bank bench lateral accretion (cf. Hickin 1979, 1986; Page & Nanson 1982). In many respects this succession resembles the point bar succession, however its upper part comprises a thick unit of muddy channel deposits which is absent in the point bar succession. This type of lateral accretion is believed to be a common phenomenon in anastomosing river systems.

All in all, it appears that various modes of lateral and vertical accretion may occur in anastomosing channels, depending on channel morphology, local flow conditions and external controls like climate and vegetation.

Avulsion-mechanisms

Anastomosing rivers can be considered as fluvial systems that are heavily dominated by avulsions. Nine avulsions during the past 3000 cal. yr were recorded within the studied cross section in the upper Columbia Valley. In the upper Inland Niger Delta, avulsion frequency seems to be lower, but at least three major avulsions of the Bani River took place since 8000 cal. yr BP, apart from the formation of a number of smaller channels. The avulsion history in the Rhine-Meuse delta was documented by Törnqvist (1994), who studied a long cross section through the central Rhine-Meuse delta. His figure 4 suggests twenty-seven avulsions of the Rhine River since 9000 cal. yr BP. These results crudely confirm the idea that avulsion frequency increases with floodplain sedimentation rate. Fewer avulsions in the upper Inland Niger Delta seem to be associated with relatively low sedimentation rates, while the more rapidly aggrading Columbia and Rhine-Meuse systems have a higher avulsion-frequency.

In current models (e.g. Mackey & Bridge 1995; Slingerland & Smith 1998), avulsion is believed to be mainly dependent on floodplain topography. Avulsion comes about when the cross-levee slope exceeds the channel slope by a critical ratio. Since floodplain sedimentation rates decrease exponentially away from the channel, these critical conditions are reached automatically after sufficient floodplain sedimentation has taken place. In a recent paper, Mack & Leeder (1998) questioned the validity of such *topography-based avulsion models*. Field data from the present study suggest that, next to the evolution in floodplain topography, the evolution in channel-capacity can help to explain avulsions.

Measurements and calculations of sediment transport in the upper Columbia River channels show that this system is unable to move coarse bed load supplied from upstream through the anastomosing reach. Low stream power results in inability of the system to erode its banks sufficiently to create space for lateral storage of the surplus of bed load in point bars. Therefore the material is stored on the channel beds which are aggrading. Bed aggradation limits channel flow capacity and forces the flow out of the channels onto the floodplain where new channels are cut. This avulsion-mechanism need not to be in conflict with the above-sketched topography-based model, but rather complements it. When overbank flooding increases due to bed aggradation, the response will be increased overbank deposition which in turn increases cross-levee slopes. Levee-growth may restore channel capacity. However, prolonged annual overbank flooding of the Columbia River indicates that bed aggradation outpaces levee aggradation, which makes the system liable to avulsions. Abandoned channels function as reservoirs for coarse bed load and often fill up with sand completely.

A similar *capacity-based avulsion model* applies to the upper Inland Niger Delta. Many levees of this system, infrequently inundated, experience little sedimentation, while old oversized channels are infilling due to significantly reduced discharge in response to climatic change. The oversized channels fill up with sand as well as abundant mud, which covers the sandy channel bars as recent levees. Subrecent eolian dunes on the channel bars are common. The relatively high width/depth ratio of the Bani River is illustrative for the channel bed aggradation. The climate is characterized by alternation of arid and humid periods. The present channel network is unable to accommodate a sharp rise in discharge, associated with a return to more humid conditions. In that case, avulsion is a plausible response of the system.

A capacity-based avulsion model was also proposed by Schumm et al. (1996) and Gibling et al. (1998) for anastomosing rivers in Australia. A crucial element of the model is a relatively low stream power, which limits increase of channel capacity by lateral erosion as well as bed load transport. Lateral erosion and accretion need not be totally absent. If in a meandering channel the surplus of bed load to be stored in the point bars, exceeds the space created by lateral erosion of floodbasin fines, bed aggradation and ultimately avulsion will be the result.

It can be concluded that a capacity-based avulsion model best explains the occurrence of avulsive anastomosing rivers in settings with a low floodplain sedimentation rate. Such a model can well be integrated into a topography-based avulsion model.

6.2   Applications of the research

River engineering
River engineers often strive for stabilization of river banks and restriction of the natural lateral migration of channels. In other words, they try to remodel braided and meandering channels into 'straight' channels (cf. section 2.2.4) by stabilizing the banks. When they succeed in doing this, sedimentary processes common in natural straight and confined meandering channels may come into play. The present study sheds light on these processes. A possible response of a meandering river to stabilization is that the channel, which is bereft of its lateral storage capacity of coarse bed load, starts to aggrade its bed more rapidly. This process in turn, demands bed regulation and improved flood protection measures to prevent crevassing and avulsion. The outlined course of events broadly parallels the long-term development of the Rhine-Meuse delta since embankment of the meandering rivers in the Late Middle Ages. In many reaches, embankment only left some space for confined lateral migration of the channel. As a result, concave-bank bench accretion became an important process. Associated phenomena have been recognized by Middelkoop (1997, p. 79-81) on the embanked floodplains in the Netherlands.

If stable channels are to be designed, the stability diagram (figure 6.4) enables a first assessment of the necessary boundary conditions. Figure 6.4 also enables an evaluation in advance of the response of fluvial channels to imposed changes. For example, a rise in sea-level will shift near-coastal meandering channels towards more lateral stability, since reduced gradients cause a decrease in stream power and therefore a shift downward in the stability diagram. Decreasing bed load transport capacity together with decreasing lateral storage of bed load will cause rapid bed aggradation, eventually leading to crevassing and avulsion. Another possibility is an increase in discharge. Nearly two decades ago, a project was proposed to divert the Kootenay River into the upper Columbia River, across the low divide near Canal Flats (figure 3.2) (Tutt 1979; B.C. Hydro 1982). The position of the Columbia River main channel in the stability diagram, suggests that there is a fair risk that a significant increase in discharge (and consequently stream power), causes a shift into the 'meandering field' of the diagram. This would imply a fundamental change in character of the upper Columbia River.

Nature restoration
Recent plans for nature restoration in the embanked floodplains in the Rhine-Meuse delta, include the re-introduction of floodplain forest and giving the river an anastomosing-like pattern by dredging of small secondary channels in order to create a more diverse ecosystem (Postma et al. 1996; Silva & Kok 1996; Sieben 1998). More trees on the embanked floodplains will certainly increase flow resistance during flooding, whereas secondary channels could compensate for the resulting loss in discharge-capacity. Hydraulically, the anastomosing upper Columbia River in many respects can be considered as a natural analogue of the planned situation in the Netherlands, along the lower reaches of the Lek, IJssel and Meuse Rivers. The present study might provide data for the scaling of secondary channels and the evaluation of the effects of vegetation.

Agriculture and rural development
In a semi-arid region like the Inland Niger Delta, abandoned channels of an anastomosing river system are very suitable for irrigated cultivation. In the Dead Delta (figure 4.1) this is put into practice on a large scale in the 'Office du Niger' irrigation project. However also in the Inland Delta proper, many of the abandoned channels appearing on the geomorphological map (appendix 2), could relatively easily be irrigated by the local population to enhance security of food production. Fish breeding could be a promising new activity. The abandoned channels are close to many villages (which are located on their levees), have a manageable size, and a less clayey soil then the extensive floodbasins. Besides, the floodbasin grasslands are traditionally reserved for grazing cattle. Large-scale geomorphological mapping of the anastomosing river floodplain coupled with shallow subsurface studies, as was carried out in the present study, is crucial for guiding such irrigation projects.

The present non-irrigated agriculture in the area is strongly dependent on frequent inundation, not only for the water, but also for the nutrient enrichment of the soils by wash load deposition. The low floodplain sedimentation rates in the Inland Delta, as demonstrated by the present study, suggest that the already marginal agriculture in this area could be seriously affected by a decrease in inundation frequency and wash load concentration that would be caused by construction of flow-regulating dams upstream or bed regulation within the Inland Delta (see also Ward 1994).

Navigability
An important function of the Inland Delta channels is that of a transport network. The traditional boats used are small and can pass the major channels until late in the dry season. However, modern commercial vessels on the Niger River are soon hindered by large sand bars. Various studies have been carried out to investigate the possibilities to

245

improve navigability of the Niger River (e.g. Nedeco 1959; IWACO/Delft Hydraulics 1996). The present study underscores that improvement in the Inland Delta will be very difficult, since channel bed aggradation is inherent to the nature of this fluvial system. Furthermore, a future shift to a more arid climate would substantially deteriorate the navigability due an increase in bed aggradation caused by a rise in eolian influx of sand, especially in the north of the Inland Delta.

Exploration of hydrocarbons and coal
A major application of the research on anastomosing rivers deposits in general is related to their potential as hydrocarbon-bearing reservoirs and the common occurrence of coal seams adjacent to the channel deposits (Smith & Putnam 1980, Smith 1983). This study clearly shows that source rock potential is limited to a certain category of anastomosing rivers, since occurrence of organic deposits and peat was strongly variable among the studied anastomosing rivers systems. The crucial factors confirmed by the present study are (1) climate, (2) base-level rise and (3) sediment supply relative to basin size. A favourable set of conditions may occur in a temperate-humid, near-coastal setting, subjected to rapid base-level (sea-level) rise, comparable to the Holocene Rhine-Meuse delta.

The present study also suggests a significant reservoir potential for the straight channel-fills commonly occurring in such environments. Although being narrow, they may form extensive networks. In addition, homogeneous sandy successions with only few mud drapes, were recorded from the many boreholes used in the present study. In contrast, considerably wider sand bodies may be less promising than they seem to be on the basis of their size, due to the presence of abundant fine-grained concave-bank bench deposits and thick mud-draped lateral accretion surfaces, which are typical features of these low-energy fluvial systems. The data from the Inland Niger Delta suggest best reservoir conditions in the laterally restricted channels sands rather than in extensive eolian sand sheets, since the latter contain significant amounts of admixed clay.

Modelling of fluvial architecture
Although not widely recognized presently, fluvial architecture models (Leeder 1978; Allen 1978; Bridge & Leeder 1979; Mackey & Bridge 1995; Heller & Paola 1996) can be applied in the petroleum industry to aid in determining the drilling strategy for exploration of potentially hydrocarbon-bearing channel sandstones. The present study suggests the following fundamental shortcomings of such models: (1) long-term coexistence of channel belts and systematic variation in the number of coexisting channels belts are not considered in the models, (2) systematic variations in channel morphology with their influence on channel sand body geometry are not taken into account, and (3) avulsion-frequency is assumed to be solely dependent on overbank sedimentation rates.

In sequence stratigraphic studies, sand body width/thickness ratio is often interpreted to be inversely related to floodplain sedimentation rate (e.g. Shanley & McCabe 1991; Mjøs & Prestholm 1993; Aitken & Flint 1995). The present study suggests that systematic variation in the number of coexisting channels of the near-coastal fluvial system (section 5.5.3) is probably an important link in this relationship. Therefore, continuing study of the sedimentology and the behaviour of modern anastomosing rivers remains of importance for accurate interpretation of fluvial sequences in the fossil record.

6.3   Conclusions

In this thesis, an anastomosing river was defined as:

a river that is composed of several interconnected channels, which enclose floodbasins.

Three river systems that conform to this definition were investigated. The conclusions arrived at for the individual river systems are pointed out below.

Upper Columbia River
- The anastomosing upper Columbia River is composed of straight channels. Lateral channel stability is caused by low stream power and erosion-resistant cohesive banks that are reinforced by vegetation.
- Anastomosis of this river system has persisted at least since 3000 cal. yr BP. Nine avulsions during this period were recorded in the studied valley-wide cross section. Channel lifetimes ranged from 800 to at least 3000 years.
- The floodplain sedimentation rate of the upper Columbia River is considerably lower than previously estimated, averaging 1.7 mm/cal. yr.
- In spite of the anastomosing morphology of the river system, the main channel of the system is by far dominant in the discharge of water and sediment.
- The river system is unable to move the bulk of the coarse bed load supplied from upstream through the anastomosing reach. Bed aggradation limits channel capacity, enhances overbank flooding and sedimentation, and promotes avulsions.

Upper Inland Niger Delta
- The channels in the upper Inland Niger delta can be classified as 'straight'. Lateral stability is caused by low stream power and erosion-resistant cohesive banks. Low bank erodibility is due to induration of the levees by strong desiccation and precipitation of ferric oxides.
- This anastomosing river system exists under relatively low floodplain sedimentation rates and in the absence of a rapid rise in base-level.
- Frequent avulsion in this river system is promoted by: (1) a very low floodplain gradient, (2) a low channel flow capacity, and (3) climate-specific avulsion triggers (eolian processes and gullying).
- The deposits of this tropical semi-arid river system are characterized by: (1) scarcity of organic matter and absence of peat, (2) the association with eolian deposits, and (3) intense bioturbation of levee deposits by termites.

Rhine-Meuse delta

- Straight, confined meandering and meandering paleochannels occurred within the anastomosing river system of the Holocene Rhine-Meuse delta. Paleochannel morphology was a function of channel stream power and subsoil erodibility (figure 5.24).
- The influence of channel stream power replaces the previously supposed direct influence of floodplain sedimentation rate (controlled by sea-level rise) on channel morphology.
- An indirect negative coupling between rate of sea-level rise and channel stream power might exist, since floodplain sedimentation rates influenced avulsion frequency and thereby the number of coexisting channels of the Rhine-Meuse system.
- The channel sand bodies of the straight, confined meandering and meandering paleochannels are each characterized by a distinct geometry and sedimentary succession (figure 6.5).
- Confined meandering channels here represent a transitional form between straight and meandering. Lateral migration of these channels was constricted by cohesive overbank sediments.
- Sedimentological data from the Schoonrewoerd system roughly confirm the patterns predicted by the Saskatchewan River avulsion model (Smith et al. 1989).

The *general conclusions*, following from a comparison of the studied anastomosing river systems are pointed out below.

- The influence of vegetation and organic material on the morphology of anastomosing rivers is of local importance only and not a universal feature of anastomosing river systems.
- The occurrence of anastomosing rivers is not necessarily associated with a rapid rise of base-level and high floodplain sedimentation rates.
- Anastomosing channels can be strongly variable in morphology, but many are of the straight (laterally stable) type.
- Straight channels not only stand out by their morphology, but also by a specific combination of stream power and grain size of bed material (figure 6.4).
- There is no standard sedimentary succession for anastomosing channel deposits. Various modes of lateral and vertical accretion occur in anastomosing channels.
- Anastomosing river systems are avulsion-dominated river systems. The current topography-based avulsion models (levee-growth avulsion functions) only partially explain the occurrence of avulsions. Decrease of channel capacity by bed aggradation is an additional important drive of avulsions.

6.4 Future research

As a sequel to the present study, future research in this field should focus on three themes: (1) hydraulic and sedimentary processes in low-energy channels, (2) avulsion-mechanisms, and (3) application of the concepts derived from modern anastomosing rivers to interpretation of the fossil record, since anastomosing river deposits generally have a high preservation potential.

A large amount of work has already been done on meandering and braided channels, when compared to straight channels. An important future step to be made is to supplement the stability diagram (figure 6.4) with new straight channel data points, for a better definition of the separation line between meandering and straight channels. The diagram would benefit much from data points for straight (laterally stable) channels with gravelly bed material. It is felt that examples of such channels can be found in anastomosing river systems in proximal montane settings. After additional field work for measuring flow structure and sedimentary processes in straight channels, a next step could be numerical modelling of straight channels. In this respect, attention should also be paid to confined meandering channels as a transitional form between straight and meandering. Identification of concave-bank bench deposits in the fossil record (no ancient examples are known to me) would be very significant for reconstruction of paleohydraulics and sedimentary environment.

The present study underscores that much remains to be done on the mechanisms governing avulsion. In current models, much is assumed but little is known. Crucial to a capacity-based avulsion model, as proposed in the present study and by various other authors (e.g. Schumm et al. 1996, Gibling et al. 1998), is channel-bed aggradation. The rate of channel-bed aggradation could be determined by sediment budget analysis in mature channel reaches of river systems that proved to be liable to avulsion in recent history. The upper Columbia River is only one example of an area were such a study could be carried out. Field data could be used to feed a future integrated avulsion-model, explaining the occurrence of avulsion as a function of a decrease in channel-capacity and an increase in cross-levee slope.

In the last decades it proved to be hard to apply the concepts derived from modern anastomosing rivers to the fossil record. A major drawback was that ancient anastomosis (coexistence of paleochannels) could rarely be proven. The present study opens up new perspectives, since it appears that channel sand body width/depth ratio varies in response to the number of coexisting channels, which in turn is linked to the rate of base-level rise (section 5.5.3). This means that fluvial systems not only respond to external changes by changing channel morphology (e.g. Schumm 1993), but also by changing the number of coexistent channels. This concept needs to be checked and refined by subsurface and outcrop studies. An important prerequisite is that sedimentation rates and their variation can be accurately estimated. This makes subrecent systems (within the range of ^{14}C-dating) most suitable. Fundamental improvements would be to implement anastomosis (and systematic variations in the number of coexisting channels) in simulation models for fluvial architecture (e.g. Mackey & Bridge 1995) and sequence stratigraphic models for continental strata (e.g. Wright & Mariott 1993; Shanley & McCabe 1993).

Summary

Anastomosing rivers; forms, processes and sediments

Introduction

The anastomosing rivers represent a major group of rivers that are currently of interest in fluvial geomorphology and sedimentology. For a long time, they were frequently confused with braided rivers, which roughly have a comparable planform. Nowadays, the term 'anastomosing' is reserved for a type of multichannel river on alluvial plains that most often seems to form under relatively low-energetic conditions (figure 1.1).

Along with the increasing number of studied modern and ancient anastomosing river systems in various parts of the world, major controversies have arisen about the controlling factors of this river type. These controversies partly reflect the lack of a precise definition and the improper classification of anastomosing rivers. There is also disagreement on the role of climate and base-level (ruling floodplain sedimentation rates) in the formation of anastomosing rivers. It is felt that the scarcity of quantitative data on hydraulic and sedimentary processes in modern anastomosing rivers considerably hinders progress in this field of research.

The *objectives* of this study are: (1) to develop a consistent definition of anastomosing rivers and to classify this type of river with respect to other types, (2) to develop a universally applicable conceptual model for the genesis of anastomosing rivers systems, and (3) to document the variability in facies and fluvial architecture of modern and subrecent anastomosing river systems to improve the interpretation of the fossil record.

The approach followed in this thesis is that of comparative research of modern and subrecent anastomosing rivers systems in various climatic and geological settings. An extensive review of literature and three field studies are the main elements of this thesis.

Literature review

It appears to be impossible to define anastomosing rivers unambiguously on the basis of channel planform only. Therefore the following definition, which couples floodplain geomorphology and channel pattern, is proposed: *an anastomosing river is composed of several interconnected channels, which enclose floodbasins* (figures 2.1 and 2.2). In this thesis, a deltaic distributary system, where bifurcating channels may not rejoin, is considered as a special case of an anastomosing river system.

In presently popular definitions of anastomosing rivers, lateral stability of channels is indissolubly coupled with its multi-channel character. In this thesis it is favoured to uncouple these two properties. At the channel-scale the terms 'straight', 'meandering' and 'braided' apply, whereas at a larger scale a river can be called anastomosing if it meets the definition given above. This means that in theory, straight, meandering and braided channels may all be part of an anastomosing river. Straight channels are defined by a sinuosity index, i.e. the ratio of the distance along the channel and the distance along the channel belt axis, lower than 1.3. They are the type of channel that most commonly occurs in combination with anastomosis. The occurrence of straight channels is favoured by low stream power, basically a product of discharge and gradient, and erosion-resistant banks.

Anastomosing rivers are formed by avulsions, which is the formation of new channels on the floodplain. Frequent avulsions cause the continued existence of anastomosing rivers, since old channels are gradually abandoned while new channels are formed. Avulsions are primarily driven by aggradation of the channel belt, and are favoured by a low floodplain gradient. Also of influence are a number of avulsion-triggers such as extreme floods, log and ice jams, and in-channel eolian dunes. Although some of these triggers are associated with a certain climate, the occurrence of anastomosis is not.

Anastomosing river deposits have a fluvial architecture characterized by a large proportion of overbank deposits, which encase laterally connected channel sand(stone) bodies. These sand(stone) bodies frequently have a ribbon-like geometry and may possess a poorly developed upward fining, as well as an abrupt, flat top. The overbank deposits commonly comprise abundant crevasse splay deposits and thick natural levee deposits. Lacustrine deposits and coal are common in association with anastomosing river deposits. None of these characteristics is unique to anastomosing river deposits and in most cases anastomosis (coexistence of channels) can not be proven in the fossil record.

The upper Columbia River
Being located in a narrow montane valley in western Canada (southeastern British Columbia), the upper Columbia River is a proximal, relatively small-scale anastomosing river system in a temperate humid climate. Previous research on the upper Columbia River primarily focused on the sedimentology of the system. Therefore, the present study involves a quantitative study of the hydraulic and sedimentary processes, with the main objective to examine the drive behind avulsions in the upper Columbia River. All data were collected in a cross profile which spanned the entire floodplain (figure 3.4). The data include ^{14}C-dates from a floodplain-wide borehole cross section, sediment trap data, and measurements of flow parameters for the 1994 flood.

The results show that anastomosis at the study location has persisted since 3000 cal. yr BP (figure 3.11). During this period, the avulsion frequency was high: nine new channels were formed within the studied cross section. Channel lifetimes were highly variable, ranging from 800 to at least 3000 cal. years. The more or less random occurrence of log jams (figure 3.9) is supposed to have interrupted the evolution of many channels, causing variable lifetimes.

The long-term average floodplain sedimentation rate appears to be significantly lower than previously assumed. Based on ^{14}C-data obtained in this study, a value of 1.7 mm/yr is estimated. During the annual flood of 1994, which was of a relatively low magnitude, on average 0.8 mm of sediment was deposited on the floodplain. This seems to be in agreement with the calculated long-term average sedimentation rate.

The multiple coexistent channels can all be classified as 'straight' and are laterally stable. This is caused by a very low specific stream power (< 3.4 W/m^2) in combination with cohesive silty banks stabilized by vegetation. Low stream power is primarily due to a low floodplain gradient (11.5 cm/km).

Of the six parallel channels that make up the anastomosing system at the study location, one channel is by far dominant for the discharge of water and sediment. Around bankfull discharge this channel carries 87 % of the flow and probably more than 95 % of the transported sediment (not including wash load).

Transported bed load by the upper Columbia River decreases longitudinally. Since the channels are laterally stable, storage of the surplus of bed load takes place on the channel beds. Bed aggradation limits channel capacity, enhances overbank flooding and sedimentation, and drives avulsions.

The upper Inland Niger Delta

The interior of West-Africa hosts a large-scale anastomosing river system, which is fed by the Niger River. The tropical semi-arid climate and the distal intracratonic setting of the Inland Niger Delta (central Mali) are the prime differences with the upper Columbia River system. The present study concentrates on the upper part of the Inland Delta, where the Bani joins the Niger River. The Bani River is the main tributary of the Niger in this region. The Inland Delta was only poorly studied previously: subsurface data were scarce and geochronometric dates were lacking. The objective of the present study is to gain insight into the genesis and sedimentary products of this anastomosing system. More specifically, attention is paid to the role of climate and the importance of floodplain sedimentation rates in the evolution of the anastomosing river system. The core of the study consists of extensive geomorphological mapping of the upper Inland Delta using aerial and satellite images. During field surveys, mapping was checked and borehole cross sections were augered. Additionally, samples were extracted for AMS ^{14}C-dating, and hydrological data were collected. The main results of the study are a geomorphological map (appendix 2) and paleogeographical reconstructions for the Holocene, illustrating the avulsion-history of the upper Inland Niger Delta (figure 4.35).

The anastomosing river system of the upper Inland Delta, exists under relatively low floodplain sedimentation rates (0.25 - 0.54 mm/yr), in the absence of a rapid rise in base-level. A number of avulsions have occurred in the study area during the Holocene. These avulsions were conduced by a very low floodplain gradient (3-4 cm/km), a low channel flow capacity, and climate-specific processes such as in-channel eolian dune formation and deflation and gullying of natural levees. Presumably, tectonic movements also influenced the avulsion-history and led to a stepwise migration of the Bani River to the east.

Large eolian dune complexes profoundly influenced the development of the hydrographical network and controlled regional base-level. Especially the level of Lake Débo, which formed downstream of the study region behind a massive dune complex, determined the base-level in the study region. A large east-west trending cordon of massive dunes was formed in the study region during the Ogolian (20,000 - 12,500 BP). Fields of smaller longitudinal dunes were formed during a mid-Holocene arid period.

The channels in the upper Inland Delta can be classified as 'straight', based on their sinuosity index. Lateral channel stability is caused by very low specific stream power (0.9

- 2.1 W/m^2) and resistant banks, due to induration of the levees by strong desiccation and precipitation of ferric oxides. Reduced discharge due to aridity led to lateral fill of the channels (figure 4.36). Presently, bed aggradation is an important process, which may eventually cause avulsion.

Deposits in the upper Inland Delta are characterized by a very low organic matter content, and the absence of peat. Besides abundant dune deposits, eolian sediments also occur as a silt/sand fraction in the Ogolian floodbasin deposits. Levee deposits typically are heavily bioturbated by termites.

The mid- to late-Holocene Rhine-Meuse delta
The Rhine-Meuse delta (central Netherlands) is a large-scale anastomosing river system in a distal coastal setting, which is dominated by a temperate humid climate. Previous studies showed that anastomosis, i.e. coexistence of multiple channels on the delta plain, persisted throughout the Holocene. The present study focuses on three subrecent paleochannels and their genetically associated deposits (termed 'fluvial systems') in the central part of the fluvial delta. The objective is to re-evaluate the factors controlling the fluvial morphology in the Rhine-Meuse delta, and especially the role of discharge, which has not been considered hitherto. The data consist of ^{14}C-dates, detailed geological maps, and sixteen borehole cross sections that are more or less evenly spaced along the studied fluvial systems (appendices 3 and 4). In two cross sections undisturbed cores were obtained for study of sedimentary structures. The three studied fluvial systems show major differences in depositional architecture.

The Schoonrewoerd system was active from 4500 to 3800 BP and comprises multiple parallel sand bodies in its upper reach (figure 5.7). Overbank deposits from the previously presumed first phase of activity of this system (5350-4700 BP) now are considered to have been deposited by the neighbouring Zijderveld system (figure 5.20). The Schoonrewoerd system is characterized by a spectacular downstream decrease in channel sand body width/thickness ratio from around 40 to 5 (figure 5.21a). This can be explained by changing paleochannel dimensions and a decrease in lateral migration. The sand body lithofacies predominantly consist of a homogeneous succession of planar cross bedded sets, while the texture shows only poorly developed upward fining. The Schoonrewoerd system is interpreted to represent a frustrated avulsion. Downstream of the avulsion node, the system shows a downstream succession of three stages in channel belt evolution (figure 5.22). Paleohydraulic reconstructions in one of the cross sections indicate that local paleodischarge (bankfull) was probably within a range of 265 to 400 m^3/s. Specific stream power was very low (between 0.7 and 3.1 W/m^2). In combination with the stiff subsoil (peat and clay), this was the cause of the lateral stability of the Schoonrewoerd paleochannel.

The Hennisdijk system was active from 3800 to 3000 BP. Sand body geometry (width/thickness ratio around 35) and lithofacies indicate substantial lateral migration of the paleochannel. Inclined heterolithic stratification (IHS), representing lateral accretion surfaces, is present in the upper part of the sand body (figures 5.14 and 5.15). Thick muddy concave-bank bench deposits systematically occur along the margins of the sand body, indicating that meandering of the paleochannel was confined. Paleodischarge (bankfull) was probably within a range of 380 to 1050 m^3/s. Specific stream power was relatively low (between 5.0 and 10.8 W/m^2), enabling only confined meandering of the paleochannel between thick packages of clayey overbank sediments.

The Echteld system was active from 2800 to 1900 BP. Based on sand body lithofacies and geometry (width/thickness ratio around 65), the paleochannel is interpreted to have been fully meandering, partly as a result of the shallow sandy Pleistocene subsoil.

It appears that paleochannel morphology can be satisfactorily explained by the factors 'stream power' and 'subsoil erodibility'. There is no direct influence of floodplain sedimentation rate (due to sea-level rise) on channel morphology in the Rhine-Meuse delta. An indirect negative coupling between the rate of sea-level rise and channel stream power probably exists.

Comparison

A comparison of the studied anastomosing river systems sheds light on the universal controls and characteristics of anastomosing rivers. Important similarities and differences are observed.

It appears that the influence of vegetation and organic material (peat) on the morphology of anastomosing rivers is not a universal feature of anastomosing river systems. The occurrence of vegetation and organic material is strongly variable among the studied anastomosing river systems, due to differences in climate, base-level rise, and sediment supply relative to the size of the sedimentary basin.

Variable rates of floodplain sedimentation and base-level rise occur among the studied anastomosing river systems, while even more variable rates were reported in literature. This indicates that anastomosing rivers are not necessarily associated with high floodplain sedimentation rates and rapid rise in base-level.

Anastomosing channels appear to be variable in morphology, but channels of the 'straight' type are most common. In a stability diagram, in which potential specific stream power is plotted versus the median grain size of bed material, the straight (laterally stable) channels from the studied systems, appear well-separated from meandering and braided channels (figure 6.4).

The borehole data from the studied anastomosing river systems show that there is no standard sedimentary succession for anastomosing channel deposits. Various modes of lateral and vertical accretion are documented, and mainly depend on channel morphology and local flow conditions (figure 6.5).

Avulsions in the studied anastomosing river systems were caused by the evolution of the floodplain topography as well as by a decreasing channel flow capacity over time. Gradually decreasing channel capacity is due to the inability of the anastomosing channels to transport the supplied bed load, causing bed aggradation. Especially in settings with a low floodplain sedimentation rate, this is an important drive of avulsions.

Samenvatting

Anastomoserende rivieren; vormen, processen en sedimenten

Inleiding

Anastomoserende rivieren staan momenteel volop in de belangstelling in het wetenschappelijk onderzoek. In het verleden werden anastomoserende rivieren vaak verward met vlechtende rivieren, die ruwweg eenzelfde geulpatroon vertonen. Tegenwoordig wordt de term 'anastomoserend' uitsluitend gebruikt voor een type rivier met meerdere parallelle geulen (zie figuur 1.1), dat zich vooral onder laag-energetische omstandigheden vormt op alluviale vlaktes. In de wetenschappelijke literatuur worden steeds meer voorbeelden van dit type rivieren beschreven. Hierbij gaat het zowel om bestaande 'actieve' rivieren, als om reconstructies van vroegere rivieren op basis van hun sedimenten. Uit deze literatuur komen zeer verschillende opvattingen naar voren over de ontstaanswijze van anastomoserende rivieren. Dit wordt voor een deel veroorzaakt door een niet-eenduidige definitie van het verschijnsel. Belangrijke geschilpunten zijn de rol van het klimaat en de erosiebasis bij het ontstaan van anastomoserende rivieren. Het onderzoek wordt vooral bemoeilijkt door een gebrek aan kwantitatieve gegevens over hydraulische en sedimentaire processen in anastomoserende rivieren.

In dit proefschrift staan de volgende doelstellingen centraal: (1) het geven van een eenduidige definitie voor anastomoserende rivieren en het rangschikken van dit riviertype ten opzichte van andere riviertypen, (2) het ontwikkelen van een universeel toepasbaar conceptueel model voor de ontstaanswijze van anastomoserende rivieren en (3) het gedetailleerd beschrijven van de afzettingen van huidige en subrecente anastomoserende rivieren om een betere interpretatie van oudere riviersedimenten van vergelijkbare oorsprong mogelijk te maken.

De benadering die in dit proefschrift wordt gevolgd is die van vergelijkend onderzoek van huidige en subrecente anastomoserende rivieren. Onderzocht zijn rivieren die sterk verschillen qua klimatologische en geologische ligging. De belangrijkste bouwstenen van dit proefschrift zijn een uitgebreid overzicht van de bestaande literatuur en veldstudies van respectievelijk: de bovenloop van de Columbia River (Canada), de Binnendelta van de Niger (Mali) en de Rijn-Maas delta (Nederland).

Conclusies uit bestaande literatuur

Uit de literatuur blijkt dat het niet mogelijk is om het anastomoserende riviertype uitsluitend op grond van het geulpatroon te definiëren. Daarom wordt in dit proefschrift een definitie voorgesteld die zowel gebaseerd is op de geomorfologie van de riviervlakte als op het geulpatroon. Deze definitie luidt: *een anastomoserende rivier bestaat uit meerdere onderling verbonden geulen die komgebieden omsluiten* (zie de figuren 2.1 en 2.2). Een rivierdelta, die vaak bestaat uit geulen die zich splitsen, maar die zich stroomafwaarts niet herenigen, wordt in dit proefschrift beschouwd als een bijzonder geval van een anastomoserende rivier. Volgens de voorgestelde definitie kunnen de individuele geulen van een anastomoserend geulenstelsel in theorie 'recht', 'meanderend' en 'vlechtend' zijn. Rechte geulen zijn in dit proefschrift gedefinieerd door middel van de sinuositeitsindex. Dit is de afstand langs de geul gedeeld door de afstand langs het midden van de stroomrug. Wanneer deze index lager is dan 1,3 wordt de geul 'recht' genoemd. Boven deze waarde is sprake van een meanderende geul.

Anastomoserende rivieren bestaan vaak uit rechte geulen. Kenmerkend voor dit type geulen is dat ze zich nauwelijks zijdelings verplaatsen door erosie van de oevers. Dit hangt samen met een gering vermogen van de stroming. Het vermogen wordt bepaald door het product van het verhang en de afvoer van de geul bij hoog water. Een andere belangrijke factor is de resistentie van de oevers tegen erosie, die afhangt van de materiaaleigenschappen: zandige oevers zijn bijvoorbeeld minder resistent dan kleiige oevers.

Anastomoserende rivieren ontstaan door stroomgordelverlegging (avulsie). Het proces van avulsie houdt in dat een nieuwe hoofdgeul gevormd wordt, door water dat dwars over de oeverwal de riviervlakte in stroomt. De oude geul raakt langzaam buiten gebruik ten gunste van de zich insnijdende geul. Avulsies zorgen voor een voortdurende verjonging van het anastomoserende riviersysteem. Een belangrijke oorzaak van avulsies ligt in het feit dat in en dichtbij een geul meer sedimentatie plaatsvindt dan verder weg op de riviervlakte. Hierdoor komen de geul en de oeverwallen steeds hoger boven de rest van de riviervlakte te liggen en neemt de kans op avulsie bij een hoge waterstand toe. Een gering verhang van de rivier is eveneens bevorderlijk voor avulsie.

Wanneer de topografie van de riviervlakte eenmaal 'gunstig' is, kan een avulsie optreden door specifieke omstandigheden zoals extreme hoogwaters en afdamming van de stroming door vastgeraakt drijfhout of ijs. In droge klimaten kan ook duinvorming een geul doen verstoppen. Hoewel elk van de genoemde fenomenen gekoppeld is aan een bepaald klimaat, komen anastomoserende rivieren in allerlei klimaatzones voor.

De afzettingen van anastomoserende rivieren worden gekenmerkt door een groot aandeel van fijnkorrelige kom- en oeverafzettingen. De grovere zandige geulafzettingen komen voor als relatief smalle lintvormige lichamen die onderling verbonden zijn tot netwerken. Deze zandige geulopvullingen zijn volledig omgeven door de fijnere afzettingen. De geulopvullingen vertonen vaak nauwelijks een verticale trend in korrelgrootte. De overgang naar de bovenliggende (fijnere) afzettingen is vaak abrupt. De oeverafzettingen van anastomoserende rivieren zijn vaak dik, terwijl ook crevasse-afzettingen veelvuldig voorkomen. Meerafzettingen en veen (of kool) worden vaak gevonden in samenhang met de afzettingen van anastomoserende rivieren. De genoemde kenmerken komen echter ook bij andere riviertypen voor. Meestal is het dan ook niet mogelijk om aan te tonen dat bepaalde fossiele rivierafzettingen zijn afgezet vanuit meerdere geulen die tegelijk actief waren.

De bovenloop van de Columbia River (West-Canada)
Het onderzochte deel van de Columbia River ligt in een smal dal in het zuidoosten van British Columbia (Canada). Er heerst hier een gematigd vochtig klimaat. De relatief kleine anastomoserende rivier wordt gekenmerkt door zijn ligging in een gebergte. Eerdere studies van de rivier waren vooral gericht op een beschrijving van de afzettingen.

Voor dit onderzoek werden kwantitatieve gegevens verzameld betreffende de hydraulische en sedimentaire processen in de rivier, met het doel het mechanisme achter de veelvuldige avulsies te achterhalen. Alle veldgegevens zijn verzameld in een dwarsprofiel over de volledige breedte van de riviervlakte (figuur 3.4). Deze gegevens omvatten onder meer boringen, ^{14}C-dateringen en metingen van de sedimentatie en de rivierafvoer tijdens het hoogwater van 1994.

Uit het onderzoek blijkt dat hier in de afgelopen 3000 jaar voortdurend sprake is geweest van meerdere gelijktijdig actieve geulen (figuur 3.11). Avulsies vonden gedurende deze periode vaak plaats: negen maal werd in het dwarsprofiel een nieuwe geul gevormd. De levensduur van de geulen was wisselend: van 800 jaar tot 3000 jaar of meer. De oorzaak van deze sterke verschillen in levensduur zou kunnen liggen in het min of meer willekeurig optreden van opstoppingen van vastgeraakt drijfhout (figuur 3.9), die leiden tot avulsie en het buiten gebruik raken van de oude geul.

Uit het onderzoek blijkt dat de gemiddelde sedimentatiesnelheid op de riviervlakte veel lager is dan tot dusverre werd aangenomen. De nieuwe ^{14}C-dateringen aan organische stof in de riviersedimenten wijzen op een gemiddelde sedimentatiesnelheid van 1,7 mm/jaar. De sedimentatiesnelheid is ook bepaald door metingen van de achtergebleven hoeveelheid sediment na het jaarlijks hoogwater in 1994. Gemiddeld bleek 0,8 mm sediment te zijn afgezet. Hierbij moet worden opgemerkt dat het hoogwater van 1994 laag was in vergelijking met andere jaren. Dit verklaart de lagere sedimentatiesnelheid vergeleken met die gemeten op langere termijn door middel van de ^{14}C-dateringen.

De geulen van de anastomoserende Columbia River zijn 'recht' (sinuositeitsindex < 1,3) en liggen ingesloten tussen stabiele, siltige oevers. Het vermogen van de stroming is gering (< 3,4 W/m^2). De oevers worden ook beschermd door de wortels van de dichte vegetatie. Het lage vermogen van stroming is voornamelijk een gevolg van het lage verhang van de riviervlakte (11,5 cm/km).

Van de zes gelijktijdig actieve geulen in het bestudeerde profiel is er één verreweg de belangrijkste, wat betreft de afvoer van water en sediment. Bij maximale geulcapaciteit ('bankfull discharge') neemt deze hoofdgeul 87% van de totale waterafvoer en zelfs 95 % van de totale sedimentafvoer (afgezien van spoeltransport) voor haar rekening.

Het beddingtransport van grof sediment neemt in de lengterichting af. Afzetting van grof materiaal dat niet verder getransporteerd kan worden vindt plaats op de bodem van de geulen. De ophoging van de bedding beperkt de capaciteit van de geulen en zorgt voor frequente overstromingen van de riviervlakte. Zo bevordert dit proces waarschijnlijk het optreden van avulsies.

De zuidelijke Binnendelta van de Niger

De Binnendelta van de Niger in Mali is een uitgestrekte overstromingsvlakte met een anastomoserend geulenstelsel in een tropisch semi-aride klimaat. Geologisch gezien wordt de Binnendelta gekenmerkt door een continentale ligging en een grote afstand tot het brongebied van de Niger. De veldstudie richtte zich op het zuidelijke, meest stroomopwaartse, deel van de Binnendelta, waar de belangrijke zijrivier de Bani zich bij de Niger voegt.

In het gebied was nog niet veel onderzoek gedaan. Er waren weinig gegevens over de opbouw van de ondiepe ondergrond en absolute ouderdomsbepalingen van de sedimenten waren geheel afwezig. In de veldstudie is de ontstaanswijze en sedimentaire opbouw van dit rivierengebied onderzocht. Er is met name aandacht besteed aan de invloed van het klimaat en de sedimentatiesnelheid op de ontwikkeling van de anastomoserende rivier.

Als eerste is het gebied geomorfologisch gekarteerd met behulp van lucht- en satellietfoto's. Gedurende veldbezoeken is deze kartering gecontroleerd en zijn grondboringen uitgevoerd. Ook zijn monsters genomen voor ^{14}C-datering en zijn hydrologische gegevens verzameld. De belangrijkste resultaten van het onderzoek zijn de geomorfologische kaart van het gebied (appendix 2) en de paleogeografische kaartjes die de ontwikkeling van het onderzochte gebied in het Holoceen laten zien (figuur 4.35).

Uit het onderzoek blijkt dat in de Binnendelta betrekkelijk lage gemiddelde sedimentatiesnelheden (0,25 - 0,54 mm/jaar) voorkomen bij een relatief stabiele erosiebasis. In de paleogeografische kaartjes is te zien dat een aantal avulsies is opgetreden tijdens het Holoceen. De belangrijkste oorzaken voor avulsies in dit gebied zijn: (1) een gering verhang van de riviervlakte, (2) onvoldoende afvoercapaciteit van de geulen en (3) enkele processen die sterk klimatologisch bepaald zijn, zoals de verstopping van geulen door duinvorming in droge perioden en aantasting van oeverwallen door winderosie en versnijding door afstromend regenwater. Opmerkelijk is dat de Bani zich stapsgewijs in oostelijke richting verlegd heeft. Dit heeft waarschijnlijk een tektonische oorzaak.

Van grote invloed op de ontwikkeling van de Binnendelta waren de grote duincomplexen die zich gedurende het Ogolien vormden. Deze intens droge periode ging vooraf aan het Holoceen en duurde van 20.000 tot 12.500 BP (= ouderdom in ^{14}C-jaren voor 1950). Deze duincomplexen blokkeerden de loop van de Niger en leidden onder andere tot vorming van het Débo-meer dat stroomafwaarts van het onderzochte gebied ligt. Het niveau van het Débo-meer vormt een lokale erosiebasis. In O-W richting ligt dwars door het onderzochte gebied een langgerekt cordon van grote duinen uit het Ogolien. Vele kleinere, eveneens langgerekte, duinen stammen uit het midden van het Holoceen.

In de zuidelijke Binnendelta komen net als in de Columbia River voornamelijk 'rechte' geulen met een lage sinuositeitsindex voor. De geringe neiging van deze geulen om zich zijdelings te verplaatsen wordt veroorzaakt door het zeer lage vermogen van de stroming (0,9 - 2,1 W/m^2) en de stevige oevers. Dit laatste wordt in de Binnendelta vooral veroorzaakt door de verharding van de sedimenten door sterke uitdroging en de verkitting door ijzeroxides. Omdat de rivierafvoer in de afgelopen duizenden jaren steeds verder afnam, zijn de rivieren enigszins gaan meanderen binnen hun te groot geworden bedding. Hierbij werd een deel van de bedding zijdelings opgevuld (figuur 4.36). Momenteel vindt snelle sedimentatie in de bedding plaats, die op den duur tot avulsie zou kunnen leiden.

De afzettingen in de zuidelijke Binnendelta zijn gekenmerkt door een zeer laag gehalte aan organische stof. Veen is volledig afwezig. Naast duinen, komen eolische afzettingen ook voor als een bijmenging van silt en zand in de kleiige komafzettingen uit het Ogolien. De oorspronkelijke structuur van de oeverwalafzettingen is in het algemeen sterk verstoord door graafactiviteiten van termieten.

De midden- tot laat-holocene Rijn-Maas delta
De Rijn-Maas delta in midden-Nederland omvat een grootschalig anastomoserend geulenstelsel met een kustnabije ligging, ver van het brongebied verwijderd. Het klimaat is gematigd vochtig. Uit eerdere studies is gebleken dat er, volgens de in dit proefschrift gehanteerde definitie, gedurende het hele Holoceen sprake was van een anastomoserend geulenstelsel in de Rijn-Maas delta. In de veldstudie zijn drie, thans niet meer actieve, rivierarmen in het centrale deel van de delta nader onderzocht. Deze paleogeulen konden worden gereconstrueerd aan de hand van boorbeschrijvingen. De paleogeulen en de hieraan gerelateerde afzettingen worden 'fluviatiele systemen' genoemd.

Het doel van deze studie was na te gaan door welke factoren de morfologie van deze paleogeulen werd bepaald. Uit voorgaande onderzoeken is gebleken dat holocene paleogeulen in de Rijn-Maas delta zowel van het 'rechte' als van het 'meanderende' type kunnen zijn. In deze studie zijn de oorzaken van deze verschillen opnieuw geëvalueerd en is met name aandacht besteed aan de rol van de paleo-afvoer. Tot dusverre was deze laatste factor buiten beschouwing gelaten.

De verzamelde gegevens bestaan uit boringen en ^{14}C-dateringen. Daarmee zijn gedetailleerde geologische kaarten en zestien geologische dwarsprofielen gemaakt (appendices 3 en 4). In twee dwarsprofielen zijn ongestoorde sedimentkernen gestoken voor een studie van sedimentaire structuren. De drie fluviatiele systemen vertonen grote verschillen in sedimentaire opbouw.

Het Schoonrewoerdse systeem was actief tussen 4500 en 3800 BP en bestaat in de bovenstroomse helft uit meerdere parallelle zandlichamen (figuur 5.7), die de opvullingen van de paleogeulen representeren. Voorheen werd verondersteld dat het Schoonrewoerdse systeem in twee fasen actief was. Uit deze studie is gebleken dat de afzettingen die de vroeger veronderstelde eerste fase van het Schoonrewoerdse systeem (5350-4700 BP) vertegenwoordigen, in feite afkomstig zijn van het naburige Zijderveldse systeem (figuur 5.20). Het zandlichaam van het Schoonrewoerdse systeem vertoont een spectaculaire stroomafwaartse afname in de breedte/dikte-verhouding van 40 tot 5 (figuur 5.21a). Dit wordt verklaard door veranderende dimensies van de paleogeul en een afname van de mogelijkheid van de paleogeul om zich zijdelings te verplaatsen. Het zandlichaam bestaat uit een vrij homogene opeenvolging van eenheden met scheve gelaagdheid. De gebruikelijke afname in korrelgrootte naar boven is in het zand slecht ontwikkeld. Het Schoonrewoerdse systeem kan worden geïnterpreteerd als het product van een 'gefrustreerde' avulsie. Stroomafwaarts van het punt waar de avulsie plaats vond, kan een ruimtelijke opeenvolging van drie stadia in de ontwikkeling van het paleogeulenstelsel waargenomen worden (figuur 5.22) die kenmerkend lijkt te zijn voor een beginnende avulsie. Hierna heeft het Schoonrewoerdse systeem zich niet verder ontwikkeld. Reconstructies van de paleo-afvoer in een van de dwarsprofielen geven aan dat bij maximale geulcapaciteit ('bankfull discharge') de afvoer van het Schoonrewoerdse systeem waarschijnlijk tussen 265 en 400 m^3/s lag. Het vermogen van de stroming was erg laag, waarschijnlijk tussen 0,7 en 3,1 W/m^2. Hierdoor én door het stevige oevermateriaal (veen en klei) kon de paleogeul niet gaan meanderen en bleef 'recht' van vorm.

Het Hennisdijkse systeem was actief tussen 3800 en 3000 BP. De dimensies van het zandlichaam (breedte/diepte-verhouding is ongeveer 35) en de sedimentaire opbouw ervan geven aan dat de paleogeul zich zijdelings heeft verplaatst. Kleiige laterale accretievlakken zijn aanwezig in het bovenste deel van het zandlichaam (figuren 5.14 en 5.15). Deze hellende kleilaagjes vertegenwoordigen voormalige posities van de oever aan de binnenbocht en wijzen derhalve op zijdelingse verplaatsing van de geul in de richting van de buitenbocht. Opvallend is ook het systematisch voorkomen van dikke pakketten kleiige afzettingen langs de rand van het zandlichaam. Dit zijn geulafzettingen die in het bovenstroomse deel van een buitenbocht gevormd worden. Dit soort afzettingen komt echter alleen voor waar een geul op één of andere manier beperkt is in zijn mogelijkheid om zijn bochten te verruimen (figuur 5.23). Het Hennisdijkse systeem kan dus 'beperkt meanderend' genoemd worden. De paleo-afvoer bij maximale capaciteit van de geul lag waarschijnlijk tussen 380 en 1050 m^3/s. Het vermogen van de stroming was betrekkelijk laag, tussen 5,0 en 10,8 W/m^2, hetgeen slechts beperkt meanderen mogelijk maakte. Een belangrijke factor hierbij was echter ook dat de smalle meandergordel van het Hennisdijkse systeem ingesloten lag tussen dikke pakketten kleiige komafzettingen.

Het Echteldse systeem was actief tussen 2800 en 1900 BP. Op grond van de dimensies van het zandlichaam (de breedte/diepte-verhouding is ongeveer 65) en de sedimentaire opbouw ervan, lijkt er sprake te zijn geweest van een sterk meanderende paleogeul. Gegevens over paleo-afvoer en het vermogen van de stroming ontbreken. Het lijkt aannemelijk dat de ondiepe aanwezigheid van een makkelijk erodeerbare, zandige pleistocene ondergrond, het meanderen van de paleogeul vergemakkelijkte.

Samenvattend kan gesteld worden dat de mate van meanderen van de bestudeerde paleogeulen afdoende verklaard kan worden door het vermogen van de stroming en de erodeerbaarheid van de oevers en ondergrond. Er lijkt geen *directe* relatie te bestaan tussen de gemiddelde sedimentatiesnelheid op de riviervlakte (gestuurd door de snelheid van zeespiegelstijging) en het type paleogeulen (recht of meanderend) in de holocene Rijn-Maas delta. Wel is het aannemelijk dat er een *indirect* verband bestaat tussen de snelheid van zeespiegelstijging en het vermogen van de stroming in de paleogeulen.

Vergelijking van de veldstudies

Bij een vergelijking van de bestudeerde anastomoserende rivieren, kunnen belangrijke overeenkomsten en verschillen worden opgemerkt. Dit leidt tot de volgende conclusies.

Het voorkomen van overvloedige vegetatie en organisch materiaal (zoals veen) is niet altijd van belang voor de ontwikkeling van anastomoserende rivieren. Door grote verschillen in de stijging van de erosiebasis, de aanvoer van sediment, en het klimaat, is het voorkomen van vegetatie en organisch materiaal sterk verschillend tussen de bestudeerde anastomoserende rivieren.

De gemiddelde sedimentatiesnelheid op de bestudeerde riviervlaktes verschilt sterk. Nog grotere verschillen zijn gerapporteerd voor andere anastomoserende rivieren. Op grond hiervan kan geconcludeerd worden dat het voorkomen van anastomoserende rivieren niet noodzakelijkerwijs gekoppeld is aan een hoge sedimentatiesnelheid en een snelle stijging van de erosiebasis.

De geulen van anastomoserende rivieren kunnen van verschillende typen zijn, maar 'rechte' geulen komen het meest voor. In een stabiliteitsdiagram waarin voor individuele geulen het 'potentiële vermogen' is uitgezet tegen de mediane korrelgrootte van het beddingmateriaal, scheidt de populatie van rechte geulen zich duidelijk af van de meanderende en vlechtende geulen (figuur 6.4).

De opvullingen van anastomoserende geulen zijn niet gekenmerkt door een eigen specifieke sedimentaire opeenvolging. Het soort opvulling hangt af van het type geul en de lokale stromingscondities. Verschillende vormen van zijdelingse en verticale opvulling komen voor (figuur 6.5).

In de bestudeerde anastomoserende rivieren worden avulsies veroorzaakt door: (1) de ontwikkeling van de topografie waardoor geulen geleidelijk hoger ten opzichte van de riviervlakte komen te liggen en (2) afname van de afvoercapaciteit in de loop van de tijd. Dit laatste is een gevolg van het onvermogen van anastomoserende geulen om het grove beddingmateriaal te transporteren, waardoor geulen ondieper worden. Vooral in gebieden waar de sedimentatiesnelheid op de riviervlakte laag is en de topografie van de riviervlakte zich dus langzaam ontwikkelt, is de geleidelijke afname van de afvoercapaciteit een belangrijke oorzaak van avulsies.

References

AITKEN, J.F. & S.S. FLINT (1995), The application of high-resolution sequence stratigraphy to fluvial systems: a case study from the Upper Carboniferous Breathitt Group, eastern Kentucky, USA. Sedimentology 42, pp. 3-30.

ALAM, M.M., K.A.W. CROOK & G. TAYLOR (1985), Fluvial herring-bone cross-stratification in a modern tributary mouth bar, Coonamble, New South Wales, Australia. Sedimentology 35, pp. 235-244.

ALEXANDER, J. & M.R. LEEDER (1987), Active tectonic control on alluvial architecture. In: F.G. Ethridge, ed., Recent developments in fluvial sedimentology. Tulsa: Society of Economic Paleontologists and Mineralogists (Special Publication 39), pp. 243-252.

ALIMEN, H. (1987), Evolution du climat et des civilisations depuis 40 000 ans du nord au sud du Sahara occidental. (Premières conceptions confrontées aux données récentes). Bulletin de l'Association française pour l'étude du Quaternaire 4, pp. 215-227.

ALLEN, J.R.L. (1965), A review of the origin and characteristics of recent alluvial sediments. Sedimentology 5, pp. 89-191.

ALLEN, J.R.L. (1970), Studies in fluviatile sedimentation: a comparison of fining-upwards cyclothems, with special reference to coarse-member composition and interpretation. Journal of Sedimentary Petrology 40, pp. 298-323.

ALLEN, J.L.R. (1978), Studies in fluviatile sedimentation: an exploratory quantitative model for the architecture of avulsion-controlled alluvial suites. Sedimentary Geology 21, pp. 129-147.

ASHLEY, G.M. (1990), Classification of large-scale subaqueous bedforms: a new look at an old problem. Journal of Sedimentary Petrology 60, pp. 160-172.

ASLAN, A. (1994), Holocene sedimentation, soil formation, and floodplain evolution of the Mississippi River floodplain, Ferriday, Louisiana. Boulder: Department of Geological Sciences, University of Colorado (Ph.D. thesis).

ASSANI, A.A. & F. PETIT (1995), Log-jam effects on bed-load mobility from experiments conducted in a small gravel-bed forest ditch. Catena 25, pp. 117-126.

ASSELMAN, N.E.M. & H. MIDDELKOOP (1995), Floodplain sedimentation: quantities, patterns and processes. Earth Surface Processes and Landforms 20, pp. 481-499.

BAKER, V.R. (1978), Adjustment of fluvial systems to climate and source terrain in tropical and subtropical environments. In: A.D. Miall, ed., Fluvial Sedimentology. Calgary: Canadian Society of Petroleum Geologists (Memoir 5), pp. 211-230.

BAKKER, J.G.M., T.W. KLEINENDORST & W. GEIRNAERT (1989), Tectonic and sedimentary history of a late Cenozoic intramontane basin (The Pitalito Basin, Colombia). Basin Research 2, pp. 161-187.

BARTH, H.K. (1977), Der geokomplex Sahel: Untersuchungen zur Landschaftsekologie im Sahel Malis als Grundlage agrar- und weidewirtschaftlicher Entwicklungsplanung. Tübingen: Geographischen Instituts der Universität Tübingen (Tübinger Geographischer Studien 71).

B.C. HYDRO (1982), Kootenay River Diversion Project, feasibility study, river regime and hydrology study. Vancouver: Hydroelectric Generation Projects Division.

BEAUDET, G., R. COQUE, P. MICHEL & P. ROGNON (1977), Y-at-il eu capture du Niger? Bulletin de l'Association de Géographes Français 445-446, pp. 215-222.

BEDAUX, R.M.A., T.S. CONSTANDSE-WESTERMANN, L. HACQUEBORD, A.G. LANGE & J.D. VAN DER WAALS (1978), Recherches archéologiques dans le Delta intérieur du Niger. Palaeohistoria 20, pp. 92-220.

BEETS, D.J., L. VAN DER VALK & M.J.F. STIVE (1992), Holocene evolution of the coast of Holland. Marine Geology 103, pp. 423-443.

BERENDSEN, H.J.A. (1982), De genese van het landschap in het zuiden van de provincie Utrecht, een fysisch-geografische studie. Utrecht: Geografisch Instituut, Rijksuniversiteit Utrecht (Utrechtse Geografische Studies 25).

BERENDSEN, H.J.A. (1984a), Quantitative analysis of radiocarbon dates of the perimarine area in the Netherlands. Geologie en Mijnbouw 63, pp. 343-350.

BERENDSEN, H.J.A. (1984b), Problems of lithostratigraphic classification of Holocene deposits in the perimarine area of the Netherlands. Geologie en Mijnbouw 63, pp. 351-354.

BERENDSEN, H.J.A. (1996), Fysisch-geografisch onderzoek; thema's en methoden. Assen: Van Gorcum.

BERENDSEN, H.J.A., E.L.J.H. FAESSEN & H.F.J. KEMPEN (1994), Zand in banen, zanddiepte-attentiekaarten van het Gelders rivierengebied. Arnhem: Provincie Gelderland.

BERENDSEN, H.J.A., W. HOEK & E.A. SCHORN (1995), Late Weichselien and Holocene river channel changes of the rivers Rhine and Meuse in the Netherlands (Land van Maas en Waal). Paläoklimaforschung 14, pp. 151-171.

BERENDSEN, H.J.A., T.E. TÖRNQVIST & H.J.T. WEERTS (1986), Degeologisch-geomorfologische kaart van de Bommelerwaard. In: H.J.A. Berendsen, ed., Het landschap van de Bommelerwaard. Amsterdam/Utrecht: Koninklijk Nederlands Aardrijkskundig Genootschap/Geografisch Instituut Rijksuniversiteit Utrecht (Nederlandse Geografische Studies 10), pp. 15-20.

BIERKENS, M.F.P. & H.J.T. WEERTS (1994), Block hydraulic conductivity of cross-bedded fluvial sediments. Water Resources Research 30, pp. 2665-2678.

BLANCK, J.P. (1968), Notice des cartes géomorphologiques de la vallée du Niger entre Tombouctou et Labbezanga (République du Mali). Strasbourg: Centre de Géographie appliquée, Université Louis Pasteur.

BLANCK, J.P. & J.L.F. TRICART (1990), Quelques effets de la néotectonique sur la géomorphologie dans la région du Delta Central du Niger (Mali). Comptes Rendus de l'Académie des Sciences (Paris) 310, Série II, pp. 309-313.

BLONG, R.J. & R. GILLESPIE (1978), Fluvially transported charcoal gives erroneous ^{14}C ages for recent deposits. Nature 271, pp. 739-741.

BOSCH, J.H.A. & H. KOK (1994), Toelichtingen bij de geologische kaart van Nederland schaal 1:50.000; blad Gorinchem West (38 W). Haarlem: Rijks Geologische Dienst.

BOWLER, J.M., E. STOCKTON & M.J. WALKER (1978), Quaternary stratigraphy of the Darling River near Tilpa, New South Wales. Melbourne: Royal Society of Victoria (Proceedings 90), pp. 79-88.

BRICE, J.C. (1964), Channel patterns and terraces of the Loup Rivers in Nebraska. Washington: U.S. Geological Survey (Professional Paper 422-D).

BRICE, J.C. (1984), Planform properties of meandering rivers. In: C.M. Elliot, ed., River meandering: Proceedings of the conference Rivers '83, New Orleans, Louisiana, October 24-26, 1983. New York: American Society of Civil Engineers, pp. 1-15.

BRIDGE, J.S. (1993), The interaction between channel geometry, water flow, sediment transport and deposition in braided rivers. In: J.L. Best & C.S. Bristow, eds., Braided rivers. London: Geological Society (Special Publication 75), pp. 13-71.

BRIDGE, J.S. & M.R. LEEDER (1979), A simulation model of alluvial stratigraphy. Sedimentology 26, pp. 617-644.

BRIDGE, J.S. & S.D. MACKEY (1993), Revised alluvial stratigraphy model. In: M. Marzo & C. Puigdefábregas, eds., Alluvial sedimentation. Oxford: Blackwell (Special Publication of the International Association of Sedimentologists 17), pp. 319-336.

BRIZGA, S.O. & B.L. FINLAYSON (1990), Channel avulsion and river metamorphosis: the case of the Thomson river, Victoria, Australia. Earth Surface Processes and Landforms 15, pp. 391-404.

BROWN, A.G. (1987), Holocene floodplain sedimentation and channel response of the lower River Severn, United Kingdom. Zeitschrift für Geomorphologie 32, pp. 293-310.

BROWNLIE, W.R. (1983), Flow depth in sand-bed channels. Journal of Hydraulic Engineering 109, pp. 959-990.

BRYANT, M., P. FALK & C. PAOLA (1995), Experimental study of avulsion frequency and rate of deposition. Geology 23, pp. 365-368.

BURNETT, A.W. & S.A. SCHUMM (1983), Alluvial river response to neotectonic deformation in Louisiana and Mississippi. Science 222, pp. 49-50.

CAIRNCROSS, B., I.G. STANISTREET, T.S. McCARTHY, W.N. ELLERY, K. ELLERY & T.S.A. GROBICKI (1988), Palaeochannels (stone-rolls) in coal seams: modern analogues from fluvial deposits of the Okavango Delta, Botswana, southern Africa. Sedimentary Geology 57, pp. 107-118.

CARSON, M.A. (1984a), The meandering-braided river threshold: a reappraisal. Journal of Hydrology 73, pp. 315-334.

CARSON, M.A. (1984b), Observations on the meandering-braided river transition, The Canterbury Plains, New Zealand: part two. New Zealand Geographer 40, pp. 89-99.

CHANG, H.H. (1979), Minimum stream power and river channel patterns. Journal of Hydrology 41, pp. 303-327.

CHURCH, M. (1983), Pattern of instability in a wandering gravel bed channel. In: J.D. Collinson & J. Lewin, eds., Modern and ancient fluvial systems. Oxford: Blackwell (Special Publication of the International Association of Sedimentologists 6), pp. 169-180.

COLEMAN, J.M. (1969), Brahmaputra River: channel processes and sedimentation. Sedimentary Geology 3, pp. 129-239.

COLLINSON, J.D. (1978), Vertical sequence and sand body shape in alluvial sequences. In: A.D. Miall, ed., Fluvial sedimentology. Calgary: Canadian Society of Petroleum Geologists (Memoir 5), pp. 577-586.

COLLINSON, J.D. (1986), Alluvial sediments. In: H.G. Reading, ed., Sedimentary environments and facies. Oxford: Blackwell, pp. 20-62.

CURRIE, P.J., G.C. NADON & M.G. LOCKLEY (1991), Dinosaur footprints with skin impressions from the Cretaceous of Alberta and Colorado. Canadian Journal of Earth Sciences 28, pp. 102-115.

DE BOER, T.A. & L.J. PONS (1960), Bodem en grasland in de Vijfheerenlanden. Wageningen: Centrum voor landbouwpublikaties en landbouwdocumentatie (Pudoc) (Verslagen van landbouwkundige onderzoekingen 66.6).

DE GROOT, Th.A.M. & W. DE GANS (1996), Facies variations and sea-level-rise response in the lowermost Rhine/Meuse area during the last 15000 years (the Netherlands). In: D.J. Beets, M.M. Fischer & W. De Gans, eds., Coastal studies on the Holocene of the Netherlands. Haarlem: Rijks Geologische Dienst (Mededelingen Rijks Geologische Dienst 57), pp. 229-250.

DE JONG, J. (1970-1971), Pollen and C14 analysis of Holocene deposits in Zijderveld and environs. Berichten van de Rijksdienst voor het Oudheidkundig Bodemonderzoek 20-21, pp. 75-88.

DEMBELÉ, M., A.M. SCHMIDT & J.D. VAN DER WAALS (1993), Prospection de sites archéologiques dans le delta intérieur du Niger. In: Vallées du Niger. (Catalogue exposition "Vallées du Niger") Paris: Editions de la Réunion des Musées Nationaux, pp. 218-232.

DNGM (1987), Ressources Minérales du Mali. Bamako: Direction Nationale de la Géologie et des Mines.

DOPPERT, J.W.Chr., G.H.J. RUEGG, C.J. VAN STAALDUINEN, W.H. ZAGWIJN & J.G. ZANDSTRA (1975), Formaties van het Kwartair en Boven-Tertiair in Nederland. In: W.H. Zagwijn & C.J. Van Staalduinen, eds., Toelichting bij geologische overzichtskaarten van Nederland. Haarlem: Rijks Geologische Dienst, pp. 11-56.

DUMONT, J.F. (1994), Neotectonics of the Amazon headwaters. In: S.A. Schumm & B.R. Winkley, eds., The variability of large alluvial rivers. New York: American Society of Civil Engineers, pp. 103-113.

DURAND, A. (1982), Oscillations of Lake Chad over the past 50.000 years: new data and new hypothesis. Palaeogeography, Palaeoclimatology, Palaeoecology 39, pp. 37-53.

EBERTH, D.A. & A.D. MIALL (1991), Stratigraphy, sedimentology and evolution of a vertebrate-bearing, braided to anastomosing fluvial system, Cutler Formation (Permian-Pennsylvanian), north-central New Mexico. Sedimentary Geology 72, pp. 225-252.

ELLIOT, T. (1974), Interdistributary bay sequences and their genesis. Sedimentology 21, pp. 611-622.

ENGELUND, F. & E. HANSEN (1967), A monograph on sediment transport in alluvial streams. Copenhagen: Teknisk Forlag.

FERGUSON, R.I. (1981), Channel form and channel changes. In: J. Lewin, ed., British Rivers. London: Allen & Unwin, pp. 90-211.

FERGUSON, R.I. (1987), Hydraulic and sedimentary controls of channel pattern. In: K.S. Richards, ed., River channels; environment and process. Oxford: Blackwell (Institute of British Geographers Special Publication 18), pp. 129-155.

FISK, H.N. (1944), Geological investigation of the alluvial valley of the lower Mississippi. Vicksburg: Mississippi River Commission, U.S. Army Corps of Engineers.

FLORES, R.M. & J.H. HANLEY, (1984), Anastomosed and associated coal-bearing fluvial deposits: Upper Tongue River Member, Palaeocene Fort Union Formation, northern Powder River Basin, Wyoming, U.S.A. In: R.A. Rahmani & R.M. Flores, eds., Sedimentology of coal and coal-bearing sequences. Oxford: Blackwell (Special Publications of the International Association of Sedimentologists 7), pp. 85-103.

FLORES, R.M. & C.L. PILLMORE (1987), Tectonic control on alluvial paleoarchitecture of the Cretaceous and Tertiary Raton Basin, Colorado and New Mexico. In: F.G. Ethridge, R.M. Flores & M.D. Harvey, eds., Recent developments in fluvial sedimentology. Tulsa: Society of Economic Paleontologists and Mineralogists (Special Publication 39), pp. 311-320.

FOLK, R.L. & W.C. WARD (1957), Brazos River bar: a study in the significance of grain size parameters. Journal of Sedimentary Petrology 27, pp. 3-26.

FRIEND, P.F. (1983), Towards the field classification of alluvial architecture or sequence. In: J.D. Collinson and J. Lewin, eds., Modern and ancient fluvial systems. Oxford: Blackwell (Special Publication of the International Association of Sedimentologists 6), pp. 345-354.

FRIEND, P.F., M.J. SLATER & R.C. WILLIAMS (1979), Vertical and lateral building of river sandstone bodies, Ebro Basin, Spain. Journal of the Geological Society of London 136, pp. 39-46.

FURON, R. (1929), L'ancien delta du Niger. Revue de Géographie physique et de Géologie dynamique 2, pp. 265-274.

GALAY, V.J., TUTT, D.B. & R. KELLERHALS (1984), The meandering distributary channels of the upper Columbia River. In: C.M. Elliot, ed., River meandering: Proceedings of the conference Rivers '83, New Orleans, Louisiana, October 24-26, 1983. New York: American Society of Civil Engineers, pp. 113-125.

GALLAIS, J. (1967), Le Delta intérieur du Niger et ses bordures; étude morphologique. Paris: Centre National de la Recherche Scientifique (Mémoires et documents, nouvelle série 3).

GALLOWAY, W.E. & D.K. HOBDAY (1983), Terrigenous clastic depositional systems; applications to petroleum, coal and uranium exploration. New York: Springer.

GARNER, H.F. (1959), Interpretation of globally distributed anastomosing channel drainages. Geological Society of America Bulletin 70, pp. 1607.

GARNER, H.F. (1967), Rivers in the making. Scientific American 216, pp. 84-94.

GASSE, F., R. TÉHET, A. DURAND, E. GIBERT & J. FONTES (1990), The arid-humid transition in the Sahara and the Sahel during the last deglaciation. Nature 346, pp. 141-146.

GEOLOGICAL SURVEY OF CANADA (1972), Map 1326A; geology; Lardeau (east half), British Columbia; scale 1:250,000. Ottawa: Geological Survey of Canada.

GEOLOGICAL SURVEY OF CANADA (1979a), Map 1501A; geology; McMurdo (east half), British Columbia; scale 1:50,000. Ottawa: Geological Survey of Canada.

GEOLOGICAL SURVEY OF CANADA (1979b), Map 1502A; geology; McMurdo (west half); British Columbia; scale 1:50,000. Ottawa: Geological Survey of Canada.

GEOLOGICAL SURVEY OF CANADA (1980), Diagrammatic structure sections (...) to accompany Map 1501A, McMurdo (east half) and Map 1502A, McMurdo (west half); scale 50,000. Ottawa: Geological Survey of Canada.

GIBLING, M.R., G.R. NANSON & J.C. MAROULIS (1998), Anastomosing river sedimentation in the Channel Country of central Australia. Sedimentology 45, pp. 595-619.

GIBLING, M.R. & B.R. RUST (1990), Ribbon sandstones in the Pennsylvanian Waddens Cove Formation, Sydney Basin, Atlantic Canada: the influence of siliceous duricrusts on channel-body geometry. Sedimentology 37, pp. 45-65.

GOHAIN, K. & G. PARKASH (1990), Morphology of the Kosi megafan. In: A.H. Rachocki & M. Church, eds., Alluvial fans: a field approach. Chichester: Wiley, pp. 151-178.

GOUDIE, A.S. (1988), The geomorphological role of termites and earthworms in the tropics. In: H.A. Viles, ed., Biogeomorphology. Oxford: Blackwell, pp. 166-192.

GOLE C.V. & S.V. CHITALE (1966), Inland delta building activity of Kosi River. Journal of the Hydraulics Division, Proceedings of the American Society of Civil Engineers 92, pp. 111-126.

GROVE, A.T. & A. WARREN (1968), Quaternary landforms and climate on the south side of the Sahara. Geographical Journal 134, pp. 194-208.

HAGEMAN, B.P. (1969), Development of the western part of the Netherlands during the Holocene. Geologie en Mijnbouw 48, pp. 373-388.

HAGEMAN, B.P. (1972), Sedimentation in the lowest part of river systems in relation to post-glacial sea level rise in The Netherlands. Proceedings of the 24th International Geological Congress, Montréal, 1972, Section 12. Montréal: 24th International Geological Congress, pp. 37-47.

HARE, F.K. & M.K. THOMAS (1974), Climate Canada. Toronto: Wiley.

HARWOOD, K. & A.G. BROWN (1993), Fluvial processes in a forested anastomosing river: flood partitioning and changing flow patterns. Earth Surface Processes and Landforms 18, pp. 741-748.

HELLER, P.L. & C. PAOLA (1996), Downstream changes in alluvial architecture: an exploration of controls on channel-stacking patterns. Journal of Sedimentary Research 66, pp. 297-306.

HICKIN, E.J. (1979), Concave-bank benches on the Squamish River, British Columbia. Canadian Journal of Earth Sciences 16, pp. 200-203.

HICKIN, E.J. (1984), Vegetation and river channel dynamics. Canadian Geographer 28, pp. 111-126.

HICKIN, E.J. (1986), Concave-bank benches in the floodplains of Muskwa and Fort Nelson rivers, British Columbia. The Canadian Geographer 30, pp. 111-122.

HICKIN, E.J. (1993), Fluvial facies models: a review of Canadian research. Progress in Physical Geography 17, pp. 205-222.

HOEFS, J. (1980), Stable isotope geochemistry. Berlin: Springer.

HOPKINS, J.C., S.W. HERMANSON & D.C. LAWTON (1982), Morphology of channels and channel-sand bodies in the glauconitic sandstone member (Upper Mannville), Little Bow area, Alberta. Bulletin of Canadian Petroleum Geology 30, pp. 274-285.

HUANG, H.Q. & G.C. NANSON (1997), Vegetation and channel variation; a case study of four small streams in southeastern Australia. Geomorphology 18, pp. 237-249.

IGN (1963), Carte internationale du monde, Feuille Tombouctou. Paris: Institut Géographique National.

IGN (1967), Carte internationale du monde, Feuille Ouagadougou. Paris: Institut Géographique National.

IWACO/DELFT HYDRAULICS (1996), Ensablement du fleuve Niger; rapport de la mission d'identification. Rotterdam/Delft: IWACO B.V. Division Projets Internationaux / Delft Hydraulics (Rapport 57.00192).

JACKSON, R.G. (1981), Sedimentology of muddy fine-grained channel deposits in meandering streams of the American Middle West. Journal of Sedimentary Petrology 51, pp. 1169-1192.

JACOBBERGER, P.A. (1987), Geomorphology of the upper Inland Niger Delta. Journal of Arid Environments 13, pp. 95-112.

JACOBBERGER, P.A. (1988a), Drought-related changes to geomorphologic processes in central Mali. Geological Society of America Bulletin 100, pp. 351-361.

JACOBBERGER, P.A. (1988b), Mapping abandoned river channels in Mali through directional filtering of Thematic Mapper data. Remote Sensing of Environment 26, pp. 161-170.

JELGERSMA, S. (1980), Late Cenozoic sea level changes in the Netherlands and the adjacent North Sea basin. In: N.-A. Mörner, ed., Earth rheology, isostasy and eustasy. Chichester: Wiley, pp. 435-447.

JOHNSON, E.A. & F.W. PIERCE (1990), Variations in fluvial deposition on an alluvial plain: an example from the Tongue River Member of the Fort Union Formation (Paleocene), southeastern Powder River Basin, Wyoming, U.S.A. Sedimentary Geology 69, pp. 21-36.

KAMATÉ, C. (1980), Climat. In: M. Traoré, ed., Atlas du Mali. Paris: Editions Jeune Afrique, pp. 14-17.

KEÏTA, M. (1980), Géologie. In: M. Traoré, ed., Atlas du Mali. Paris: Editions Jeune Afrique, pp. 10-11.

KEVRAN, L. (1959), Le cours fossile du Niger. Notre Sahara 10, pp. 53-58.

KELLER, E.A. & A. BROOKES (1984), Consideration of meandering in channelization projects: selected observations and judgements. In: C.M. Elliot, ed., River meandering: Proceedings of the conference Rivers '83, New Orleans, Louisiana, October 24-26, 1983. New York: American Society of Civil Engineers, pp. 384-397.

KING, W.A. & I.P. MARTINI (1984), Morphology and recent sediments of the lower anastomosing reaches of the Attawapiskat River, James Bay, Ontario, Canada. Sedimentary Geology 37, pp. 295-320.

KIRSCHBAUM, M.A. & P.J. McCABE (1992), Controls on the accumulation of coal and on the development of anastomosed fluvial systems in the Cretaceous Dakota Formation of southern Utah. Sedimentology 39, pp. 581-598.

KNIGHT, M.J. (1975), Recent crevassing of the Erap River, Papua New Guinea. Australian Geographical Studies 13, pp. 77-84.

KNIGHTON, A.D. (1984), Fluvial forms and processes. London: Arnold.

KNIGHTON, A.D. (1987), River channel adjustment; the downstream dimension. In: K.S. Richards, ed., River channels; environment and process. Oxford: Blackwell (Institute of British Geographers Special Publication 18), pp. 98-128.

KNIGHTON, A.D. & G.C. NANSON (1993), Anastomosis and the continuum of channel pattern. Earth Surface Processes and Landforms 18, pp. 613-625.

KOCURECK, G.A. (1996), Desert aeolian systems. In: H.G. Reading, ed., Sedimentary Environments: processes, facies and stratigraphy. Oxford: Blackwell, pp. 125-153.

KONERT M. & J. VANDENBERGHE (1997), Comparison of laser grain size analysis with pipette and sieve analysis: a solution for the underestimation of the clay fraction. Sedimentology 44, pp. 523-535.

KRUIT, C. (1955), Sediments of the Rhône Delta; grain size and microfauna. Groningen: Rijksuniversiteit Groningen (Ph.D. thesis)

KUMAR, R. & S.K. TANDON (1985), Sedimentology of Plio-Pleistocene late orogenic deposits associated with intraplate subduction, the Upper Siwalik Subgroup of a part of Panjab sub-Himalaya, India. Sedimentary Geology 42, pp. 105-158.

LANGFORD, R.P. (1989), Fluvial-aeolian interactions: part I, modern systems. Sedimentology 36, pp. 1023-1035.

LE BLANC SMITH, G. & K.A. ERIKSSON (1979), A fluvioglacial and glaciolacustrine deltaic depositional model for Permo-Carboniferous coals of the northeastern Karoo basin, South Africa. Palaeogeography, Palaeoclimatology, Palaeoecology 27, pp. 67-84.

LECCE, S.A. (1997), Spatial patterns of historical overbank sedimentation and floodplain evolution, Blue River, Wisconsin. Geomorphology 18, pp. 265-277.

LEEDER, M.R. (1973), Fluviatile fining-upward cycles and the magnitude of palaeochannels. Geological Magazine 110, pp. 265-276.

LEEDER, M.R. (1978), A quantitative stratigraphic model for alluvium, with special reference to channel deposit density and interconnectedness. In: A.D. Miall, ed., Fluvial Sedimentology. Calgary: Canadian Society for Petroleum Geologists (Memoir 5), pp. 587-596.

LEOPOLD, L.B. & M.G. WOLMAN (1957), River channel patterns: braided, meandering and straight. Washington: U.S. Geological Survey (Professional Paper 282-B).

LÉZINE, A.M. (1989a), Late Quaternary vegetation and climate of the Sahel. Quaternary Research 32, pp. 317-334.

LÉZINE, A.M. (1989b), Le Sahel: 20.000 ans d'histoire de la végétation. Bulletin de la Société géologique de France 5, pp. 35-42.

LÉZINE, A.M. & J. CASANOVA (1989), Pollen and hydrological evidence for the interpretation of past climates in tropical west Africa during the Holocene. Quaternary Science Reviews 8, pp. 45-55.

LOCKING, T. (1983), Hydrology and sediment transport in an anastomosing reach of the upper Colombia River, B.C. M.Sc.thesis, Calgary: Department of Geography, University of Calgary. (M.Sc. thesis)

LOUWE KOOIJMANS, L.P. (1974), The Rhine/Meuse delta; four studies on its prehistoric occupation and Holocene geology. Leiden: Instituut voor Prehistorie, Rijksuniversiteit Leiden (Analecta Praehistorica Leidensia 7).

LUNDEGARD, P.D. & N.D. SAMUELS (1980), Field classification of fine-grained sedimentary rocks. Journal of Sedimentary Petrology 50, pp. 781-786.

MACK, G.H. & M.R. LEEDER (1998), Channel shifting of the Rio Grande, southern Rio Grande rift: implications for alluvial stratigraphic models. Sedimentary Geology 117, pp. 207-219.

MACKEY, S.D. & J.S. BRIDGE (1995), Three-dimensional model of alluvial stratigraphy: theory and application. Journal of Sedimentary Research B65, pp. 7-31.

MACKIN, J.H. (1948), Concept of a graded river. Geological Society of America Bulletin 59, pp. 463-511.

MAKASKE, B. (1994), Un bassin fluvial entre forêt équatoriale et désert. In: R.M.A. Bedaux & J.D. van der Waals, ed., Djenné; une ville millénaire au Mali. Leiden/Gent: Rijksmuseum voor Volkenkunde/Snoeck Ducajou, pp. 34-40.

MAKASKE, B. & R.L. NAP (1995), A transition from a braided to a meandering channel facies, showing inclined heterolithic stratification (Late Weichselian, central Netherlands). Geologie en Mijnbouw 74, pp. 1-8.

MAKASKE, B. & M. TERLIEN (1996), Le développement géomorphologique du Delta intérieur du Niger méridionale. Utrecht: Interuniversitair Centrum voor Geo-ecologisch Onderzoek (ICG)/Vakgroep Fysische Geografie, Universiteit Utrecht (ICG-rapport 96/2).

MALEY, J. (1982), Dust, clouds, rain types and climatic variations in tropical north Africa. Quaternary Research 18, pp. 1-16.

MANSIKKANIEMI, H. (1985), Sedimentation and water quality in the flood basin of the river Kyrönjoki in Finland. Fennia 163, pp. 155-194.

McCABE, P.J. (1984), Depositional environments of coal and coal-bearing strata. In: R.A. Rahmani & R.M. Flores, eds., Sedimentology of coal and coal-bearing sequences. Oxford: Blackwell (Special Publications of the International Association of Sedimentologists 7), pp. 13-42.

McCARTHY, T.S. (1993), The great inland deltas of Africa. Journal of African Earth Sciences 17, pp. 275-291.

McCARTHY, T.S., W.N. ELLERY & J.G. STANISTREET (1992), Avulsion mechanisms on the Okavango fan, Botswana: the control of a fluvial system by vegetation. Sedimentology 39, pp. 779-795.

McINTOSH, R.J. (1983), Floodplain geomorphology and human occupation of the upper Inland Delta of the Niger. Geographical Journal 149, pp. 182-201.

McINTOSH, R.J. (1993), The pulse model: genesis and accomodation of specialization in the Middle Niger. Journal of African History 34, pp. 181-220.

McINTOSH, R.J. & S.K. McINTOSH (1981), The Inland Delta before the empire of Mali: evidence from Jenne-jeno. Journal of African History 22, pp. 1-22.

McINTOSH, S.K. & R.J. McINTOSH (1980), Prehistoric investigations in the region of Jenne, Mali. Oxford: British Archaeological Reports (Cambridge Monographs in African Archaeology 2).

McMANUS, J. (1988), Grain size determination and interpretation. In: M.E. Tucker, ed., Techniques in sedimentology. Oxford: Blackwell, pp. 63-85.

McTAINSH, G.H., NICKLING, W.G. & A.W. LYNCH (1997), Dust deposition and particle size in Mali, West-Africa. Catena 29, pp. 307-322.

MERTES, L.A.K. (1994), Rates of flood-plain sedimentation onthe central Amazon River. Geology 22, pp. 171-174.

MIALL, A.D. (1985), Architectural-element analysis: a new method of facies analysis applied to fluvial deposits. Earth-Science Reviews 22, pp. 261-308.

MIALL, A.D. (1992), Alluvial deposits. In: R.G. Walker & N.P. James, eds., Facies Models; response to sea level change. St. John's: Geological Association of Canada, pp. 119-142.

MIALL, A.D. (1996), The geology of fluvial deposits; sedimentary facies, basin analysis and petroleum geology. Berlin: Springer.

MIDDELKOOP, H. (1997), Embanked floodplains in the Netherlands; geomorphological evolution over various time scales. Utrecht: Koninklijk Nederlands Aardrijkskundig Genootschap/Faculteit Ruimtelijke Wetenschappen, Universiteit Utrecht (Nederlandse Geografische Studies 224).

MIKE, K. (1975), Utilization of the analysis of ancient river beds for the detection of Holocene crustal movements. Tectonophysics 29, pp. 359-368.

MILLER, J.R. (1991), Development of anastomosing channels in south-central Indiana. Geomorphology 4, pp. 221 - 229.

MJØS, R. & E. PRESTHOLM (1993), The geometry and organization of fluviodeltaic channel sandstones in the Jurassic Saltwick Formation, Yorkshire, England. Sedimentology 40, pp. 919-935.

MOLLARD, J.D. (1973), Airphoto interpretation of fluvial features. In: Fluvial processes and sedimentation. Proceedings of hydrology symposium held at the University of Alberta, Edmonton, May 8-9, 1973. Ottawa: National Research Council of Canada, pp. 341-380.

MOOK, W.G. & H.J. STREURMAN (1983), Physical and chemical aspects of radiocarbon dating. In: W.G. Mook & H.T. Waterbolk. eds., Proceedings of the first international symposium ^{14}C and archeology, Groningen, 1981. Strasbourg: Groupe européen d'études pour les techniques physiques, chimiques, biologique et mathématiques appliquées à l'archéologie, Conseil de l'Europe (PACT 8), pp. 31-55.

MULDERS, M.A. (1969), The arid soils of the Balikh Basin (Syria). Utrecht: Rijksuniversiteit Utrecht. (Ph.D. thesis)

NADON, G.C. (1988), Tectonic controls on sedimentation within a foreland basin: the Bearpaw, Blood Reserve and St. Mary River Formations, southwestern Alberta. Canadian Society of Petroleum Geologists' field guide to Sequences, Stratigraphy, Sedimentology: Surface and Subsurface Technical Meeting, September 14-16, Calgary, Alberta. Calgary: Canadian Society of Petroleum Geologists.

NADON, G.C. (1994), The genesis and recognition of anastomosed fluvial deposits: data from the St. Mary River Formation, southwestern Alberta, Canada. Journal of Sedimentary Research B64, pp. 451-463.

NANSON, G.C. (1980), Point bar and floodplain formation of the meandering Beatton River, northeastern British Columbia, Canada. Sedimentology 27, pp. 3-29.

NANSON, G.C., X.Y. CHEN & D.M. PRICE (1995), Aeolian and fluvial evidence of changing climate and wind patterns during the past 100 ka in the western Simpson Desert, Australia. Palaeogeography, Palaeoclimatology, Palaeoecology 113, pp. 87-102.

NANSON, G.C. & J.C. CROKE (1992), A genetic classification of floodplains. Geomorphology 4, pp. 459-486.

NANSON, G.C., T.J. EAST & R.G. ROBERTS (1993), Quaternary stratigraphy, geochronology and evolution of the Magela Creek catchment in the monsoon tropics of northern Australia. Sedimentary Geology 83, pp. 277-302.

NANSON, G.C. & H.Q. HUANG (in press), Anabranching rivers: divided efficiency leading to fluvial diversity. In: A. Miller & A. Gupta, eds., Varieties of fluvial form. New York: Wiley.

NANSON, G.C. & A.D. KNIGHTON (1996), Anabranching rivers: their cause, character and classification. Earth Surface Processes and Landforms 21, pp. 217-239.

NANSON, G.C. & K.J. PAGE (1983), Lateral accretion of fine-grained concave benches on meandering rivers. In: J. Collinson & J. Lewin eds., Modern and ancient fluvial systems. Oxford: Blackwell (Special Publication of the International Association of Sedimentologists 6), pp. 133-143.

NANSON, G.C., B.R. RUST & G. TAYLOR (1986), Coexistent mud braids and anastomosing channels in an arid-zone river: Cooper Creek, Central Australia. Geology 14, pp. 175-178.

NEDECO (1959), River studies and recommendations on improvement of Niger and Benue. Amsterdam: North-Holland.

NEDERLANDS NORMALISATIE INSTITUUT (1989), NEN 5104: Geotechniek; classificatie van onverharde grondmonsters. Delft: Nederlands Normalisatie-instituut.

NELLER, R.J., J.S. SALO, & M.E. RÄSÄNEN (1992), On the formation of blocked valley lakes by channel avulsion in upper Amazon foreland basins. Zeitschrift für Geomorphologie 63, pp. 401-411.

NORDSETH, K. (1973), Floodplain construction on a braided river; the islands of Koppangöyene on the river Glomma. Norsk geografisk Tidsskrift 27, pp. 109-126.

OELE, E., W. APON, M.M. FISCHER, R. HOOGENDOORN, C.S. MESDAG, E.F.J. DE MULDER, B. OVERZEE, A. SESÖREN & W.E. WESTERHOFF (1983), Surveying The

Netherlands: sampling techniques, maps and their application. Geologie en Mijnbouw 62, pp. 355-372.

ORSTOM (1970a), Monographie hydrologique du bassin du Niger;partie 1: le Niger supérieur et le Bani. Paris: Office de la Recherche Scientifique et Technique Outre-Mer.

ORSTOM (1970b), Monographie hydrologique du bassin du Niger, Partie 2: La cuvette lacustre. Paris: Office de la Recherche Scientifique et Technique Outre-Mer.

OUCHI, S. (1985), Response of alluvial rivers to slow active tectonic movement. Geological Society of America Bulletin 96, pp. 504-515.

PAGE, K.J. (1983), Concave bench evolution and sedimentation on the Manawatu River, New Zealand. New Zealand Geographer 39, pp. 59-63.

PAGE, K.J. & G.C. NANSON (1982), Concave-bank benches and associated floodplain formation. Earth Surface Processes and Landforms 7, pp. 529-543.

PAGE, K.J. & G.C. NANSON (1996), Stratigraphic architecture resulting from Late Quaternary evolution of the Riverine Plain, south-eastern Australia. Sedimentology 43, pp. 927-945.

PALAUSI, G. (1955), Au sujet du Niger fossile dans la région de Tombouctou. Revue de Géomorphologie dynamique 6, pp. 217-218.

PENG, S. (1990), Fundamental characteristics of the anastomosing fluvial system on complex deltaic plain. Chinese Science Bulletin 35, pp. 835-839.

PESSENDA, L.C.R., R. AVARENA, A.J. MELFI, E.C.C. TELLES, R. BOULET, E.P.E. VALENCIA & M. TOMAZELLO (1996a), The use of carbon isotopes (^{13}C, ^{14}C) in soil to evaluate vegetation changes during the Holocene in Central Brazil. Radiocarbon 38, pp. 191-201.

PESSENDA, L.C.R., E.P.E. VALENCIA, P.B. CAMARGO, E.C.C. TELLES, L.A. MARTINELLI, C.C. CERRI, R. ARAVENA & K. ROZANSKI (1996b), Natural radiocarbon measurements in Brazilian soils developed on basic rocks. Radiocarbon 38, pp. 203-208.

PETIT-MAIRE, N. (1988), Climate change and man in the Sahara. In: J. Bower & D. Lubell, eds., Prehistoric cultures and environments in the Late Quaternary of Africa. Oxford: British Archaeology Reports (Cambridge Monographs in African Archaeology 26), pp. 19-42.

PETIT-MAIRE, N., D. COMMELIN, J. FABRE & M. FONTUGNE (1990), First evidence for Holocene rainfall in the Tanezrouft hyperdesert and its margins. Palaeogeography, Palaeoclimatology, Palaeoecology 79, pp. 333-338.

PONS, L.J. (1957), De geologie, de bodemvorming en de waterstaatkundige ontwikkeling van het Land van Maas en Waal en een gedeelte van het Rijk van Nijmegen. Wageningen: Stichting voor Bodemkartering (Mededelingen van de Stichting voor Bodemkartering, Bodemkundige Studies 3).

POSTMA, R., M.J.J. KERKHOFS, G.B.M. PEDROLI & J.G.M. RADEMAKERS (1996), Een stroom natuur. Watersysteemverkenningen 1996. Een analyse van de problematiek in aquatisch milieu. Natuurstreefbeelden voor Rijn en Maas. Arnhem: RIZA/Delft Hydraulics, Zeist: Grontmij.

PUTNAM, P.E. (1982), Aspects of petroleum geology of the Lloydminster heavy oil fields, Alberta and Saskatchewan. Bulletin of Canadian Petroleum Geology 30, pp. 81-111.

PUTNAM, P.E. (1983), Fluvial deposits and hydrocarbon accumulations: examples from the Lloydminster area, Canada. In: J.D. Collinson & J. Lewin, eds., Modern and ancient fluvial systems. Oxford: Blackwell (Special Publication of the International Association of Sedimentologists 6), pp. 517-532.

PUTNAM, P.E. (1993), A multidisciplinary analysis of Belly River-Brazeau (Campanian) fluvial channel reservoirs in west-central Alberta, Canada. Bulletin of Canadian Petroleum Geology 41, pp. 186-217.

PUTNAM, P.E. & T.A. OLIVER (1980), Stratigraphic traps in channel sandstones in the Upper Mannville (Albian) of east-central Alberta. Bulletin of Canadian Petroleum Geology 28, pp. 489-508.

READING, H.G., ed. (1986), Sedimentary environments and facies. Oxford: Blackwell.

RECLUS, E. (1887), Nouvelle géographie universelle, t. XII; l'Afrique occidentale. Paris: Hachette.

REINECK, H.-E. & I.B. SINGH (1980), Depositional sedimentary environments. Berlin: Springer.

RICHARDS, K.S. (1982), Rivers; form and process in alluvial channels. London: Methuen.

RIJKSWATERSTAAT (1996), Jaarboek monitoring rijkswateren 1994. Den Haag: Rijkswaterstaat.

RIJNBEEK, J. (1996), Togué en Sabé, een fysisch-geografisch onderzoek naar opvallende heuvels in de zuidelijke Binnendelta van de Niger, Mali. Utrecht: Vakgroep Fysische Geografie, Universiteit Utrecht.

RILEY, S.J. (1975), The channel shape-grain size relation in eastern Australia and some paleohydrologic implications. Sedimentary Geology 14, pp. 253-258.

RILEY, S.J. & G. TAYLOR (1978), The geomorphology of the Upper Darling River System with special reference to the present fluvial system. Melbourne: Royal Society of Victoria (Proceedings 90), pp. 89-102.

RISER, J. & N. PETIT-MAIRE (1986), Paléohydrographie du bassin d'Araouane à l'Holocène. Revue de Géologie dynamique et de Géographie physique 27, pp. 205-212.

ROGNON, P. (1976), Essai d'interprétation des variations climatiques au Sahara depuis 40.000 ans. Revue de Géographie physique et de Géologie dynamique 18, pp. 251-282.

ROGNON, P. (1993), L'évolution des vallées du Niger depuis 20000 ans. In: Vallées du Niger. (Catalogue exposition "Vallées du Niger") Paris: Editions de la Réunion des Musées Nationaux, pp. 40-62.

RUSSELL, R.J. (1954), Alluvial morphology of Anatolian rivers. Annals of the Association of American Geographers 44, pp. 363-391.

RUST, B.R. (1978), A classification of alluvial channel systems. In: A.D. Miall, ed., Fluvial Sedimentology. Calgary: Canadian Society of Petroleum Geologists (Memoir 5), pp. 187-198.

RUST, B.R. (1981), Sedimentation in an arid-zone anastomosing fluvial system: Cooper's Creek, Central Australia. Journal of Sedimentary Petrology 51, pp. 745-755.

RUST, B.R., M.R. GIBLING & A.S. LEGUN (1984), Coal deposition in an anastomosing-fluvial system: the Pennsylvanian Cumberland Group south of Joggins, Nova Scotia, Canada. Oxford: Blackwell (Special Publication of the International Association of Sedimentologists 7), pp. 105-120.

RUST, B.R. & A.S. LEGUN (1983), Modern anastomosing-fluvial deposits in arid Central Australia, and a Carboniferous analogue in New Brunswick, Canada. In: J.D. Collinson & J. Lewin, eds., Modern and ancient fluvial systems. Oxford: Blackwell (Special Publication of the International Association of Sedimentologists 6), pp. 385-392.

RUTHERFURD, I.D. (1994), Inherited controls on the form of a large, low energy river: the Murray River, Australia. In: S.A. Schumm & B.R. Winkley, eds., The variability of large alluvial rivers. New York: American Society of Civil Engineers, pp. 177-197.

RUTTEN, M.G. (1967), Flat-bottomed glacial valleys, braided rivers and the beaver. Geologie en Mijnbouw 46, pp. 356-360.

SAUCIER, R.T. (1994), Geomorphology and Quaternary geologic history of the Lower Mississippi Valley. Vicksburg: Mississippi River Commission, U.S. Army Corps of Engineers.

SAVAT, J. (1975), Some morphological and hydraulic characteristics of river-patterns in the Zaire Basin. Catena 2, pp. 161-180.

SAWICKI O. & D.G. SMITH (1992), Glacial Lake Invermere, upper Columbia River valley, British Columbia: a paleogeographic reconstruction. Canadian Journal of Earth Sciences 29, pp. 687-692.

SCHMIDT, A.M. (1993), Le 'Projet Toguèrè' dans le Delta intérieur du Niger, Mali. In: C. Bakels, ed., The end of our third decade; papers written on the occasion of the 30th anniversary of the Institute of Prehistory, volume II. Leiden: Instituut voor Prehistorie, Rijksuniversiteit Leiden (Analecta Praehistorica Leidensia 26), pp. 207-211.

SCHOUTE, J.F.Th. (1984), Vegetation horizons and related phenomena, a palaeoecological-micromorphological study in the younger coastal Holocene of the Northern Netherlands (Schildmeer area). Vaduz: Gantner. (Dissertationes Botanicæ 81)

SCHUMANN, R.R. (1989), Morphology of Red Creek, Wyoming, an arid-region anastomosing channel system. Earth Surface Processes and Landforms 14, pp. 277-288.

SCHUMM, S.A. (1968a), River adjustment to altered hydrologic regimen; Murrumbidgee River and paleochannels, Australia. Washington: U.S. Geological Survey (Professional Paper 598).

SCHUMM, S.A. (1968b), Speculations concerning paleohydraulic controls on terrestrial sedimentation. Geological Society of America Bulletin 79, pp. 1573-1588.

SCHUMM, S.A. (1977), The fluvial system. New York: Wiley.

SCHUMM, S.A. (1981), Evolution and response of the fluvial system, sedimentological implications. In: F.G. Ethridge & R.M. Flores, eds., Recent and ancient nonmarine depositional environments: models for exploration. Tulsa: Society of Economic Paleontologists and Mineralogists (Special Publication 31), pp. 19-29.

SCHUMM, S.A. (1985), Patterns of alluvial rivers. Annual Review of Earth and Planetary Sciences 13, pp. 5-27.

SCHUMM, S.A. (1988), Variability of the fluvial system in space and time. In: T. Rosswall, R.G. Woodmansee & P.G. Risser, eds., Scales and global change. New York: Wiley, pp. 225-250.

SCHUMM, S.A. (1993), River response to baselevel change: implications for sequence stratigraphy. The Journal of Geology 101, pp. 279-294.

SCHUMM, S.A. & H.R. KHAN (1972), Experimental study of channel patterns. Geological Society of America Bulletin 83, pp. 1755-1770.

SCHUMM, S.A., W.D. ERSKINE, & J.W. TILLEARD (1996), Morphology, hydrology, and evolution of the anastomosing Ovens and King Rivers, Victoria, Australia. Geological Society of America Bulletin 108, pp. 1212-1224.

SELBY, M.J. (1977), Pluvials in northern and East Africa and their relations to glacial climates in Europe. Johannesburg: University of the Witwatersrand, Department of Geography and Environmental Studies (Occasional Paper 19).

SHANLEY, K.W. & P.J. McCABE (1991), Predicting facies architecture through sequence stratigraphy, an example from the Kaiparowits Plateau, Utah. Geology 19, pp. 742-745.

SHANLEY, K.W. & P.J. McCABE (1993), Alluvial architecture in a sequence stratigraphic frame-work: a case history from the Upper Cretaceous of southern Utah, USA. In: S.S. Flint & I.D. Bryant, eds., The geological modelling of hydrocarbon reservoirs and outcrop analogues. Oxford: Blackwell (Special Publication of the International Association of Sedimentologists 15), pp. 21-56.

SIEBEN, J. (1998), Geulen in de Gamerense uiterwaard, aanvullende analyse van morfologische effecten. Arnhem: RIZA (RIZA rapport 98.032).

SILVA, W. & M. KOK (1996), Integrale Verkenning inrichting Rijntakken. Hoofdrapport 'Een weegschaal voor rivierbeheer'. Arnhem: RIZA/Delft Hydraulics (IVR rapport 1).

SLINGERLAND, R. & N.D. SMITH (1998), Necessary conditions for a meandering-river avulsion. Geology 26, pp. 435-438.

SMITH, D.G. (1973), Aggradation of the Alexandra-North Saskatchewan River, Banff Park, Alberta. In: M. Morisawa, ed., Fluvial geomorphology: a proceedings volume of the 4th annual geomorphology symposia series held at Binghamton, New York, September 27-28, 1973. Binghamton: State University of New York, pp. 201-219.

SMITH, D.G. (1976), Effect of vegetation on lateral migration of anastomosed channels of a glacier meltwater river. Geological Society of America Bulletin 87, pp. 857-860.

SMITH, D.G. (1983), Anastomosed fluvial deposits: modern examples from Western Canada. In: J. Collinson & J. Lewin, eds., Modern and ancient fluvial systems. Oxford: Blackwell (Special Publication of the International Association of Sedimentologists 6), pp. 155-168.

SMITH, D.G. (1984), Vibracoring fluvial and deltaic sediments: tips on improving penetration and recovery. Journal of Sedimentary Petrology 54, pp. 660-663.

SMITH, D.G. (1986), Anastomosing river deposits, sedimentation rates and basin subsidence, Magdalena River, northwestern Colombia, South America. Sedimentary Geology 46, pp. 177-196.

SMITH, D.G. & P.E. PUTNAM (1980), Anastomosed river deposits: modern and ancient examples in Alberta, Canada. Canadian Journal of Earth Sciences 17, pp. 1396-1406.

SMITH, D.G. & N.D. SMITH (1980), Sedimentation in anastomosed river systems: examples from alluvial valleys near Banff, Alberta. Journal of Sedimentary Petrology 50, pp. 157-164.

SMITH, N.D. (1975), Sedimentary environments and Late Quaternary history of a "low-energy" mountain delta. Canadian Journal of Earth Sciences 12, pp. 2004-2013.

SMITH, N.D., T.A. CROSS, J.P. DUFFICY & S.R. CLOUGH (1989), Anatomy of an avulsion. Sedimentology 36, pp. 1-23.

SMITH, N.D., T.S. MCCARTHY, W.N. ELLERY, C.L. MERRY & H. RÜTHER (1997), Avulsion and anastomosis in the panhandle region of the Okavango Fan, Botswana. Geomorphology 20, pp. 49-65.

SMITH, N.D. & M. PÉREZ-ARLUCEA (1994), Fine-grained splay deposition in the avulsion belt of the lower Saskatchewan River, Canada. Journal of Sedimentary Research B64, pp. 159-168.

STANISTREET, I.G., B. CAIRNCROSS & T.S. MCCARTHY (1993), Low sinuosity and meandering bedload rivers of the Okavango Fan: channel confinement by vegetated levées without fine sediment. Sedimentary Geology 85, pp. 135-156.

STANISTREET, I.G. & T.S. MCCARTHY (1993), The Okavango Fan and the classification of subaerial fan systems. Sedimentary Geology 85, pp. 115-133.

STERNBERG, H.O'R. (1959), Radiocarbon dating as applied to a problem of Amazonian morphology. Comptes rendus du XVIIIe Congrès International de Géographie, Rio de Janeiro, 1956, Tome 2. Rio de Janeiro: Comité National du Brésil, Union Géographique Internationale, pp. 399-424.

STICHTING VOOR BODEMKARTERING (1959), Alblasserwaard; bodemkundige overzichtskaart schaal 1:10.000. Wageningen: Stichting voor Bodemkartering.

STOUTHAMER, E. & H.J.A. BERENDSEN (1997), Holocene avulsions in the Rhine-Meuse delta, The Netherlands. In: Abstracts, 6th International Conference on Fluvial Sedimentology, 22-26 September 1997, Cape Town. Cape Town: University of Cape Town, p. 200.

STREET, F.A. & A.T. GROVE (1976), Environmental and climatic implications of late Quaternary lake-level fluctuations in Africa. Nature 261, pp. 385-389.

STREET, F.A. & A.T. GROVE (1979), Global maps of lake-level fluctuations since 30,000 yr B.P. Quaternary Research 12, pp. 83-118.

STUIVER, M., A. LONG & R.S. KRA, eds. (1993), Calibration 1993. Radiocarbon 35, pp. 1-244.

TALBOT, M.R. (1980), Environmental responses to climatic change in West African Sahel over the past 20,000 years. In: M.A.J. Williams en H. Faure, eds., The Sahara and the Nile. Rotterdam: Balkema, pp. 37-62.

TAYLOR, G. & K.D. WOODYER (1978), Bank deposition in suspended-load streams. In: A.D. Miall, ed., Fluvial Sedimentology. Calgary: Canadian Society of Petroleum Geologists (Memoir 5), pp. 257-275.

THOMAS, M.F. (1994), Geomorphology in the tropics; a study of weathering and denudation in low latitudes, Wiley, Chichester, 460 p.

THOMAS, R.G., D.G. SMITH, J.M. WOOD, J. VISSER, E.A. CALVERLEY -RANGE & E.H. KOSTER (1987), Inclined heterolithic stratification: terminology, description, interpretation and significance. Sedimentary Geology 53, pp. 123-179.

TÖRNQVIST, T.E. (1993a), Holocene alternation of meandering and anastomosing fluvial systems in the Rhine-Meuse delta (central Netherlands) controlled by sea-level rise and subsoil erodibility. Journal of Sedimentary Petrology 63, pp. 683-693.

TÖRNQVIST, T.E. (1993b), Fluvial sedimentary geology and chronology af the Holocene Rhine-Meuse delta, The Netherlands. Utrecht: Koninklijk Nederlands Aardrijkskundig Genootschap/Faculteit Ruimtelijke Wetenschappen, Universiteit Utrecht (Nederlandse Geografische Studies 166).

TÖRNQVIST, T.E. (1994), Middle and late Holocene avulsion history of the River Rhine (Rhine-Meuse delta, Netherlands). Geology 22, pp. 711-714.

TÖRNQVIST, T.E. (1998), Longitudinal profile evolution of the Rhine-Meuse system during the last deglaciation: interplay of climate change and glacio-eustacy? Terra Nova 10, pp. 11-15.

TÖRNQVIST, T.E., A. ASLAN & W.E. AUTIN (1994), Holocene fluvial styles of the Lower Mississippi River, a preliminary assessment. Abstracts 14th International Sedimentological Congress. Recife: International Association of Sedimentologists, pp. D79-D81.

TÖRNQVIST, T.E. & M.F.P. BIERKENS (1994), How smooth should curves be for calibration of radiocarbon ages? Radiocarbon 36, pp. 11-26.

TÖRNQVIST, T.E., J.S. BRIDGE & N.E.M. ASSELMAN (1996), Quantitative analysis of overbank deposition in the Rhine-Meuse and Mississippi deltas: implications for 3-d modelling of alluvial architecture. In: Programma en abstracts lezingen, 3^e Nederlands Aardwetenschappelijk Congres, 2-3 mei 1996, Veldhoven. Koninklijk Nederlands Geologisch Mijnbouwkundig Genootschap/Koninklijke Nederlandse Akademie van Wetenschappen/ Nederlandse Organisatie voor Wetenschappelijk Onderzoek, lezing 45.

TÖRNQVIST, T.E., A.F.M. DE JONG, W.A. OOSTERBAAN & K. VAN DER BORG (1992), Accurate dating of organic deposits by AMS ^{14}C measurement of macrofossils. Radiocarbon 34, pp. 566-577.

TÖRNQVIST, T.E. & G.J. VAN DIJK (1993), Optimizing sampling strategy for radiocarbon dating of Holocene fluvial systems in a vertically aggrading setting. Boreas 22, pp. 129-145.

TÖRNQVIST, T.E., M.H.M. VAN REE & E.L.J.H. FAESSEN (1993), Longitudinal facies architectural changes of a Middle Holocene anastomosing distributary system (Rhine-Meuse delta, central Netherlands). Sedimentary Geology 85, pp. 203-220.

TÖRNQVIST, T.E., M.H.M. VAN REE, R. VAN 'T VEER & B. VAN GEEL (1998), Improving methodology for high-resolution reconstruction of sea-level rise and neotectonics by paleoecological analysis and AMS ^{14}C dating of basal peats. Quaternary Research 49, pp. 72-85.

TÖRNQVIST, T.E., H.J.T. WEERTS & H.J.A. BERENDSEN (1994), Definition of two new members in the upper Kreftenheye and Twente Formations (Quaternary, the Netherlands): a final solution to persistent confusion? Geologie en Mijnbouw 72, pp. 251-264.

TRICART, J. (1959), Géomorphologie dynamique de la moyenne vallée du Niger (Soudan). Annales de Géographie 68, pp. 333-343.

TRICART, J. (1965), Rapport de la mission de reconnaissance géomorphologique de la vallée moyenne du Niger (Janvier-Avril 1957). Dakar: Institut Fondamental d'Afrique Noire. (Mémoire de l'Institut Fondamental d'Afrique Noire 72).

TUTT, D.B. (1979), Kootenay River Diversion Project, river regime and morphology studies. Proceedings of the 4th National Hydrotechnical Conference, Vancouver.

URVOY, Y. (1942), Les bassins du Niger; étude de géographie physique et de paléogéographie. Paris: Librairie Larose. (Ph.D. thesis)

VAN DE MEENE, E.A. (1977), Toelichtingen bij de geologische kaart van Nederland schaal 1:50.000; blad Arnhem Oost (40 O). Haarlem: Rijks Geologische Dienst.

VAN DE MEENE, E.A., J. VAN DER STAAY, & TEOH LAY HOCK (1979), The Van der Staay suction-corer; a simple apparatus for drilling in sand below groundwater table. Haarlem: Rijks Geologische Dienst.

VAN DE MEENE, E.A., M. VAN MEERKERK & J. VAN DER STAAY (1988), Toelichtingen bij de geologische kaart van Nederland schaal 1:50.000; blad Utrecht Oost (31 O). Haarlem: Rijks Geologische Dienst.

VAN DEN BERG, J.H. (1995), Prediction of alluvial channel pattern of perennial rivers. Geomorphology 12, pp. 259-279.

VAN DEN BERG, J.H. & A. VAN GELDER, (1993) Prediction of suspended bed material transport in flows over silt and very fine sand. Water Resources Research 29, pp. 1393-1404.

VAN DE PLASSCHE, O. (1982), Sea-level change and water-level movements in the Netherlands during the Holocene. Amsterdam: Vrije Universiteit. (Ph.D. thesis)

VAN DER PLICHT (1993), The Groningen radiocarbon calibration program. Radiocarbon 35, pp. 231-237.

VAN DER WOUDE, J.D. (1979), Chronology of the perimarine fluviatile depositional phases at Molenaarsgraaf. Geologie en Mijnbouw 58, pp. 381-382.

VAN DER WOUDE, J.D. (1983), Holocene paleoenvironmental evolution of a perimarine fluviatile area; geology and paleobotany of the area surrounding the archeological excavation at the Hazendonk river dune (Western Netherlands). Leiden: Instituut voor Prehistorie, Rijksuniversiteit Leiden (Analecta Praehistorica Leidensia 16).

VAN DER WOUDE, J.D. (1984), The fluviolagoonal palaeoenvironment in the Rhine/Meuse deltaic plain. Sedimentology 31, pp. 395-400.

VAN DIJK, G.J., H.J.A. BERENDSEN & W. ROELEVELD (1991), Holocene water level development in The Netherlands' river area; implications for sea level reconstruction. Geologie en Mijnbouw 70, pp. 311-326.

VAN GELDER, A., J.H. VAN DEN BERG, G. CHENG & C. XUE (1994), Overbank and channelfill deposits of the modern Yellow River delta. Sedimentary Geology 90, pp. 293-305.

VAN RIJN, L.C. (1984a), Sediment transport, part I: bed load transport. Journal of Hydraulic Engineering 110, pp. 1431-1456.

VAN RIJN, L.C. (1984b), Sediment transport, part II: suspended load transport. Journal of Hydraulic Engineering 110, pp. 1613-1641.

VAN RIJN, L.C. (1984c), Sediment transport, part III: bed forms and alluvial roughness. Journal of Hydraulic Engineering 110, pp. 1733-1754.

VAN RIJN, L.C. (1993), Principles of sediment transport in rivers, estuaries and coastal seas. Amsterdam: Aqua Publications.

VERBRAECK, A. (1970), Toelichtingen bij de geologische kaart van Nederland schaal 1:50.000; blad Gorkum Oost (38 O). Haarlem: Rijks Geologische Dienst.

VERBRAECK, A. (1984), Toelichtingen bij de geologische kaart van Nederland schaal 1:50.000; blad Tiel West (39 W), blad Tiel Oost (39 O). Haarlem: Rijks Geologische Dienst.

VERBRAECK, A., H. KOK & M. VAN MEERKERK (1974), The genesis and age of the riverdunes (donken) in the Alblasserwaard. Haarlem: Rijks Geologische Dienst (Mededelingen Rijks Geologische Dienst 25), pp. 1-8.

VERBRUGGEN, M. (1992), Geoarchaeological prospection of the Rommertsdonk. In: C. Bakels, ed., The end of our third decade; papers written on the occasion of the 30th anniversary of the Institute of Prehistory, volume I. Leiden: Instituut voor Prehistorie, Rijksuniversiteit Leiden, (Analecta Praehistorica Leidensia 25), pp. 117-128.

VERNET, R. (1993), Le Sahel. In: Vallées du Niger. (Catalogue exposition "Vallées du Niger") Paris: Editions de la Réunion des Musées Nationaux, pp. 75-82.

VINK, T. (1926), De Lekstreek; een aardrijkskundige verkenning van een bewoond deltagebied. Amsterdam: H.J. Paris. (Ph.D. thesis)

VOUTE, C. (1962), Geological and morphological evolution of the Niger and Benue Valleys. Annalen van het Koninklijk Museum voor Midden-Afrika, Tervuren; reeks in-8°; wetenschappen van de mens 40, pp. 189-205.

WARD, J.O. (1994), The Niger River: geomorphic considerations for future development. In: S.A. Schumm & B.R. Winkley, eds., The variability of large alluvial rivers. New York: American Society of Civil Engineers, pp. 423-439.

WARWICK, P.D. & R.M. FLORES (1987), Evolution of fluvial styles in the Eocene Wasatch Formation, Powder River Basin, Wyoming. In: F.G. Ethridge, R.M. Flores & M.D. Harvey, eds., Recent developments in fluvial sedimentology. Tulsa: Society of Economic Paleontologists and Mineralogists (Special Publication 39), pp. 303-310.

WATER SURVEY OF CANADA (1991a), Historical streamflow summary, British Columbia, 1990. Ottawa: Water Survey of Canada.

WATER SURVEY OF CANADA (1991b), Historical streamflow summary, Manitoba, 1990. Ottawa: Water Survey of Canada.

WEERTS, H.J.T. (1996), Complex confining layers; architecture and hydraulic properties of Holocene and Late Weichselian deposits in the fluvial Rhine-Meuse delta, The Netherlands. Utrecht: Koninklijk Nederlands Aardrijkskundig Genootschap/Faculteit Ruimtelijke Wetenschappen, Universiteit Utrecht (Nederlandse Geografische Studies 213).

WEERTS, H.J.T. & H.J.A. BERENDSEN (1995), Late Weichselian and Holocene fluvial palaeogeography of the southern Rhine-Meuse delta (the Netherlands). Geologie en Mijnbouw 74, pp. 199-212.

WEERTS, H.J.T. & M.F.P. BIERKENS (1993), Geostatistical analysis of overbank deposits of anastomosing and meandering fluvial systems, Rhine-Meuse delta, central Netherlands. Sedimentary Geology 85, pp. 221-232.

WELLS, N.A. & J.A. DORR, Jr. (1987), Shifting of the Kosi River, Northern India. Geology 15, pp. 204-207.

WHITE, W.R., E. PARIS & R. BETTES (1979), A new general method for predicting the frictional characteristics of alluvial streams. Wallingford: Hydraulic Research Station. (Report No. IT 187)

WINSPEAR, N.R. & K. PYE (1995), The origin and significance of boxwork clay coatings on dune sand grains from the Nebraska Sand Hills, USA. Sedimentary Geology 94, pp. 245-254.

WOODYER, K.D., G. TAYLOR & K.A.W. CROOK (1979), Depositional processes along a very low-gradient suspended-load stream: the Barwon River, New South Wales. Sedimentary Geology 22, pp. 97-120.

WRIGHT, V.P. & S.B. MARRIOTT (1993), The sequence stratigraphy of fluvial depositional systems: the role of floodplain sediment storage. Sedimentary Geology 86, pp. 203-210.

YONECHI, F. & W. MAUNG (1986), Subdivision on the anastomosing river channel with a proposal of the Irrawaddy type. The Science Reports of the Tohoku University, 7th Series (Geography) 36, pp. 102-113.

Appendix 1 Sediment transport functions

The three sediment transport functions applied in chapter 3 are given below. The meaning the of the characters and symbols used can be found at the end of this appendix.

1. **The Engelund & Hansen (1967) function**

$$q_t = \frac{\rho_s \, 0.05 \overline{u}^5}{(s-1)^2 \, g^{0.5} \, d_{50} \, C^3}$$

2. **The Van Rijn (1984a, 1984b) function**

$$q_t = q_s + q_b$$

in which

$$q_s = \rho_s \, F \, \overline{u} \, h \, C_a$$

and

$$q_b = 0.053 \rho_s (s-1)^{0.5} g^{0.5} (d_{50})^{1.5} (D_*)^{-0.3} T^{2.1}$$

However, if $T \geq 3$ then

$$q_b = 0.1 \rho_s (s-1)^{0.5} g^{0.5} (d_{50})^{1.5} (D_*)^{-0.3} T^{1.5}$$

The following relationships apply to the various parameters in these formulae:

a. *The grain size parameter*

$$D_* = d_{50} \left(\frac{(s-1)g}{v^2}\right)^{1/3}$$

b. *The excess bed shear parameter*

$$T = (\theta - \theta_{cr})/\theta_{cr}$$

in which the bed shear parameter is defined as

$$\theta = \overline{u}^2(C')^{-2}\{(s-1)d_{50}\}^{-1}$$

in which the grain-related Chézy coefficient is defined as

$$C' = 18 \log(12h/3d_{90})$$

while the critical bed shear parameter is defined as

$\theta_{cr} = 0.24\ D_*^{-1}$	for	1	< D_* ≤	4
$\theta_{cr} = 0.14\ D_*^{-0.64}$	for	4	< D_* ≤	10
$\theta_{cr} = 0.04\ D_*^{-0.1}$	for	10	< D_* ≤	20
$\theta_{cr} = 0.013\ D_*^{0.29}$	for	20	< D_* ≤	150
$\theta_{cr} = 0.055$	for		D_* >	150

c. *The reference concentration*

$$C_a = 0.0015(d_{50}/a)(T^{1.5}/D_*^{0.3})$$

d. *The shape factor*

$$F = \frac{(a/h)^{Z'} - (a/h)^{1.2}}{(1 - a/h)^{Z'}(1.2 - Z')}$$

in which the suspension number is defined as

$$Z' = Z + \phi$$

in which the stratification correction of the suspension number is defined as

$$\phi = 2.5(w_s/u_*)^{0.8}(C_a/C_0)^{0.4}$$

in which the overall bed shear velocity is defined as

$$u_* = (g^{0.5}/C)\ \overline{u}$$

in which the overall Chézy-coefficient is defined as

$$C = 18 \log(12h/k_s)$$

The uncorrected suspension number is defined as

$$Z = w_s /(\beta \kappa u_*)$$

in which the ratio of sediment and fluid mixing coefficient is defined as

$$\beta = 1 + 2(w_s /u_*)^2 \quad (with \ \beta_{max} = 2)$$

in which the fall velocity of suspended sediment is defined as

$$w_s = \frac{(s-1)g \ d_s^2}{18v} \quad (for \ 1 < d_s \leq 100 \ \mu m)$$

or

$$w_s = 10v/d_s \ [\sqrt{(1 + \frac{0.01 \ (s-1) \ g \ d_s^3}{v^2})} - 1] \quad (for \ 100 < d_s < 1000 \ \mu m)$$

in which the representative grain size of suspended bed material is defined as

$$d_s = [1 + 0.011 \ (\sigma_s - 1)(T - 25)] \ d_{50} \quad (however \ d_s = d_{50} \ for \ T \geq 25)$$

in which the gradation coefficient of the bed material is defined as

$$\sigma_s = 1/2 \ (d_{84} /d_{50} + d_{50} /d_{16})$$

A numerical program (TRANSPOR) was used for the computations. This program may compute sediment transport in current and in wave direction. A full description of the program is given in Van Rijn (1993, Appendix A). For the current-alone case the following input data are required: h, ū, d_{50}, d_{90}, d_s, k_s, water temperature (ranging from 15 to 18° C in our case) and the fluid salinity (0 ‰ in our case).

3. The modified Van Rijn function (Van den Berg & Van Gelder 1993)

Leaving the basic formulae intact, Van den Berg & Van Gelder proposed three modifications concerning the following parameters in the formulae:

a. The excess bed shear parameter (T)
For the range $D_* \leq 6$ they they proposed to use the following definition of critical bed shear parameter:

$$\theta_{cr} = 0.109 \ D_*^{-0.5}$$

b. The near bed reference concentration of suspended bed material (C_a)
They proposed the following different equation:

$$C_a = 0.053 \ d_{50} T \ D_*^{-0.3} a^{-1}$$

c. The shape factor (F)
Taking into account hindered settling effects, they proposed a different equation for the stratification correction of the suspension number:

$$\phi = 3.5 \ Z^{0.8} (\frac{a \ C_a}{0.05hC_0})^{0.4}$$

They also proposed a different equation for the fall velocity of suspended sediment:

$$w_s = w_0 \ [1 - (a/0.05h)C_a]^4$$

in which w_0 represents the fall velocity of a sediment particle in a clear, still fluid:

$$w_0 = \frac{(s-1)g \ d_s^2}{18v} \quad (for \ 1 < d_s \leq 100 \ \mu m)$$

or

$$w_0 = 10v/d_s \ [\sqrt{(1 + \frac{0.01 \ (s-1) \ g \ d_s^3}{v^2})} - 1] \quad (for \ 100 < d_s < 1000 \ \mu m)$$

Notation

a	=	reference level above the mean bed (m), equal to half the bed form height or k_s, while $0.01h \leq a \leq 0.05h$
C	=	overall Chézy-coefficient ($m^{0.5}/s$)
C'	=	grain-related Chézy-coefficient ($m^{0.5}/s$)
C_a	=	near bed reference concentration of suspended bed material load (-)
C_0	=	maximum volumetric concentration of the bed (= 0.65)
D_*	=	grain size parameter (-)
d_{50}	=	median grain size of the bed material (m)
d_{16}, d_{84} and d_{90}	=	grain sizes in a distribution , for which 16, 84 and 90 percent, by weight, respectively are finer (m)
d_s	=	representative grain size of suspended bed material (m)
F	=	shape factor, a correction factor for suspended bed material load in the Van Rijn bed load transport function (-)
g	=	acceleration of gravity (m/s^2)
h	=	flow depth (m)
k_s	=	Nikuradse roughness height (m)
R	=	hydraulic radius (m)
s	=	specific density (ρ/ρ_s) (-)
T	=	excess bed shear parameter (m)
$\bar{u}$	=	depth-averaged flow velocity (m/s)
u_*	=	overall bed-shear velocity (m/s)
w_0	=	particle fall velocity in a clear, still fluid (m/s)
w_s	=	fall velocity of suspended sediment particles in a mixture of fluid and suspended load (m/s)
q_b	=	bed load transport per unit width (kg/m/s)
q_s	=	suspended bed material transport per unit width (kg/m/s)
q_t	=	total bed material transport per unit width (kg/m/s)
Z	=	suspension number (-)
Z'	=	corrected suspension number (-)
β	=	ratio of sediment and fluid mixing coefficient (-)
Θ	=	bed shear parameter (-)
Θ_{cr}	=	critical bed shear parameter (-)
κ	=	constant of Von Kármàn for clear fluid (= 0.4)
ν	=	kinematic viscosity coefficient (m^2/s)
ρ_s	=	sediment density (= 2650 kg/m^3)
ρ	=	fluid density (kg/m^3)
σ_s	=	gradation coefficient of the bed material (-)
ϕ	=	correction factor for the suspension number (-)

Curriculum vitae

Bart Makaske was born on May 8, 1965 in Doornspijk (the Netherlands). In June 1983 he finished secondary school ('VWO') at the "Johannes Fontanus College" in Barneveld, after which he was educated in journalism in Amersfoort for one year. In September 1984 he started the study of physical geography at Utrecht University. He specialized in process-modelling in physical geography and completed his M.Sc. in June 1991. During the M.Sc. studies, fieldwork was carried out in the Rhône-Delta to investigate the morphodynamics and sedimentology of the beach face. The study program included fluid mechanics, sedimentology and palynology. For the latter two subjects, fieldwork was carried out in Spain and Portugal. Practical work also comprised a field study of the geomorphological history of the upper Inland Niger Delta in Mali. This study was part of an archeological research project, executed within the framework of development cooperation.

After his military service, Bart Makaske returned to the Department of Physical Geography of the Utrecht University in 1992. He then started a study of anastomosing rivers that resulted in this Ph.D. thesis. As a part of the Ph.D. research, he was funded by the Netherlands Ministry of Foreign Affairs to participate again in the above-mentioned development project in Mali. He is presently involved in ongoing research in the western part of the Netherlands, aiming at reconstructing relative sea-level movements during the Holocene. Next to his research activities, he supervised many students during their field studies.

Bart Makaske is an enthusiastic speedskater. He is an active member of the skating-club "Het Biltsche Meertje" and completed the 'elfstedentocht' (eleven cities tour) of 1986 and 1997.